MRS WARREN'S PROFESSION

broadview editions
series editor: L.W. Conolly

Shaw in 1898,
the year he published *Mrs Warren's Profession*

MRS WARREN'S PROFESSION

Bernard Shaw

edited by L.W. Conolly

broadview editions

Library and Archives Canada Cataloguing in Publication

Shaw, Bernard, 1856-1950
   Mrs. Warren's profession / Bernard Shaw ; edited by L.W. Conolly.

(Broadview editions)
ISBN 1-55111-627-8

I. Conolly, L. W. (Leonard W.)   II. Title.   III. Series.

PR5363.M7 2005   822'.912   C2005-904531-0

Broadview Press Ltd. is an independent, international publishing house, incorporated in 1985. Broadview believes in shared ownership, both with its employees and with the general public; since the year 2000 Broadview shares have traded publicly on the Toronto Venture Exchange under the symbol BDP.

We welcome comments and suggestions regarding any aspect of our publications—please feel free to contact us at the addresses below or at broadview@broadviewpress.com.

Broadview Press Ltd. gratefully acknowledges the financial support of the Government of Canada through the Book Publishing Industry Development Program for our publishing activities.

North America:

PO Box 1243, Peterborough, Ontario,
Canada K9J 7H5

PO Box 1015, 3576 California Road,
Orchard Park, NY, USA 14127

Tel: (705) 743-8990;
Fax: (705) 743-8353
E-mail: customerservice@
broadviewpress.com

UK, Ireland, and continental Europe:

NBN Plymbridge
Estover Road
Plymouth PL6 7PY UK

Tel: 44 (0) 1752 202301
Fax: 44 (0) 1752 202331
Fax Order Line: 44 (0) 1752 202333
Customer Service:
cservs@nbnplymbridge.com
Orders: orders@nbnplymbridge.com

Australia and New Zealand:

UNIREPS,
University of New South Wales
Sydney, NSW, 2052
Australia

Tel: 61 2 9664 0999
Fax: 61 2 9664 5420
E-mail: info.press@unsw.edu.au

www.broadviewpress.com

This book is printed on acid-free paper containing 100% post-consumer fibre.

Book design and composition by George Kirkpatrick

PRINTED IN CANADA

For
Eugene Benson
Colleague, Mentor, Collaborator, and — above all — Dear Friend

Contents

Acknowledgements

The advice and support of numerous friends, colleagues, students, and family members have made this edition far better than it would otherwise have been, and I warmly thank them all for their interest and generosity. Kathryn Yam provided valuable research assistance on the 1905 New Haven and New York productions of *Mrs Warren's Profession*. Another former student, Matthew Griffis, expertly input the text of the play. Canadian, British, and American friends and colleagues have unstintingly guided, corrected, and supplemented my work on the play. I express deep appreciation in particular to Alan Andrews, Michel Pharand, Peter Wearing, John Burbidge, Denis Johnston, Jeremy Crow, Eugene Benson, and Dan H. Laurence. It is a pleasure as well to acknowledge the leadership and energy of Richard Dietrich in establishing and presiding over the International Shaw Society, an organisation that has facilitated worldwide cooperation among Shaw scholars. And as on previous occasions of this kind, I again express my appreciation to the Warden and Fellows of Robinson College, Cambridge, for welcoming me as a senior member of the College and providing such a congenial environment for work and leisure. During my frequent visits to the Dan H. Laurence Shaw Collection at the University of Guelph Library, Lorne Bruce and the staff of Archival and Special Collections have again proved unfailingly courteous and helpful. I am also indebted to many people at Broadview Press for good and cheerful counsel; Don LePan and Julia Gaunce deserve special thanks for their encouragement and enthusiasm at all stages of my work on this book, as do George Kirkpatrick, Judith Earnshaw, Tara Lowes, Anne Hodgetts, and Piper-Lee Bradford for giving me the benefit of their expertise and advice.

My family has somehow tolerated my intimate relationship with Shaw for several years, and I thank my wife and children for their forbearance—past, present, and future. In particular, I thank my son James for his serene resolution of many stressful disputes between me and my computer, my daughter Rebecca for finding recondite matters of English grammar and usage as vitally life-enhancing as I do, and my wife Barbara for bringing her formidable publishing skills to bear for the betterment of this book.

The definitive text (see below, A Note on the Text, p. 80) of *Mrs Warren's Profession* and all Bernard Shaw quotations in this Broadview edition are used by permission of the Society of Authors, on behalf of the Bernard Shaw Estate. Copyright © 1898, 1913, 1926, 1930, 1933, 1941, George Bernard Shaw. Copyright © 1905, Brentano's. Copyright © 1957, The Public Trustee as Executor of the Estate of George Bernard Shaw.

Extracts in Appendix D1 from *The Unknown Mayhew* are reprinted by permission of the Merlin Press, PO Box 30705, London WC2E 8QD (www.merlinpress.co.uk).

Extracts in Appendix D4 from *A Newnham Anthology* are reprinted by permission of Cambridge University Press.

All extracts in Appendix H are reprinted by permission of Carolyn Christensen Nelson and Broadview Press.

Introduction

Mrs Warren's Profession in America

"The most shockingly immoral dialogue ever publicly repeated ... the words, suggestions—the whole rotten mess of immoral suggestions—have no place on the public platform."[1] Thus was Bernard Shaw's *Mrs Warren's Profession* greeted by the theatre critic of the *New Haven Leader* on its North American première at the Hyperion Theatre, New Haven, on Friday 27 October 1905. His colleague at the *New Haven Register* heartily agreed; this "repulsive" play, he wrote, should not "under any circumstances be given before a mixed audience." He wished it "a speedy exit from the boards, here and elsewhere."

It had been a rowdy night at the Hyperion. There had been a football game between Yale and Princeton that day (Yale won), and a thousand students packed the galleries, anticipating—from the publicity generated by the already notorious play about an unrepentant prostitute—a couple of hours of bawdy entertainment. Mary Shaw (no relation to the author), who played the role of Mrs Warren, reported that "in the very first act speeches that had no significance beyond their literal meaning were greeted with laughter and exclamations," and as the second act progressed it was "plain to all of us that there was going to be trouble." In the scene in Act 2 where Vivie demands to know the identity of her father, "pandemonium broke loose in the upper galleries." Mary Shaw found it impossible to proceed. The "staid professors and responsible people in the lower part of the house" started hissing and calling for quiet from the raucous students. While she was waiting for order to be restored, Mary Shaw decided that a new approach to the part of Kitty Warren was needed:

---

1   My account of the New Haven events is drawn from the *New York Times*, 29 October 1905, and Mary Shaw, "My 'Immoral' Play." For further accounts from the New York press, see also Innes 225-29; George E. Wellwarth, "Mrs Warren Comes to America, or the Blue-Noses, the Politicians and the Procurers," *Shaw Review* 2.8 (1959): 8-16; and John H. Houchin, *Censorship of the American Theatre in the Twentieth Century* (Cambridge: Cambridge UP, 2003) 52-57.

... a sudden conviction came upon me that it was going to be impossible to play Kitty Warren as Kitty Warren should be played, in the vulgar cockney dialect to which she reverted in strong feeling. Knowing something of the methods of controlling mob spirits in audiences, I strode to the head of the table, took on the manner of Lady Macbeth, and played the entire scene in loud, sonorous tones with menace in every one of them. An appalling silence fell upon the theater. There was no more trouble of any kind from the undergraduates, and when the curtain fell upon the second act they paid the tribute that cowards always pay the courageous, and gave us ten curtain calls.

Early the next day, however, phone calls and delegations alerted the New Haven mayor, John P. Studley, that there was some kind of problem. He hadn't been at the performance, and he certainly hadn't read the play (or even heard of Bernard Shaw), but what he was now hearing convinced him that there was "something improper" about it "that had shocked the sensibilities of the audience." The mayor called the producer of the play, Arnold Daly,[1] to his office. Daly did his best to explain who Shaw was and what *Mrs Warren's Profession* was about. The mayor seemed to think that the whole thing was a tempest in a teapot, but his political instincts got the better of him and he told Daly "I guess I will have to shut this thing up; there seems to be a lot of noise about it, and the wisest thing to do would be just to cut it out." At noon he ordered the chief of police to revoke the licence of the Hyperion Theatre as long as *Mrs Warren's Profession* was scheduled to be performed there. Daly and his company promptly left New Haven "in high dudgeon" to mount the play in New York, leaving behind sold out performances for the Saturday matinée and evening performances.

New York was waiting. Anthony Comstock, an indefatigable crusader against allegedly obscene literature, and founder of

---

1 Daly (1875-1927) had previously introduced several Shaw plays to American audiences: *Candida*, *The Man of Destiny*, *How He Lied to Her Husband*, *You Never Can Tell*, and *John Bull's Other Island*. Daly played the role of Frank in the New Haven and New York productions of *Mrs Warren's Profession*.

the New York Society for the Suppression of Vice,[1] had already warned Daly that he would face legal action if he went ahead with the production of this "filthy" play. Daly responded that Comstock's epithet was "decorative, but not descriptive," and invited him to a rehearsal at the Garrick Theatre, where *Mrs Warren's Profession* was scheduled to open on 30 October (*New York Times*, 25 October 1905). Comstock declined, but William McAdoo, the city's Police Commissioner, was not so reticent about getting involved. As soon as Daly arrived in town McAdoo demanded the prompt-book for the play and proceeded to blue-pencil "those few phrases and expressions that he thought might be a little dangerous." Most of the cuts came in speeches by Mrs Warren, and Mary Shaw was given instructions by Daly to adhere strictly to McAdoo's expurgated text.

The play duly opened on 30 October. The *New York Times* reported on the morning of the opening that "every single line which is capable of double construction will be either eliminated entirely or so changed as to convey directly the meaning intended." Daly confirmed that "some of the lines have been cut or changed, but nowhere has the impression which Mr Shaw meant to convey been clouded." And the reports of an expurgated text did nothing to quell audience interest. Mary Shaw describes her journey to the theatre:

... as I approached the corner of Thirty-fifth Street and Broadway, I saw huge crowds of people packing solidly the whole length of Thirty-fourth Street, and I thought at first there must be a fire. I was told by a policeman that they were people who were trying to get into the Garrick Theater. I found it impossible to make any headway from Broadway, and I turned back, intending to go around the other way to the back door. This approach, if anything, was more terribly

---

1   Comstock (1844-1915) was said to have been responsible for the destruction of "more than fifty tons of indecent books, 28,425 pounds of plates for the printing of such books, almost four million obscene pictures, and 16,900 negatives for such pictures." He also claimed the dubious distinction of having caused the suicide of fifteen people (Haney 20).

crowded and blocked than the other. A cordon of police were endeavoring to keep the people out of the streets, so that traffic might pass. Ticket speculators were shrieking out impossible prices for seats. I saw tickets handed along through the crowd, and one man in an automobile secured seats in the back of the balcony for sixty dollars each.

I turned again, and made my way back to the Broadway side, and there I begged a policeman to get me through the crowd, telling him I was to play Mrs Warren, and that there would be no play until I could get in. Taking his billy out of its sheath, he brandished it in the air, and, assisted by another policeman, he dragged me through this struggling mass of people, who were shrieking and howling and bidding for seats and behaving generally like maniacs. It took me fully ten minutes after I reached my dressing-room to recover my composure.

The Garrick Theatre was packed—a full house of 963 people—and between two and three thousand others were turned away. McAdoo was in the audience, but when Mary Shaw glanced in his direction during the key scene between Mrs Warren and her daughter, she saw McAdoo "placidly sleeping" in his box. But several of his staff were there as well, two of whom were ordered to inspect the prompt-book after the show to make sure that Daly hadn't deviated from the version approved by McAdoo. Unlike in New Haven, there were no disturbances during the performance, but according to an exit poll conducted by the *New York World* about a third of the audience thought the play unfit for performance.[1]

Press reaction next day was mostly hostile,[2] and if McAdoo thought that his tampering with the text of *Mrs Warren's Profession* would keep the lid on things he was gravely mistaken. There was an extraordinary flurry of activity the day (Tuesday 31 October 1905) after the opening. The press was full of condemnatory edi-

---

1   The *World* distributed a ballot that asked audience members to say whether the play was "fit" or "unfit" for performance. Of the 563 completed ballots, 304 voted fit, 272 voted unfit (about 50 votes fewer than the *World*'s calculation of a third of the audience).
2   See, for example, Appendices C3 and C4.

torials and letters, and McAdoo (albeit asleep during the performance) had decided that even the censored version of the play was "revolting, indecent, and nauseating where it was not boring" (*New York Times*, 1 November 1905). After consulting with New York's Mayor George McClellan, McAdoo told the manager of the Garrick Theatre, Samuel W. Gumpertz, that not only were further performances of *Mrs Warren's Profession* banned, but everyone associated with the first performance was going to be arrested, including the cast, and charged with "offending public decency." A warrant was issued and served later that day. Mary Shaw seems to have been oblivious to all of this until she went to the theatre at four o'clock that afternoon to collect her mail and saw a notice announcing the ban. On the Wednesday morning Gumpertz picked her up at her hotel to take her, with other members of the cast, to Jefferson Market Court for the hearing. As Mary Shaw tells the story, however, there was yet more excitement to come:

> Just as we came within sight of Jefferson Market, a man who had been on the lookout for us jumped into the front of the hansom, and, giving directions to the driver, hung on while he turned swiftly and swung in the opposite direction. When we asked him what this meant, he told us that they had decided to hold no examination that morning, and that he was trying to get us away from the camera fiends who were swarming in front of Jefferson Market. For four or five blocks excited men with cameras kept rushing out ahead of us, and in their efforts to snap-shot us were very nearly run down by the horses.

The hearing had been postponed. The new one was set for a week later, 9 November. Various legal manoeuvres and delays followed until the case finally came before the New York Court of Special Sessions on 6 July 1906, by which time charges against all but Daly and Gumpertz had been dropped.

The court proved to be enlightened, and was certainly more insightful about *Mrs Warren's Profession* than most of the New Haven and New York critics:

It appears that instead of exciting impure imagination in the mind of the spectator, that which is really excited is disgust; that the unlovely, the repellant, the disgusting in the play, are merely accessories to the main purpose of the drama, which is an attack on certain social conditions relating to the employment of women, which, the dramatist believes, as do many others with him, should be reformed.

As regards the law, the court found no evidence of criminality in "the acts of these defendants in publicly producing" the play, and Daly and Gumpertz were duly acquitted.[1]

The acquittal was the first good news Shaw had heard in the whole sorry débâcle. From the outset, Shaw had cautioned Daly about producing *Mrs Warren's Profession* without adequate preparation of the public, and then—in the light of Comstock's opposition, and so fearing, justifiably, that a fair hearing for the play would be impossible—he had expressly (but unsuccessfully) countermanded the New York performance (Laurence II, 573). Shaw subsequently witnessed the whole affair from across the Atlantic in some despair. Once battle had been joined, however, he was not averse to engaging in long-distance combat.

Shaw's participation was facilitated by the New York press—particularly *The Sun*—which was eager to get his take on events. He told readers of *The Sun* (1 November 1905) that he was "extremely proud" of *Mrs Warren's Profession*, and that the play "has made me more friends than any other work of mine, especially among women." Whose interests, Shaw wondered, were being protected by the suppression of the play? "It will be seen more and more clearly that the police, doubtless with the best intentions, are protecting not public morality but the interest of the most dangerous class, namely, the employers who pay women less than subsistence wages and overwork them mercilessly to grind profits for themselves out of the pith of the nation." Shaw later (*The Sun*, 12 November 1905) lambasted McAdoo for the "contradictions, confusions and reckless inaccuracy" of his public pronouncements on *Mrs Warren's Profession* and decried the "public scandal" of a

---

1   *Wilshire's Magazine*, August 1906, as qtd. in Laurence II, 631-32.

Catherine Countess as Vivie Warren, and Mary Shaw as Mrs Warren, Manhattan Theatre, New York, 1907.

police officer "using his reports and correspondence as copy for the newspapers and writing them accordingly in the style of the yellowest of yellow journalism."[1]

But when Daly and Gumpertz were acquitted Shaw was quick to praise the American judicial system. In response to a request from the *New York American* for a statement on the court's decision, Shaw took the opportunity to admonish the New York press—"every conceivable insult and outrage was heaped on me"—but applauded a system that allowed for due process in determining the legal status of his play: "My case has been heard and my play restored to the stage with its motives. My character and that of Mr Daly and his company has been publicly vindicated" (Laurence II, 633). *Mrs Warren's Profession* was performed again—unmolested this time—at the Manhattan Theatre in New York in March 1907, again with Mrs Warren

---

1 Shaw's cables to *The Sun* are quoted in Shaw, *The Bodley Head Bernard Shaw*, 357-62.

played by Mary Shaw, who subsequently took the play on a national tour. There were, to be sure, some tense moments on the tour—the clergy in Lincoln, Nebraska, who took exception to Vivie asking her mother to identify her father ("Isn't it a terrible thing for a girl to ask her mother who her father was?"), and two Jesuit priests in post-earthquake San Francisco demanding deletion of lines by George Crofts in Act 3 that allude to questionable church investments in property developments. But Mary Shaw kept the show on the road by a strategy of careful preparation of her audiences (through meetings, for example, with women's organizations) and appeasement (i.e. agreeing to deleting a line here and a word there).[1]

Thus it was that *Mrs Warren's Profession*, after a turbulent initiation, had a strong performance history in the United States long before it received its first public performance in England in 1925. There was a production as well in Canada (Winnipeg) many years before the English première—though the critics mauled it (see Appendix C5)—and several throughout Europe, where it was normally greeted without the moral fluster and bluster of early productions in North America.[2]

Shaw's Early Career

By 1905 Shaw was no stranger to controversy. There was little, however, in his family background or early career that hinted at how frequently during his life he would be embroiled in theatrical, intellectual, social, and political controversies big and small, profound and trivial, earnest and whimsical. Born in Dublin on 26 July 1856 to an alcoholic grain merchant father and a frustrated amateur mezzo-soprano mother, Shaw left school at fifteen to take a mundane

---

1 Shaw, "My 'Immoral Play'," 692-93.
2 A comprehensive listing of international productions of *Mrs Warren's Profession* has not yet been compiled, though several productions are mentioned in Conolly and Pearson, *passim*. French productions and criticism are discussed in Michel W. Pharand, *Bernard Shaw and the French* (Gainesville: UP of Florida, 2000), *passim*. See also Wendi Chen, "The First Shaw Play on the Chinese Stage: the Production of *Mrs Warren's Profession* in 1921," *SHAW: The Annual of Bernard Shaw Studies* 19 (1999): 99-118.

clerical position with a Dublin property agency, while in his spare time continuing to immerse himself in the many cultural amenities of Dublin—a practice he had begun as a schoolboy: the National Gallery and the Theatre Royal were among his favourite havens. He also gained a broad if somewhat unconventional musical education by attending the lessons and rehearsals of his mother's eccentric singing teacher, Vandeleur Lee; while he was still a schoolboy Shaw could recognize and sing or whistle all the principal works of Handel, Haydn, Mozart, Beethoven, Rossini, Bellini, Donizetti, and Verdi (Laurence I, 4). He also read widely and avidly (especially Shakespeare), and began experimenting as a writer himself.

New opportunities opened up for Shaw when his mother finally gave up on her husband and followed Lee to London in June 1873. Shaw stayed with his father for nearly three more years, strained though the relationship was, but at the end of March 1876 he too had had enough both of his father and of Dublin. He resigned from his job and sailed for England, arriving in London on April Fool's Day with nothing but uncertain prospects. "Here am I, in London," he wrote to his Dublin friend Edward McNulty on 3 June 1876, "without the credentials of a peasant immigrant and I still bear traces of the Shaw snobbery which considers manual work contemptible, and on no account will I enter an office again" (Laurence I, 19).

Vandeleur Lee paid Shaw to ghost-write musical criticism for him for a periodical called *The Hornet* for several months in 1876 and 1877, but later (November 1879) Shaw broke the vow he had made to McNulty and took a job in London with the Edison Telephone Company. Initially hired to persuade property owners to allow Edison to erect structures on their rooftops to support telephone wires, Shaw was later promoted to a managerial position, but shortly after Edison merged with Bell Telephone in June 1880 he resigned (Gibbs 38-39). What little income he now had came from a few articles in the press and occasional hand-outs from his father. His father also sent him a few curses as well: "You are an illnatured cur that you would not once in a way [while], say 6 or 12 months, drop me a few lines no matter whether you have anything to say or not" (Laurence I, 17). Shaw depended almost entirely on his mother, with whom he continued to live: "I did not throw myself into the struggle for life: I threw my mother into it. I was not a staff to my father's old age: I hung on his coat tails," he quipped in the preface to his novel *The Irrational Knot* (Laurence I, 17). *The Irrational Knot* was but one of five novels Shaw wrote between 1879 and 1883, all rejected—some several times—by London publishers (though all were eventually published once Shaw had established his reputation as a critic and playwright). When not writing his novels, Shaw busied himself studying French, seeing plays, gaining entrées to London society (the home of Lady Wilde, Oscar's mother, for example), falling in love, and, most importantly, reading voraciously in the library of the British Museum. It was there that Shaw first read (in a French translation) Marx's *Das Kapital*, a work that powerfully stimulated his political sensibilities, though not always in ways that Marx would have welcomed.

Shaw also actively participated in various debating clubs and literary societies in London, and in May 1884 he attended his first meeting of the Fabian Society, a socialist advocacy group formed in London earlier that year. The Fabian Society remains active in England, though its influence has waned considerably since the heady days when it counted some of England's leading writers and thinkers—H.G. Wells, Beatrice and Sydney Webb, Shaw (he joined in September 1884)—among its members. Named after Fabius Maximus (c. 260-203 BCE), a Roman general famous for his military caution, the Fabian Society was committed to radical social and political reform, but through the means of rational debate and gradual rather than revolutionary change. The society gave the young Shaw an increasingly important platform as a writer (he wrote many of the Fabian Society's famous "tracts") and orator, and helped him formulate many of the ideas that he expressed in his plays as well as in his political writings and speeches.

The year 1884, then, was significant for Shaw politically, but it was also the year in which his creative work took a new direction—from fiction to drama. The person who pointed Shaw in the new direction was someone he had first met in the British Museum, probably in the fall of 1883. His name was William

Archer (1856-1924), one of London's leading theatre critics and the translator and advocate of the Norwegian playwright Henrik Ibsen (1828-1906), whose provocative plays (*A Doll's House, Ghosts,* and *Hedda Gabler,* for example) Shaw also came to admire, champion, and, in his own way, emulate. (One of Shaw's earliest books— *The Quintessence of Ibsenism* published in 1891, but originally an 1890 lecture to the Fabian Society— is an analysis and defence of Ibsen's work.) Archer helped Shaw secure posts as music and art critic with major periodicals (the *Dramatic Review* and *The World*), but, more significantly, suggested a plot outline for the play that eventually was performed and published as *Widowers' Houses,* Shaw's first play.

Shaw worked on the play in November 1884, and returned to it periodically over the next several years, leaving it untouched, however, for long periods. By 1884, after eight years in London, his life was becoming astonishingly full and busy. He was one of London's most active critics, adding the *Pall Mall Gazette* (as literary critic) and *The Star* (as music critic, using the impressive pseudonym "Corno di Bassetto") to the publications he wrote for, and his reputation as a compelling and entertaining lecturer on political and a miscellany of other topics meant that by the mid-1880s he was giving a hundred or so lectures a year in London and the provinces. He took part in political demonstrations, he travelled in Europe, he wrote pamphlets for the Fabian Society (and edited *Fabian Essays in Socialism,* 1889), he met writers (Oscar Wilde, William Butler Yeats), he went to the theatre, and he pursued and fended off women—young and not-so-young, single, married, and widowed. By 1891 Shaw had become, as Dan Laurence (I, 106) puts it, "something of a celebrity." "Everybody in London knows Shaw," said the *Sunday World*: "Fabian, Socialist, art and musical critic, vegetarian, ascetic, humourist, artist to the tips of his fingers, man of the people to the tips of his boots. The most original and inspiring of men—fiercely uncompromising, full of ideas, irrepressibly brilliant—an Irishman" (qtd. in Laurence I, 106-107).

No wonder Shaw found little time for finishing *Widowers' Houses.* But in late July 1892 he returned to it, and by the end of October it was completed. The incentive to return to—and finish— *Widowers' Houses* was provided by the formation in 1891 in London of an organization called the Independent Theatre Society, of which Shaw— always eager to join a club or society of like-minded individuals— was a founding member. Headed by a Dutch-born critic and playwright named Jacob Thomas Grein (1862-1935), the Independent Theatre Society was established to produce plays that because of their experimental or avant-garde nature, or because they dealt with sensitive political or social issues, had little chance of being accepted by managers of commercial theatres. As Shaw pointed out in his preface to Archer's *The Theatrical 'World' of 1894*, the reality of London theatre was that it was dominated and controlled by actor-managers such as Henry Irving (1838-1905) at the Lyceum Theatre, Beerbohm Tree (1853-1917) at the Haymarket, and Charles Wyndham (1837-1919) at the Criterion, all of whom tended to select plays on the basis of a good leading part for themselves and the expectation of solid financial returns. Unless, Shaw calculated, "a London manager sees some probability of from 50,000 to 75,000 people paying him an average five shillings apiece within three months, he will hardly be persuaded to venture."[1]

The Independent Theatre, however, was not constrained by the commercial considerations of a large theatre organization, or by the necessity of satisfying the egos of prominent actor-managers. Moreover, as a private club, whose productions were open to members only, it was not subject to Britain's censorship laws (see below, pp. 53-54), and thus could produce plays that had been denied a licence for public performance, or, on account of their subject matter, stood little or no chance of receiving the necessary licence. Thus it was that the first production of the Independent Theatre Society was Ibsen's *Ghosts*, a play about social and family diseases, symbolic and literal— including venereal disease, a subject that guaranteed the play's inadmissibility to Britain's public theatres. In a translation by William Archer, *Ghosts* was

---

1 William Archer, *The Theatrical 'World' of 1894* (London: Walter Scott, 1895) xix. Irving, Tree, and Wyndham were all knighted for their services to theatre (beginning with Irving in 1895), an indication of the acceptability of their theatrical values to royalty and government. See George Rowell, *Theatre in the Age of Irving* (Oxford: Blackwell, 1981) for an introduction to the theatre of this period.

produced by the Independent Theatre Society at the Royalty Theatre, Soho, on 13 March 1891.[1] Shaw was in the audience and wrote to Archer that he found the evening "simply a tremendous success" (Laurence I, 285). But in that same letter (14 March 1891) Shaw also predicted that "the gloves will be off" among the critics who attended the performance. He was right. In an article called *"Ghosts* and Gibberings" *(Pall Mall Gazette*, 8 April 1891, qtd. in Egan 209-14) Archer himself provided a summary of the critical abuse hurled at Ibsen and his play: "An open drain: a loathsome sore unbandaged; a dirty act done publicly.... Absolutely loathsome and fetid.... Gross, almost putrid indecorum" *(Daily Telegraph)*; "Revoltingly suggestive and blasphemous" *(Daily Chronicle)*; "putrid" *(Academy)*; "As foul and filthy a concoction as has ever been allowed to disgrace the boards of an English theatre" *(Era)*.

That was the kind of stormy arena that Shaw found irresistible, and when Grein told Shaw that he would welcome a new play by a British playwright for his second season of plays at the Independent Theatre Shaw jumped at the opportunity and quickly provided him with the manuscript of *Widowers' Houses*. Grein promptly accepted it, and the play opened at the Royalty Theatre on 9 December 1892, followed by a second (matinée) performance on 13 December 1892.

Widowers' Houses defined the kind of playwright Shaw wanted to be — at least in the early years of his playwriting career — and the reaction of the critics to the play heralded the kind of hostility that would dog Shaw for much of his career. Structured as a social comedy, with deliberately conventional stock characters and a happy ending (the marriage of a young couple after apparently insurmountable obstacles have been overcome to the satisfaction of all concerned), *Widowers' Houses* undermines convention by tackling an ugly and pervasive social problem head on. Drawing on his first-hand knowledge of the slums of Dublin (including collecting rents from slum residents), and reflecting his resolute political convictions, Shaw denounces in *Widowers' Houses* the iniquities of slum housing, not by showing the slums and their

---

1   The Royalty Theatre was a rented venue; the Independent Theatre Society did not have its own theatre.

tenants, but by exposing the moral sophistry and corruption of the beneficiaries of slum housing—the middle-class landlords, the upper-class holders of mortgages on slum properties, and even a working-class former rent collector turned property owner. Or, as Shaw himself put it, "I have shewn middle-class respectability and younger son gentility fattening on the poverty of the slum as flies fatten on filth" (see Appendix A1).

While this "topical lecture" and "homily" might elicit a sympathetic reaction on moral or social grounds, *Widowers' Houses* was not, according to the anonymous critic of the *Daily Telegraph*, much of a play, its plot unconvincing and its characters simply Shaw's "puppets" (10 December 1892, qtd. in Evans 41-44). William Archer, too, was disappointed with what Shaw had made of his original suggestion for the play. The lovers, said Archer, are "not human beings at all," Shaw's middle-classes are "strangely bloodless," his world has "no breath of humanity" (*The World*, 14 December 1892, qtd. in Holroyd I, 284). And some members of the audience on that opening night at the Royalty Theatre weren't too taken with the play either—hissing their disapproval. Shaw took to the stage at the end of the play to confront them, and, to his own way of thinking at least, convinced them that *Widowers' Houses* deserved their approval: "I have appeared before the curtain amid transcendent hooting & retired amid cheers," he wrote to fellow Fabian and actor-manager Charles Charrington (1860?-1926) on 14 December 1892 (Laurence I, 372). In his letter Shaw also praised theatre critic Moy Thomas (1828-1910), whose review in the *Daily News* (10 December 1892, qtd. in Evans 45) argued that *Widowers' Houses* "exhibits many of the qualities which go to the making of a dramatist of the first rank," and that "those who infer that this is only a Fabian pamphlet or a succession of Socialistic tirades and rhetorical speeches, uttered by mere abstractions attired in human clothing, will fall into a great mistake." The critical debate about Shaw—a maker of puppets who spout, often tediously, his theories, or a creator of vibrant and complex characters who *live* his ideas—continued to his death, and much beyond.

Widowers' Houses was published in May 1893, but did not receive its public première until a production on 7 October 1907 at the Midland Theatre in Manchester. By then, Shaw had completed some of his best and most enduring plays: *The Philanderer, Arms and the Man, The Man of Destiny, Candida, You Never Can Tell, The Devil's Disciple, Caesar and Cleopatra, Man and Superman, John Bull's Other Island, Major Barbara,* and *The Doctor's Dilemma* among them[1]—a range, quality, and volume of work unmatched by any of his theatrical contemporaries. And with productions in Europe and the United Sates as well as London and the English provinces, Shaw's reputation was now international. And while playwriting had become Shaw's major preoccupation (and a source of significant income), it could hardly be said that he had retired from other interests: writing criticism, supporting lost causes (such as Oscar Wilde during his trial and imprisonment for gross indecency in 1895), meeting and marrying (in 1898) Irish heiress Charlotte Payne-Townshend, learning to ride a bicycle (and having a collision with Bertrand Russell), cruising on the *Lusitania* long before it gained notoriety when sunk by a German U-boat in 1915, being elected to the St Pancras Borough Council in 1897 and defeated when running for election to the London County Council in 1904, advocating women's rights, writing for and arguing with the Fabians, travelling in Europe, sitting for a bust by French sculptor Auguste Rodin in 1906, and almost drowning while swimming off the coast of Wales in 1907.

And by 1907 Shaw had also long since completed *Mrs Warren's Profession,* his third play,[2] written between 20 August and 2 November 1893 (Holroyd I, 291-93).

---

1 See the Chronology (pp. 75-78) for the dates of these plays. Productions of several of them at the Court Theatre in London under the management of Harley Granville Barker (1877-1946) and J.E. Vedrenne (1867-1930) established Shaw's reputation as a leading playwright. Between 1904 and 1907 eleven Shaw plays were mounted at the Court for a total of 701 performances.

2 Shaw's second play, *The Philanderer,* was written in 1893. Described by Shaw as a "topical comedy," the play exposes "the grotesque sexual compacts made between men and women under marriage laws which represent to some of us a political necessity (especially for other people), to some a divine ordinance, to some a romantic ideal, to some a domestic profession for women, and to some that worst of blundering abominations, an institution which society has outgrown but not modified, and which 'advanced' individuals are therefore forced to evade" (Shaw, *The Bodley Head Bernard Shaw,* 19, 33).

From Slums to Prostitutes

As with the situation in *Widowers' Houses*, Shaw had some hands-on (as it were) experience to draw on in writing about prostitution, the subject (or one of them) of *Mrs Warren's Profession*. He was once accosted by a prostitute while walking in central London in the early hours of the morning: "she attached herself so devotedly to me," Shaw said, "that I could not without actual violence shake her off. At last I made a stand at the end of Old Bond Street. I took out my purse; opened it; and held it upside down. Her countenance fell, poor girl! She turned on her heel with a melancholy flirt of her skirt, and vanished."[1] And during his term as an elected member of the St Pancras Borough Council (1897-1903) Shaw became aware that in the borough there were "long sections of main streets in which almost every house was a brothel."[2] That prostitution, like slum housing, was a major social concern in late Victorian society is evident from the extensive press coverage (often of court cases involving prostitutes and brothel keepers) and a large number of surveys and studies, some of which attempted to calculate the number of prostitutes working in London and the provinces. Some estimates put the number of prostitutes in Victorian London at about 80,000, while the respected medical journal, the *Lancet*, estimated in 1857 that one in sixty houses in London was a brothel and one in every sixteen females was a prostitute (Pearl 36). Police evidence presented in 1881 to a Parliamentary committee suggested that daytime solicitation in central London was common, while at night some 500 prostitutes were active in the area of Piccadilly Circus (Innes 200). Figures such as these were often speculative, but they reflect what one social historian has described as "the frustration deeply felt in the face of a social problem seemingly of

---

1 From the preface to Shaw's second novel, *The Irrational Knot* (1905), xvi. Shaw was probably referring to this incident (and perhaps similar ones) in a long letter he wrote in support of a 1917 petition to remove the ban in England on public performances of *Mrs Warren's Profession*: "I became familiar not only with the mask of affection, but with the cynical frankness with which it is dropped when it is no use." The letter is printed in full in Conolly 69-71.

2 Bernard Shaw, "The Unmentionable Case for Women's Suffrage," *The Englishwoman*, 1:2 (March 1909): 120.

Max Beerbohm, "The Iconoclast's One Friend" (c. 1902). "*A Member of Mrs Warren's Profession*: 'Mr Shaw, I have long wished to meet you and grasp you by the hand... God bless you!... I understand that the Army and Navy, the Church, the Stage, the Bar, the Faculty, the Literary Gents, the Nobility and Gentry, and all the Royal Family, will have nothing more to do with you. Never mind! *My* house will always be open to you.' (*Exit, dashing away a tear.*)" Courtesy Burgunder Collection, Cornell University Library.

intractable size and unmalleable character" (Nield [3]).[1] There was as much disagreement about the causes of prostitution as there was about the numbers of prostitutes, and there were many debates and arguments about what to do to alleviate the problem. For perhaps a majority of Victorian social reformers prostitution was a moral issue. Hence William Acton's definition of a prostitute:

> She is a woman with half the woman gone, and the half containing all that elevates her nature, leaving her a mere instrument of impurity; degraded and fallen she extracts from the sins of others the means of living, corrupt and dependent on corruption, and therefore interested directly in the increase of immorality — a social pest, carrying contamination and foulness to every quarter to which she has access.... (Appendix D4)

In so far as prostitutes were perceived as "fallen" or "corrupt," the appropriate response was punishment. While prostitution itself was not illegal in Victorian England, legislation such as the Contagious Diseases Acts of 1864, 1866, and 1869 enabled magistrates to order the medical examination of women suspected by the police of being infected with venereal disease. Any women found to be infected could be detained in a locked hospital ward for treatment.[2] Prostitutes could also be prosecuted — and frequently were — as "vagrants" under the 1824 Vagrancy Act; under this and other legislation 7,537 prosecutions were recorded in England in 1896 (Bartley 2).[3] A more compassionate attitude was taken by organisations such as

---

1 There is a concise summary of some statistical data in Nelson 358-59.
2 The rationale for the Contagious Diseases Acts was the widespread occurrence of venereal disease among military personnel stationed in Britain's garrison towns. It was estimated that about 20% of the army was infected in any given year (Nield [5]). The blatant discrimination against women in such legislation — men faced no similar constraints — was recognised (under pressure from reformers such as Josephine Butler [1828-1906] and her Ladies National Association) by government repeal of the Acts in 1886. See Paul McHugh, *Prostitution and Victorian Social Reform* (London: Croom Helm, 1980) for a comprehensive discussion of the Contagious Diseases Acts and the successful efforts of Butler and others to repeal them.
3 Bartley (202) provides a useful summary of Victorian legislation to control prostitution. See also Fisher 80-94, 112-37.

the Salvation Army, whose "rescue homes" provided shelter and support for women whose foray into prostitution had led only to destitution and helplessness (see Appendix D7).

Prostitutes also had a measure of protection against procurers and brothel keepers under legislation such as the 1885 Criminal Law Amendment Act, which allowed for fines and prison terms (with or without hard labour), including, in some cases (e.g. procurement of girls under thirteen years of age) life imprisonment (see Appendix D6). The 1885 act also made it a criminal offence to "procure any woman or girl to leave the United Kingdom, with intent that she may become an inmate of a brothel elsewhere," but the law did little to slow down the "White Slave Trade" that lured women and girls into European brothels, where they were rarely treated as benevolently as Mrs Warren's employees (see Appendix D5).

For Shaw, however, punishment, succour, and legal intervention were ineffective ways of dealing with prostitution. It was necessary, he argued, to identify and respond to the root causes of prostitution, causes that had much more to do with economics than with morality. Victorian social reformers identified many causes of prostitution—moral turpitude, alcohol, seduction, sexual abuse, poverty[1]—but for Shaw the "fundamental condition of the existence of this traffic is that society must be so organized that a large class of women are more highly paid and better treated as prostitutes than they would be as respectable women."[2] Responsibility for prostitution, in Shaw's view, lay not with any particular segment of society—and certainly not with the

---

1 The *Encyclopaedia Britannica*, 11th ed. (1910-11), identified the following causes of prostitution: "difficulty of finding employment; excessively laborious and ill-paid work; harsh treatment of girls at home; promiscuous and indecent mode of living among the overcrowded poor; the aggregation of people together in large communities and factories, whereby the young are brought into constant contact with demoralized companions; the example of luxury, self-indulgence and loose manners set by the wealthier classes; demoralizing literature and amusements; the arts of profligate men and their agents" (vol. 22, p. 458).

2 All quotations from Shaw in this paragraph are from his essay "The Root of the White Slave Traffic," *Fabian Feminist. Bernard Shaw and Woman*, ed. Rodelle Weintraub (University Park: Penn State UP, 1977) 255-59. The essay was first published in *The Awakener*, November 1912.

prostitutes themselves—but with society as a whole, particularly those whose perceived respectability appeared to distance them from such sordid matters: "ladies and gentlemen, clergymen, bishops, judges, Members of Parliament, highly connected ladies leading society in Cathedral towns, peers and peeresses, and pillars of solid middle-class Puritanism." The connection between such people and prostitution was that they supported and profited from "industrial enterprises which employ women and girls ... [on] wages which are insufficient to support them." Most young working-class women are "saved from the streets" by husbands or parents, but "there are always orphans and widows and girls from the country and abroad who have no families and no husbands; and these must submit to the blackest misery that a slum garret and an income of from eighteenpence to a shilling a day can bring to a lonely, despised, shabby, dirty, underfed woman, or else add to their wages by prostitution."

Evidence provided by working-class women themselves amply supports Shaw's contention. A young woman trying to support her elderly widowed mother and herself in the 1840s on earnings of less than ten shillings a week reported that "not one young girl that works at slop work [i.e. in clothes manufacturing] ... is virtuous, and there are some thousands in the trade." With mothers and fathers to support them, "they may be virtuous, but not without," she said. "I've heard of numbers who have gone from slop work to the streets altogether for a living, and I shall be obliged to do the same thing myself unless something better turns up for me" (Appendix D1). Even William Acton's harsh moral condemnation of prostitutes (above, 30) did not blind him to the fact that many women were driven into the profession "by cruel biting poverty." "It is," he wrote, "a shameful fact, but no less true, that the lowness of wages paid to workwomen in various trades is a fruitful source of prostitution: unable to obtain by their labour the means of procuring the bare necessities of life, they gain, by surrendering their bodies to evil uses, food to sustain and clothes to cover them" (Appendix D4). Whereas a wage of ten shillings a week scarcely bought these "bare necessities" (see Appendix D8 for basic living costs), an income of twenty to thirty pounds a week (fifty or sixty times higher) was achievable by many prostitutes (Laurence, "Victorians Unveiled," 39).[1]

Few can escape responsibility, Shaw charged, for sustaining the conditions of intolerably low pay for women in manufacturing and service industries: "The wages of prostitution are stitched into your buttonholes and into your blouse, pasted into your matchboxes and your boxes of pins, stuffed into your mattress, mixed with paint on your walls,[2] and stuck between the joints of your water-pipes." "There is," Shaw concluded, "one remedy, and one alone" for prostitution: "Make it impossible, by the enactment of a Minimum Wage law and by proper provision for the unemployed, for any woman to be forced to choose between prostitution and penury, and the White Slaver [i.e. procurers and brothel keepers] will have no more power over the daughters of laborers, artisans, and clerks than he ... has over the wives of bishops."

Shaw was much ahead of his time—as he was in so many things—in advocating a minimum wage and unemployment benefits (especially for women). He was not quite so alone in his conviction that there was a firm link between prostitution and the economic plight of many working women,[3] but no-one in late-

---

1   The economic causes of prostitution were stressed again by Shaw in *Everybody's Political What's What?* (London: Constable, 1944) where he defined prostitution as "an economic phenomenon produced by an underpayment of honest women so degrading, and an overpayment of whores so luxurious, that a poor woman of any attractiveness actually owed it to her self-respect to sell herself in the streets rather than toil miserably in a sweater's den sixteen hours a day for twopence an hour, or risk phosphorous poisoning in a match factory for five shillings a week, or the like" (196). "It is easy," Shaw also pointed out, "to ask a woman to be virtuous; but it is not reasonable if the penalty of virtue be starvation, and the reward of vice immediate relief" (*The Intelligent Woman's Guide to Socialism and Capitalism* [New York: Brentano's, 1928] 199).

2   One of Mrs Warren's half-sisters has died from lead poisoning caused by working in a paint factory (Act 2). See Appendices D1, D3, and D8 for accounts of working conditions and incomes for women in Victorian England.

3   See, for example, comments by James Miller (Appendix D2) and William Booth (Appendix D7), though neither Miller nor Booth is as emphatic as Shaw on the issue. In his 1929 novel *The Midnight Bell* (London: Constable), Patrick Hamilton has one prostitute ask another, "Jever hear of Bernard Shaw?" "Yes," is the reply, "I've heard of him. He's one of them Great Writers, ain't he?" "Yes. Well, he wrote a book called *Mrs Warren's Profession*—an' showed it was all economics." There is a pause. "Well," is the response, "I guess he was just about *right*." (Courtesy Alan Andrews.)

Victorian England could match the audacious and provocative way in which Shaw chose to make this point to the British public.

The Drama of Prostitution

Shaw explained in a letter to the *Daily Chronicle* (30 April 1898, qtd. in Bullough 340) that Janet Achurch[1] once told him the plot of Guy de Maupassant's 1885 short story, *Yvette*. After hearing it, Shaw determined to "work out the real truth about that mother some day." The mother in question in the Maupassant story is a courtesan whose eighteen-year old daughter, appalled by the discovery of her mother's profession, attempts (unsuccessfully — she is revived by her paramour) to commit suicide by a drug overdose. At Shaw's suggestion, Achurch herself adapted *Yvette* for the stage. Her version, *Mrs Daintree's Daughter*, was performed in Manchester in May 1903, but she followed (again at Shaw's suggestion) "the original romantic lines" of what Shaw described as an "ultra-romantic" story (*Daily Chronicle*, 30 April 1898).[2] Shaw's own disposition was towards something less conventional than other contemporary portrayals of prostitutes and courtesans — portrayals, for instance, such as those in two plays that opened in London in May 1893, just a few weeks before Shaw began to write *Mrs Warren's Profession*.

The two plays were an adaptation of *La Dame aux Camélias*, an 1848 novel by Alexandre Dumas *fils* (1824-95), and a new play by the popular British playwright Arthur Wing Pinero (1855-1934), *The Second Mrs Tanqueray*.[3] The "dame" of *La Dame aux Camélias*, Marguerite Gautier, is a Parisian courtesan (with a passion for camellias) who begins a new life in the country with her lover, only to abandon him (under pressure from his outraged father)

---

1 Achurch (1864-1916) was a leading actor of her time, praised by Shaw for her Ibsen roles. She played Candida in the first public production of *Candida* in 1897.

2 *Mrs Daintree's Daughter* was not published, but there is a summary (from the manuscript text in the Lord Chamberlain's Papers in the British Library) in Bullough 350-55.

3 *La Dame aux Camélias*, starring the famous Italian actress Eleonora Duse (1858-1924), opened at the Lyric Theatre on 24 May 1893. *The Second Mrs Tanqueray*, starring Mrs Patrick Campbell (1865-1940) — subsequently to have an intimate relationship with Shaw and to play Eliza in the British première of *Pygmalion* in 1914 — opened at St James's Theatre on 27 May 1893.

because she believes that her reputation from her former life is an insurmountable obstacle to their happiness. A consumptive, Marguerite dies in her lover's arms after he locates her again in Paris.

In Pinero's play, Paula Tanqueray, after a promiscuous past with a series of well-off and socially well-placed lovers, has given up her profession to become the second wife of the respected and respectable Aubrey Tanqueray. Tanqueray is aware of his new wife's past, though his daughter, Ellean, from his first marriage is not. When one of Mrs Tanqueray's former lovers—ignorant through absence abroad of her new situation in life—falls in love with Ellean, Mrs Tanqueray feels bound to identify him to her husband and stepdaughter. The only resolution to the ensuing domestic crisis, Paula concludes, is suicide, which she dutifully and discreetly commits (by means unspecified) in the privacy of her bedroom.

The issue, then, in late-Victorian England, was not so much whether prostitution and promiscuity should be presented on stage, but *how* they should be presented. Public performances of plays such as *La Dame aux Camélias* and *The Second Mrs Tanqueray* were accepted and welcomed because they presented the more glamorous side of prostitution (neither Marguerite Gautier nor Paula Tanqueray were ever common streetwalkers such as the one encountered by Shaw) and because, most importantly, they showed *repentant* prostitutes. Marguerite and Paula are remorseful and contrite for their past, and they both pay with their lives for their transgressions. Victorian audiences could leave the theatre reassured that all was well in the moral order: the wages of sin are, indeed, death (Romans 6.23). As Shaw put it, "members of Mrs Warren's profession shall be tolerated on the stage only when they are beautiful, exquisitely dressed, and sumptuously lodged and fed," and at the end of the play they are expected to "die of consumption to the sympathetic tears of the whole audience, or step into the next room to commit suicide, or at least be turned out by their protectors and passed on to be 'redeemed' by old and faithful lovers who have adored them in spite of all their levities" (Shaw, "Author's Apology" x–xi).

This kind of approach did not sit at all well with Shaw,

especially as he witnessed it in *The Second Mrs Tanqueray*, which he read (in a privately printed edition) in August 1893 (Gibbs 111) and saw at St James's Theatre on 11 December that year (Gibbs 113). He read the play again when it was published (1894) in his capacity as theatre critic for the *Saturday Review* (a position he held from January 1895 to May 1898). In his review (23 February 1895) Shaw criticized Pinero for failing to rise above "the conventional system of morals." Pinero, he said, "is no interpreter of character, but simply an adroit describer of people as the ordinary man sees and judges them."

By the time that Shaw wrote this review, he had completed his own take on prostitution, initially prompted to do so both by Janet Achurch's account of Maupassant's *Yvette* (above) and by a suggestion from his Fabian colleague Beatrice Webb (1858-1943) that he "put on the stage a real modern lady of the governing class—not the sort of thing that the theatrical and critical authorities imagine such a lady to be" (*Daily Chronicle*, 30 April 1898). The "real modern lady" emerged as Vivie Warren, Mrs Warren's daughter, but Shaw also acknowledged—in a letter to William Archer on 30 August 1893—the influence of *The Second Mrs Tanqueray*.[1] Both plays turn on a daughter's (stepdaughter's in Pinero's case) shocking discovery of a hitherto hidden and unsuspected aspect of her mother's life, but Shaw's Mrs Warren is far less obliging than Pinero's Mrs Tanqueray in acquiescing in conventional morality.

A Play for Women

In his preface to *Mrs Warren's Profession*, Shaw stresses that the play is "for women ... written for women" (Appendix A2). It is also a play *about* women, about women in general and about two women in particular. Kitty Warren and her daughter Vivie share a commanding

---

1   Laurence I, 403. In the same letter Shaw also acknowledges the influence of Shelley's play *The Cenci*, published in 1819, but not performed (in a private production by the Shelley Society) until 1886. The incestuous father-daughter relationship in the play caused it to be banned from public theatres in England until 1922 (Johnston 75-76). The connection between *The Cenci* and *Mrs Warren's Profession* arises from the potential incestuous relationship between Vivie and Frank (Act 3).

presence in the play, albeit outnumbered four to two by male characters. There is nothing very subtle or complex about the male characters, but they serve their purpose both in helping to move the plot along and, more importantly, in representing values that reveal how complicit the middle-classes are in condoning—through ignorance, indifference, or exploitation—the problems that drove Mrs Warren into prostitution.

The origins of the friendship between Praed (the first man we encounter in the play) and Mrs Warren are left fuzzy by Shaw, but Praed's unwillingness to see or talk about anything beyond the "Gospel of Art" (149)[1] makes clear enough the aesthete's irrelevance both to the ugliness of Mrs Warren's world and to the realities of the professional world that Vivie chooses to embrace. The bumbling, hapless Reverend Samuel is a comic turn who would rather forget and ignore the consequences of his fling with Mrs Warren—just as, Shaw seems to be suggesting, the church generally would rather not be reminded of the source of some of its property revenues (see, for example, Crofts' comments to Vivie in Act 3 [139]). The "old stick-in-the-mud" Gardner (see Appendix A2), says Shaw, also serves as a "mordant contrast" with the entrepreneurial Mrs Warren, while his son Frank—idle, dissolute, irresponsible, and supportive of Vivie only so far as his own self-interest is at stake—is, as Shaw succinctly puts it, "a cynically worthless member of society" (Appendix A2).

Crofts is as one-dimensional as the other male characters, but he has a more prominent role in the play than the others, featuring centrally in several conversations, particularly the crucial one with Vivie in Act 3 in which he attempts to buy her in marriage. Vivie flatly rejects his calculating appeal to her pecuniary self-interest, but the conversation gives Shaw the opportunity to expose the capitalist values that both cause and sustain prostitution. For Crofts, the only criterion for a business investment is the financial return. "If you are going to pick and choose your acquaintances on moral principles," he tells Vivie, "youd[2] better clear out of this

---

1   Page references are to the text of the play in this edition.
2   Shaw often omits the apostrophe in contractions such as "youd", "dont", "Ive", and "doesnt". See A Note on the Text (below, p. 80).

country, unless you want to cut yourself out of all decent society" (140). It is this "decent society" that allows Crofts' brother, a Member of Parliament (he doesn't appear in the play), to earn a 22% return on his investment in "a factory with 600 girls in it, and not one of them getting wages enough to live on" (139), while Crofts himself makes a handsome 35% from his investment in Mrs Warren's brothels. "As long as you dont fly openly in the face of society, society doesnt ask any inconvenient questions," he explains (140).

Crofts' problem with Vivie is that she *does* ask inconvenient questions, and she doesn't like the answers. She also asks many inconvenient questions of her mother, the redoubtable Kitty Warren, and it is those questions—and Mrs Warren's answers—that supply the play's intellectual core as well as its dramatic tension.

Kitty Warren

There is no overt recognition in either *La Dame aux Camélias* or *The Second Mrs Tanqueray* of prostitution as a social problem. Having set his direction as a playwright (and as a socialist) with *Widowers' Houses* and *The Philanderer*, it is not surprising that Shaw should want to go beyond Dumas and Pinero and examine the social and economic as well as personal and domestic ramifications of prostitution in *Mrs Warren's Profession*. His principal vehicle for doing so is Kitty Warren.

Margaret Rhondda, Viscountess of Llanwern (Lady Rhondda, 1883-1958), a leading feminist and political commentator, said in 1930 that "of all the men who have written during the past thirty or forty years, Shaw has undoubtedly come nearest to drawing flesh-and-blood women with real reactions and real individualities."[1] This worthwhile rebuke to those who insist on dismissing Shaw's characters as mere mouthpieces for his ideas is particularly relevant to Kitty Warren.

Our first impressions of Mrs Warren are predominantly unsympathetic. "*Rather spoilt and domineering, and decidedly vulgar,*

---

1 "The Shavian Everywoman," *Time and Tide* (14 March 1930): 331.

but, on the whole, a genial and fairly presentable old blackguard of a woman," is how Shaw introduces her (95), and her behaviour bears out much of this description. A largely absentee mother, she has attended to her daughter's material and educational needs, but she takes exception to Praed's suggestion that she should treat Vivie with respect ("Treat my own daughter with respect! What next, pray!" [97]). She soon demonstrates this lack of respect by unilaterally rejecting Frank as Vivie's suitor when she discovers he doesn't have any money (110), her concern about money overriding the objections of Crofts and the Reverend Samuel to Frank's courtship of Vivie, both Crofts and Gardner suspecting that Frank and Vivie might be half-siblings. A bossy, blowsy woman, Mrs Warren can, nonetheless, indulge in bouts of self-pity when the going gets emotionally tough, as it does when Vivie starts asking awkward questions about her mother's past ("Who are you? What are you?" [119]). Lear-like, Mrs Warren starts uttering empty threats ("Take care. I shall do something I'll be sorry for after, and you too" [119])[1] as Vivie pursues the subject, but then she tries to take shelter in whimpering and (Shaw's stage direction) *"throwing herself on her knees"* (119).

At this stage (early in Act 2) there have been a number of hints of Mrs Warren's sexual proclivities, personal and professional. In Act 1 (95) Praed starts to explain to Vivie something "very difficult" about her mother, but is interrupted by the arrival of Mrs Warren and Crofts; shortly afterwards Crofts and Praed discuss the mystery of the identity of Vivie's father ("for all I know *I* might be her father," says Crofts [98]); we know by the end of Act 1 that Kitty Warren (then known as "Miss Vavasour") and the Reverend Samuel have had a sexual relationship; and at the beginning of Act 2 a flirtatious conversation between Mrs Warren and Frank ends with Mrs Warren kissing him, her dismissal of it as "a motherly kiss" (107) fooling neither of them (nor the audience). But only in the crucial conversation with Vivie later in Act 2

---

1   See Lear's threat to his daughters Regan and Goneril: "I will do such things—/ What they are, yet I know not; but they shall be/The terrors of the earth!" (2.4.275-77). John Bertolini has drawn interesting parallels between Mrs Warren and Lear; see his introduction to *Man and Superman and Three Other Plays* (New York: Barnes & Noble, 2004) xviii-xxv.

(from where Frank leaves them alone [117] to the end of the act) does the nature of Mrs Warren's profession become clear. When Mrs Warren vehemently denies that George Crofts is Vivie's father ("I'm certain of that, at least" [120]), she inadvertently reveals her past promiscuity, and that's enough for Vivie to want to put an end to the conversation and go to bed. Mrs Warren, however, then takes the initiative, and demands that Vivie hear more about the circumstances of her upbringing. In the course of this long and gripping explanation both the audience and Vivie come to a full (and now sympathetic) understanding of Kitty Warren's past, and Shaw succeeds brilliantly—without ever using the words "prostitute," "prostitution," or "brothel"—in highlighting poverty as a major cause of prostitution in England.

One of four children, Kitty Warren has witnessed the contrasting fates of her two "respectable" half-sisters, one dying of lead poisoning after working in a paint factory twelve hours a day for nine shillings a week, the other raising three children on eighteen shillings a week until her husband "took to drink" (122).[1] Kitty herself has had a series of menial and ill-paying jobs, including "fourteen hours a day serving drinks and washing glasses for four shillings a week and my board" in a bar at Waterloo station (123). It is while working here that she is visited by her sister, Lizzie, dressed in "a long fur cloak, elegant and comfortable, with a lot of sovereigns in her purse" (123). While still at school, Lizzie "went out one night and never came back" (122), and is now saving money to open a brothel in Brussels. Declaring her sister a "little fool" for "wearing out your health and your appearance for other people's profit" (123), Lizzie loans Kitty money to set herself up in business, and Kitty eventually makes enough money "pleasing men" to pay back Lizzie and become her partner in Brussels.

Although Mrs Warren apparently treats her employees in Brussels well ("a much better place for a woman to be in," she says, "than the factory where Anne Jane got poisoned" [124]),[2]

---

1   See a Note on British Currency (below, p. 79) and Appendices D1 and D8 for some sense of the value of nine shillings and eighteen shillings a week.

2   Brothels were illegal in England (see Appendix D6), but not in most continental countries. And while Mrs Warren may have been a benevolent employer, most owners and managers of European brothels were not (see Appendix D5.)

she (and, of course, Shaw) doesn't gloss over the sordidness of prostitution: "Ive often pitied a poor girl, tired out and in low spirits, having to try to please some man that she doesnt care two straws for—some half-drunken fool that thinks he's making himself agreeable when he's teasing and worrying and disgusting a woman so that hardly any money could pay her for putting up with it" (125). The point, however, of *Mrs Warren's Profession* is not to stress what for Shaw was obvious—that prostitution is a squalid and degrading business—but that prostitution is made necessary by an economic structure that undervalues and underpays work done by women.[1] For a "poor girl," Mrs Warren points out to Vivie, prostitution is "far better than any other employment open to her." Mrs Warren has always thought, she continues, that "that oughtnt to be": "It c a n t[2] be right, Vivie, that there shouldnt be better opportunities for women. I stick to that: it's wrong. But it's so, right or wrong; and a girl must make the best of it" (125). And making the best of it is also (paradoxically so, it might at first appear) an issue of self-respect, for "How could you keep your self-respect in ... starvation and slavery? And whats a woman worth? whats life worth? without self-respect!" (125).

Mrs Warren's position is not an argument *in favour* of prostitution. Shaw explains in his preface that the case she makes "is no defence at all of the vice which she organizes." "It is no defence of an immoral life," he says, "to say that the alternative offered by society collectively to poor women is a miserable life, starved, overworked, fetid, ailing, ugly." While he defends Mrs Warren's choice of "the least immoral alternative," it is "none the less infamous of society to offer such alternatives," for "the alternatives offered are not morality and immorality, but two sorts

---

1   Germaine Greer misses the point when she criticizes Shaw for not revealing "the whole or any part of the truth about a way of life beset by police persecution, illness, exploitation by pimps and protection rackets, clients who exact humiliating and painful liberties and then refuse to pay, landlords who rack-rent to the trade, and the prostitutes' own guilt and shame" (Greer 165). Apart from the constraints of censorship on what could be openly shown and discussed in the theatre about prostitution, Shaw quite deliberately focuses on the *causes* of prostitution.

2   The spacing between the letters is Shaw's way of indicating a stress on the word. See A Note on the Text (p. 80).

of immorality." For Shaw, "starvation, overwork, dirt, and disease are as anti-social as prostitution ... they are the vices and crimes of a nation, and not merely its misfortune" (Appendix A2).

Vivie has remained largely silent during her mother's revelations and explanations, but by the end of them she is totally convinced of the appropriateness—the inevitability almost—of Mrs Warren's chosen direction, calling her "a wonderful woman: stronger than all England" (126). It remains only for Mrs Warren to dismiss any notion that she is ashamed of her profession, and then Vivie, after admiring the "*radiance of the harvest moon*," bids goodnight, with a kiss, to her "dear old mother" and Act 2 ends.

Where next? A rapprochement has been reached between mother and daughter, and, through Kitty Warren, Shaw has forcefully made his point about the economic causes of prostitution. Vivie doesn't seem concerned any more about the identity of her father, and the only potential plot development seems to lie with Vivie's choice of a husband—Frank or Crofts (or neither), with maybe a bit more fun at the bumbling rector's expense. The prospect of two acts of light romantic comedy to finish off the play is perhaps attractive enough to bring the audience back after an intermission (which is normally taken at this point), but it's not exactly a gripping prospect, and it's not, happily, what Shaw has in mind.

The most significant revelation in the second half of the play is that Mrs Warren, despite now being comfortably off, has continued to manage a chain of brothels in Europe. It was Vivie's (unspoken) assumption that her mother, like her aunt Lizzie, had retired—Lizzie, Mrs Warren has told Vivie, is living in Winchester, "one of the most respectable ladies there" (123). Vivie has come to terms with her mother's past partly because of the compelling explanation provided by Mrs Warren, and partly because it is the *past*. When Vivie discovers that Mrs Warren's past is also her present, her perceptions and her judgement of her mother are turned upside down. And so are the audience's. Thus it is that Mrs Warren transcends the role of Shaw's mouthpiece and becomes, as Lady Rhondda put it, one of those "flesh-and-blood women with real reactions and real individualities."

The new information about Mrs Warren comes abruptly and—for Vivie—shockingly. His crass marriage proposal (a bribe of money and status) to Vivie having been firmly rebuffed, Sir George Crofts tries to blackmail her into marriage by revealing his business relationship with Mrs Warren (a £40,000 investment) and darkly urging Vivie to "think of all the trouble and the explanations it would save if we were to keep the whole thing in the family, so to speak." "Ask your mother," he says, "whether she'd like to have to explain all her affairs to a perfect stranger" (137). Vivie is not initially fazed by the threat because she understands "that the business is wound up, and the money invested" (137). When Crofts disabuses her of this notion ("Wound up! Wind up a business thats paying 35 per cent in the worst years! Not likely" [137]), Vivie, "*her color quite gone*," has to sit down, and then, "*sickened*," she listens as Crofts gives his account of the business and Mrs Warren's ongoing and "indispensable" role as managing director (138). By the time Crofts has finished his paean to capitalism—having during the course of it reminded Vivie that her education and "the dress you have on your back" (138) have been paid for from the profits of the business—Vivie has recovered her equilibrium, and is able to tell Crofts "how helpless nine out of ten young girls would be in the hands of you and my mother!" She then dismisses them both as "the unmentionable woman and her capitalist bully" (141). As a parting gesture, and as Frank, responding to Vivie's call for assistance, intervenes to restrain the furious Crofts, Crofts drops another bombshell as he mockingly "introduces" Frank to his "half-sister, the eldest daughter of the Reverend Samuel Gardner," and Vivie to her "half-brother," Samuel Gardner's son.

Kitty Warren doesn't appear at all in Act 3, yet in some ways she is the central figure in the act. Despite not having seen or heard her, the audience's perception of Mrs Warren has altered enormously since the end of Act 2. From being sympathetically viewed as a woman driven into prostitution by dire economic circumstances—a victim of capitalism's ruthless exploitation of women—Mrs Warren is now under suspicion (is Crofts' account true?) as a willing ally of capitalism: the oppressor, not the victim, "the personification of the capitalist," as one critic has put it (Whitman 194). She has a lot of questions to answer, and it is those questions—and her answers—that give the play powerful momentum into the final act.[1]

By the beginning of Act 4 Vivie has fled the emotional and moral maelstrom of Haslemere for the professional calm of her friend's office in London. She is visited there by Frank and Praed, neither of whom know the full truth about Mrs Warren until Vivie—unable to bring herself to speak the words—writes her mother's "qualifications" on a piece of paper for them (151).[2] It is not surprising that Vivie is dismissive of a close relationship with either of them. She has made it clear to Praed in Act 1 that she does not share his passion for art, and as regards Frank—whose main source of income now seems to be gambling—she views a dispassionate and distant brother-sister relationship with him as "very suitable" (146). But Shaw sensibly saves the real tension of the play's final act for the arrival of Mrs Warren. After courteous goodbyes from Frank and Praed, Vivie and her mother are again alone, their first meeting since the end of Act 2.

Vivie has already judged her mother, and it's a harsh judgement: "From this time I go my own way in my own business and among my own friends. And you will go yours. [*She rises.*] Goodbye" (156). In response to her mother's bewilderment at Vivie's changed attitude towards her—"But I explained"—Vivie responds, "You explained how it came about. You did not tell me that it is still going on" (156), which captures exactly the mixed feelings that many audience members and readers have at this point, though, unlike Vivie, some, at least, want to hear Mrs Warren's explanation before judging her. Mrs Warren's initial explanation for remaining in the business is blatantly self-indulgent. Continuing to work "means a new dress every day; it means theatres and balls every night; it means having the pick of all the gentlemen in Europe at your feet; it means a lovely house and plenty of servants; it means everything

---

1   An act in which one critic surprisingly concludes that Mrs Warren, after managing "wonderfully well for three acts," is "mysteriously dropped" by Shaw, demonstrating that he was "at bottom, an allegorist, intent not on realizing a character, but on working out a doctrine" (Valency 94-95).

2   See below, p. 150, note 1, for the words written by Vivie.

you like, everything you want, everything you can think of" (156). And then she tries to put the responsibility on Vivie, arguing that she needs to maintain her connections with "the big people, the clever people, the managing people" so that she can use her money and her influence to help keep Vivie "respectable," though Mrs Warren's sense of "respectability" (social status and wealth) differs radically from Vivie's: "I shouldnt enjoy trotting about the park to advertise my dressmaker and carriage builder, or being bored at the opera to shew off a shopwindowful of diamonds," Vivie insists (158). And when Vivie again puts the crucial question—"Tell me why you continue your business now that you are independent of it"(158)— there seems little hope that Mrs Warren can regain the sympathy she has been rapidly losing.

She doesn't help her case by losing control of her emotions, then her temper—"melodramatic displays of motherly outrage and self-pity" that make her "as tainted and contemptible as Paula Tanqueray in her efforts to be what she is not," according to one modern critic (Wiley 120). Shaw's stage directions for Mrs Warren in the final few minutes of the play are important: her voice is "*stifled in tears*," she lapses "*recklessly*" into her cockney dialect, she speaks "*violently*" before "*screaming*," and utters almost her last words to Vivie "*sulkily*." And then after looking at Vivie "*fiercely*" and "*with a savage impulse to strike her*," she leaves, "*slamming the door behind her*" (161).

Another stage door had famously slammed in Henrik Ibsen's *A Doll's House*, whose English première Shaw had attended on 7 June 1889 (Gibbs 88). In Ibsen's play a young married woman leaves her husband and children in a desperate and courageous attempt to find some meaning and direction for her life beyond the stifling confines of domesticity and marital subservience. Nora's slamming of the door at the end of *A Doll's House* signifies a new beginning for her, and, symbolically, for women generally. Kitty Warren's exit doesn't have the same symbolic reverberations, and her situation in life is quite different from Nora's. Yet the endings of the two plays conjure similar dilemmas for audiences: how *could* Nora desert her family in such an irresponsible and selfish way; how *could* Kitty choose to remain in such a corrupting and demeaning profession long after her financial needs have been satisfied?

One of the consequences of Mrs Warren's losing her temper is that it causes her to abandon attempts to defend her profession by, for example, disingenuously claiming that she isn't doing "any real harm" (159) — has she forgotten the "disgusting" experiences she described to Vivie in Act 2? — and to win Vivie's sympathy ("Who is to care for me when I'm old?" [159]). Rather, knowing that Vivie is resolute in her determination to sever relations with her, she is freed from the need to persuade or manipulate, thus empowering her to speak with an honesty (and intensity)[1] that has much more chance of winning respect and understanding than her earlier efforts:

> Oh, the injustice of it! the injustice! I always wanted to be a good woman. I tried honest work; and I was slave-driven until I cursed the day I ever heard of honest work. I was a good mother; and because I made my daughter a good woman she turns me out as if I was a leper. Oh, if I only had my life to live over again! I'd talk to that lying clergyman[2] in the school. From this time forth, so help me Heaven in my last hour, I'll do wrong and nothing but wrong. And I'll prosper on it. (160)

Just as to blame Nora for leaving her husband and children is to prioritize symptom over cause, so to condemn Mrs Warren for continuing to work is to invoke conventional moral judgement while disregarding the circumstances that drove her into prostitution in the first place. Denied access to education as a young woman, Mrs Warren now has limited options: continue to work, or follow her sister Liz to the empty life of "being a lady," which would drive her "melancholy mad." "And what else is there for me to do? The life suits me: I'm not fit for anything else" (158). And a

---

1   In his introduction to *Plays Unpleasant* (London: Penguin, 2000), playwright David Edgar describes Mrs Warren's arguments in Act 2 justifying her decision to become a prostitute as "cogent and convincing"; in Act 4, he says, her arguments for continuing to run her brothels "are neither, but they are compelling, because they are about her limits as a human being and her fears of growing old alone" (xix).

2   The one who got Mrs Warren a job as a scullery maid (p. 123). Mrs Warren's sense of injustice in this speech echoes Edmund's speech in *King Lear* (1.1.1-22); her final comment ("I'll prosper on it") parallels Edmund's "I grow, I prosper."

repentant Mrs Warren—the Pinero expedient—is the last thing that Shaw wanted. Critics could—and did—huff and puff all they liked about Mrs Warren's decision, but it provided a double benefit for Shaw: it sustains interest in the "flesh-and-blood" (to return to Lady Rhondda's phrase) protagonist, and, by spurning easy outcomes, it keeps the focus on Shaw's concerns about the causes *and* consequences of prostitution. As one critic has perceptively put it, we see here not Shaw's condemnation of Mrs Warren's decision, but his "outrage against the civilization ultimately to blame for her maimed vitality." The "waste" of her talents is "tragic rather than disgusting" (Turco 73).[1]

Vivie Warren

It is a mistake to interpret the conclusion of *Mrs Warren's Profession* as a contest between Mrs Warren and Vivie to win the sympathy and support of the audience. The issues—and the characters—are more complex than that. Not surprisingly, then, critical reaction to Vivie has been as varied and as contradictory as the reaction to Mrs Warren. Vivie is the "moral conscience" of the play (Crompton 10), despite her "sexually and emotionally troubled core" (Gainor 40). Her actions at the end of the play "convey an almost palpable sense of wasted vitality" (Carpenter 58), but she is also "in a state of self-knowledge, purgation, and peace with herself, constituting salvation" (Berst 11). Vivie is "forlorn" (Morgan 45), "incomplete as a person and social force" (Whitman 195), or "hardly credible as a human being" (Wiley 121), while for another critic Vivie simply "remains mysterious throughout the play" because "Shaw did not know quite what to make of her" (Valency 99).

But Shaw knew exactly what he was making of Vivie. She was, he told a correspondent in November 1895, "the highly educated, capable, independent young woman of the governing class as we know her today, working, smoking, preferring the society of men

---

1   This conclusion about Mrs Warren is very much at odds with that of some other critics. Charles A. Berst, for example, in language reminiscent of the New York press in 1905, harshly says of her, "The staunchness and vision required for the struggle up through the slime have not led to fresh air, but rather to a diving back into the filth" (Berst 10).

to that of women simply because men talk about the questions that interest her and not about servants & babies, making no pretence of caring much about art or romance, respectable through sheer usefulness & strength, and playing the part of the charming woman only as the amusement of her life, not as its serious occupation" (Laurence I, 566-67). While Vivie expresses no overt political views (e.g. about women's suffrage) or articulates a reasoned philosophical or moral basis for her values and actions, she is, in short, an early representative of the "New Woman," a phrase coined by novelist and essayist Sarah Grand (Frances Elizabeth Clarke McFall, 1854-1943) in March 1894 to denote those women who rejected their traditional maternal and domestic role and demanded the same opportunities (political, social, educational, cultural, professional) as men.[1] Thus it is that Vivie shocks the easily shockable Praed with her rejection of "romance" and "beauty" in favour of "working and getting paid for it" and, after work, "a comfortable chair, a cigar, a little whisky, and a novel with a good detective story in it" (92). She hates holidays, is bored by Beethoven and Wagner, only worked hard at Cambridge to win a bet, and has entered the decidedly unromantic profession of "actuarial calculations and conveyancing" (92).

Vivie's comments about her experience at Cambridge are revealing. Academically, she has been outstandingly successful, but it has meant "grind, grind, grind for six to eight hours a day at mathematics, and nothing but mathematics.... Outside

---

1   See Carolyn Christensen Nelson, ed., *A New Woman Reader: Fiction, Articles, and Drama of the 1890s* (Peterborough, ON: Broadview Press, 2001). The drama in Nelson's anthology is a satire, *The New Woman* (also included in Chothia) by Sydney Grundy (1848-1914), first produced at the Comedy Theatre, London, on 1 September 1894. In her introduction, Nelson explains that a "stereo-typed image of the New Woman quickly took hold on the public imagination. She was educated at Girton College, Cambridge, rode a bicycle, insisted on rational dress, and smoked in public: in short, she rejected the traditional role for women and demanded emancipation" (p. ix). Nelson adds that while the "women of the nineties held a variety of opinions on social and political issues," what they did share "was a rejection of the culturally defined feminine role and a desire for increased educational and career opportunities that would allow them to be economically self-sufficient" (p. x). See Appendix H for further context on Vivie's New Woman characteristics.

mathematics, lawn-tennis, eating, sleeping, cycling, and walking, I'm a more ignorant barbarian than any woman could possibly be who hadnt gone in for the tripos" (92).[1] Praed, "*revolted*," exclaims in response: "What a monstrous, wicked, rascally system! I knew it! I felt at once that it meant destroying all that makes womanhood beautiful" (92). Many of Shaw's early readers and audiences would certainly have picked up the irony in Praed's view of "monstrous, wicked, rascally" Cambridge. In reality, it deserved these epithets, not because it destroyed all that made womanhood "beautiful," but because—unlike most other British (and North American) universities at this time—it denied women the educational opportunities offered to men. Vivie excelled at Cambridge, but, as a woman, she was not awarded a degree; she leaves Cambridge as plain Vivie Warren, not Vivie Warren B.A.[2] In many other respects she would have encountered prejudice and exclusion at Cambridge. Women students were tolerated (barely) in Vivie's time—accommodated in two women's colleges: Girton (founded in 1869) and Newnham, Vivie's College (founded in 1871)—but the governing bodies of the university were exclusively male and typically reacted with horror and dismay—and sometimes violence—whenever efforts were made to improve the status of women at the university. Proposals in 1896, for example, to admit women to degrees occasioned heated debate in the all-male Senate as well as violent street demonstrations both before and after the proposals were rejected. When women were finally allowed to take degrees (in 1921), Vivie's college was attacked by a mob of male undergraduates. (See Appendix G for more information on Vivie's Cambridge.)

To survive, let alone excel, in such an intimidating environment demanded extraordinary commitment and single-mindedness from Vivie, as Shaw and his contemporaries would have recognized. And Vivie would need those attributes even more

---

1 For an explanation of "the tripos" see p. 91, note 2.

2 Vivie would have faced the same discrimination at Oxford, but all other English universities admitted women to degrees, as did the Scottish universities and the University of Wales. Trinity College, Dublin, did not.

to establish herself and to prosper in the professional world she enters after leaving Cambridge—a world dominated, of course, like Cambridge, by men.

Out of a childhood shaped by boarding schools, a mostly absent mother, and a completely absent (and unknown) father, followed by a restricting rather than liberating experience at Cambridge, Vivie Warren has devised a coping mechanism of self-sufficiency that allows little space for emotional involvement and social niceties. Hence her brusque treatment of Praed in the opening scene, and her indifference to how her mother will get from the station to the cottage ("She knows the way," she curtly tells Praed [89]). It is a mechanism that allows for some mild (and temporary) flirtation with Frank, but it is also one that unequivocally rejects what she perceives as the aimlessness and self-indulgence of her mother and her coterie: "If I thought that *I* was like that—that I was going to be a waster, shifting along from one meal to another with no purpose, and no character, and no grit in me, I'd open an artery and bleed to death without one moment's hesitation" (113). The life she has devised for herself at Cambridge and in her chosen profession is one characterized by order, predictability, and logic. These parameters serve her well enough until she is confronted with the revelation of her mother's own profession in the middle of Act 2.

Vivie fends off the initial shock with a cold "Well, that is enough for tonight. At what hour would you like breakfast?" (120), and continues to resist her mother's charged appeals ("People are always blaming their circumstances for what they are. I dont believe in circumstances" [121]) until Mrs Warren's account (which Vivie is hearing for the first time) of her family background. By the end of this speech (the one about Lizzie in the whitelead factory [122]) Vivie is no longer dismissive—and here again Shaw's stage directions are important—but *"thoughtfully attentive"* (122), and then, over the next few minutes, *"intensely interested"* (124), *"more and more deeply moved"* (125), and *"fascinated"* (126), at which point Vivie praises her mother as a "wonderful woman … stronger than all England" (126). The act ends with mother and daughter in each other's arms.

This is a Vivie we haven't seen before, probably a Vivie that no-one has seen before. It is, in an important sense, a more complete Vivie, a Vivie whose life and values now have acquired, at least temporarily, a previously absent emotional dimension. When we next see Vivie (the following morning) she has her arm around her mother's waist as they enter the rectory garden (131-32), and she staunchly defends her against Frank's accusation that she's "a bad lot, a very bad lot" (134).

But in a play of many twists and turns, Vivie's emotional equanimity is soon sorely tested by Crofts' disclosure that Mrs Warren is still in business—contrary to Vivie's assumption that since her mother is now financially independent she has retired—and, as if that were not a big enough blow, Crofts also reveals that Vivie and Frank are probably half-siblings (141-42). Vivie's retreat into her actuarial shell is almost instantaneous. Even before the bombshell about the possible identity of her father, Vivie has rejected her mother as "the unmentionable woman" and Crofts as "her capitalist bully" (141). Frank is next—"You make all my flesh creep" (142)—before she flees to the sanctuary of Honoria Fraser's chambers in London.

When Frank visits her there at the beginning of Act 4 (two days later) she tells him that she has recovered "all [her] strength and self-possession" (145). Frank reckons she looks "quite happy," quickly adding "And as hard as nails" (145). She is newly committed to a life of actuarial calculations, a "brother and sister" relationship with Frank, and "no beauty and no romance" (148). "I must be treated as a woman of business, permanently single [to Frank] and permanently unromantic [to Praed]" (149). After the definitiveness of that statement, there remains only her relationship with her mother to resolve, although the outcome of the argument between them that ends the play is by no means a foregone conclusion, especially since Vivie is not quite as firmly in control of her emotions as she would like Frank and Praed to believe—witness her momentary relapse after she has written down the "two words" that describe her mother's "qualifications" (151). Throughout the final argument, however, Vivie retains full control of her emotions, in marked contrast to her mother, provoking Mrs Warren to describe Vivie as a "pious, canting, hard, selfish woman" (159-60), a judgement that critics and audiences frequently endorse.[1] Unconvinced by her mother's explanation of why she has continued to run her chain of brothels, and appalled—understandably so—by the prospect of the "worthless" life her mother would wish for her, "trotting about the park to advertise my dressmaker and carriage builder, or being bored at the opera to shew off a shopwindowful of diamonds" (158)—Vivie cuts all ties with her. She refuses even to shake hands as Mrs Warren finally leaves. Vivie's sense of personal integrity and her determination to be a fully independent woman leave no room for compromise.

There is no doubting Mrs Warren's unhappiness as she leaves; she resists, Shaw tells us, *"a savage impulse"* to strike Vivie before she slams the door behind her (161). Vivie, on the other hand, has an expression of *"joyous content,"* she lets out *"a half sob, half laugh of intense relief,"* goes *"buoyantly"* to her desk, and *"goes at her work with a plunge"* as the play ends (161). The contrast is stark, but it is surely a contrast that calls for an understanding of the position of both women rather than condemnation of Mrs Warren for continuing in her profession, or of Vivie for her "pride and prejudices," as her mother puts it (160). If any judgement is appropriate it is not one that disparages Mrs Warren as "tainted and contemptible" (Wiley 120) or praises Vivie as "genuinely better than her mother" (Baker 102), but one that condemns the circumstances that have led inexorably to the discord between mother and daughter, that is, the overwhelming inequities and injustices—economic, social, political, educational—that so limited the choices available to women in late Victorian England. As Shaw says in his preface, "society, and not any individual, is the villain of the piece" (Appendix A2).[2]

---

1 She is "an iceberg of contempt," wrote G.K. Chesterton (*George Bernard Shaw* [London: John Lane, 1909] 138).

2 In his 1920 novel, *Mrs Warren's Daughter* (London: Chatto & Windus), Harry Johnston takes Vivie from the end of the play through law school (disguised as a man), reconciliation with her mother, a vigorous suffragette campaign (imprisoned and force-fed), the First World War (as a nurse), and finally into a comfortable marriage as a "womanly woman." See F.L. Radford, *"Lady Chatterley's Second Husband and Mrs Warren's Daughter," Shaw Review* 23.2 (1980): 57-62.

The Suppression of *Mrs Warren's Profession*

A year after J.T. Grein had produced Shaw's first play — *Widowers' Houses* — in December 1892 (see above, 25), he expressed interest in *Mrs Warren's Profession*, which Shaw had recently finished. Shaw responded by writing to Grein on 12 December 1893 to outline the play, describing Mrs Warren as "a woman of bad character, proprietress of two *maisons tolérées* in Brussels, and of similar establishments in other continental cities." Shaw also cautioned Grein that "I do not think there is the least chance of the play being licensed" (Laurence I, 412-13).

Shaw's brief reference to the licensing of the play was but the beginning of a lengthy and stormy battle between Shaw and officialdom over the suitability of *Mrs Warren's Profession* for public performance in England, a battle that quickly came to encompass principles of freedom of expression for British playwrights as well as the particular case of Shaw's play.

In 1737, in response to political satires by Henry Fielding (1707-54) and others, the government of Robert Walpole (1676-1745) introduced the Stage Licensing Act, which stipulated that every new play must be licensed for public performance. The licence was issued by the Lord Chamberlain, the senior official of the royal household (through whom all theatres had to be licensed as well). The Lord Chamberlain's authority to license plays was normally delegated to an official known as the Examiner of Plays, whose responsibility it was to read all new plays and determine their suitability for public performance (see Appendix F2). Originally intended to prevent political attacks on the government, the legislation also restricted the ability of playwrights to deal critically with political, moral, or religious issues in general.[1] The legislation was intentionally vague on

---

1 For an account of the 1737 legislation and its early implementation see L.W. Conolly, *The Censorship of English Drama, 1737-1824* (San Marino: The Huntington Library, 1976). For later periods (including Shaw's) see John Russell Stephens, *The Censorship of English Drama, 1824-1901* (Cambridge: Cambridge UP, 1980), Steve Nicholson, *The Censorship of British Drama, 1900-1932*, Volume 1, 1900-1932 (Exeter: U of Exeter P, 2003), and Nicholas de Jongh, *Politics, Prudery & Perversions: The Censoring of the English Stage, 1901-1968* (London: Methuen, 2000). John Johnston's *The Lord Chamberlain's Blue Pencil* (London: Hodder & Stoughton, 1990) is a more general survey.

what the Lord Chamberlain might or might not allow, the 1843 amended version of the Act (the one in force when Shaw wrote *Mrs Warren's Profession* [see Appendix F1]) giving him (it was always a man) the authority to ban anything that might, in his judgement, threaten the "preservation of good manners, decorum, or ... the public peace." The Lord Chamberlain's decision was final and absolute; no appeal was allowed. It was this system that Shaw was referring to in his letter to Grein.

Prior to that, however, Grein disappointed Shaw by refusing to produce the play privately.[1] Convinced that there was no hope of getting the play licensed, Shaw made other efforts to have the play produced privately in England or publicly in Ireland, which was outside the Lord Chamberlain's jurisdiction. When those efforts failed, Shaw faced something of a dilemma. He wanted to publish the play — which the Lord Chamberlain could not prevent — but copyright law required performance as well as publication of a play to establish the playwright's ownership of copyright. Shaw finally decided, then, to submit *Mrs Warren's Profession* for a licence for a copyright performance of the play (essentially a staged reading) at the Victoria Hall in suburban Bayswater, anticipating a refusal but hoping that the Examiner of Plays (George Redford, a former bank manager) would identify any parts of the play that he deemed objectionable and license the rest. Redford refused to cooperate, simply telling the manager of the Victoria Hall (in a letter dated 11 March 1898) that the play could not be licensed. Frustrated, but not defeated, Shaw proceeded to censor himself, drastically cutting and revising the play to remove all possible offence. In what Shaw described as his "mutilated" version of the play, Mrs Warren's profession is changed from prostitute to pickpocket, a "female Fagin" as Shaw put it (see Appendix B). Redford had no problem with this version, and duly licensed the play for the copyright performance on 30 March 1898. Publication of the full text quickly followed, appearing simultaneously in English

---

1 Grein's dislike of *Mrs Warren's Profession* is expressed in his review of the 1902 Stage Society production (Appendix C2). Unless otherwise noted, the account of the suppression of *Mrs Warren's Profession* given here is drawn from my much longer account in *SHAW: The Annual of Shaw Studies* (see Sources Cited in the Introduction, below, p. 72).

and American editions on 19 April 1898.[1] But well over four years after Shaw had finished *Mrs Warren's Profession* there still hadn't been a full production.

It wasn't that the Lord Chamberlain was averse to licensing plays about prostitutes—there had been no problem, for example, with Pinero's *The Second Mrs Tanqueray*, and Shaw claimed (with a forgivable degree of exaggeration) in a letter to *The Nation* (16 November 1907) that "licensed drama positively teems with prostitutes and procuresses."[2] The problem was that Mrs Warren is not a *repentant* prostitute, nor by the end of the play is she a *dead* prostitute. Far from it. At the end of the play she is bruised by her daughter's rejection, but otherwise she is alive and well and looking forward to managing her brothels enthusiastically, efficiently, and indefinitely. It is hard to know if Redford found all of this endangered "good manners" or "decorum" or "the public peace"—perhaps all three. And there was also the little matter of incest.

Among the many horrors of the "morally rotten" *Mrs Warren's Profession* identified by the *New York Herald* on 31 October 1905 (Appendix C4), the "worst of all" was "the revolting form of degeneracy" countenanced by the play's "flippantly discussing the marriage of brother and sister, father and daughter." It is more likely that Vivie and Frank are half-siblings (i.e. that the Reverend Samuel is the father of both, as claimed by Crofts in Act 3 [141-42]), than that Crofts is Vivie's father (which Mrs Warren denies [120], although Crofts concedes that it is possible [98]). Shaw leaves it uncertain, though in the letter to *The Nation* quoted above, he refers only to the half-sibling possibility when discussing incest ("And the two [Vivie and Frank] have to face the question, Is he her half-brother? only to find it unanswerable.")

---

1   *Mrs Warren's Profession* was included in volume 1 of *Plays Pleasant and Unpleasant*, published in London by Grant Richards and in Chicago and New York by Herbert S. Stone. Also included in volume 1 (the "unpleasant" plays) were *Widowers' Houses* and *The Philanderer*. The "pleasant" plays (volume 2) were *Arms and the Man*, *Candida*, *The Man of Destiny*, and *You Never Can Tell*. For full bibliographical information see Dan H. Laurence, *Bernard Shaw: A Bibliography* (Oxford: Clarendon Press, 1983) I:33-36.

2   This letter, and a further letter to *The Nation* (8 February 1908) on censorship, are reprinted in Bernard Shaw, *Agitations. Letters to the Press 1875-1950*, ed. Dan H. Laurence and James Rambeau (New York: Frederick Ungar, 1985) 93-105.

At the time that Shaw wrote *Mrs Warren's Profession* incest was not a criminal offence, though by 1908, after intense political debate (see Appendices E2, E3), it had become so, and half-siblings were included in the new legislation—under the 1908 legislation Frank would have been subject to up to seven years in prison had he been convicted of "carnal knowledge" of Vivie (see Appendix E4). Biblical teaching (see Appendix E1) and canon law, moreover, were clear in their condemnation of incest, and no church in England would have married Frank and Vivie (let alone Vivie and Crofts) if there had been even a whiff of suspicion of an incestuous relationship. For most of Shaw's contemporaries incest was, as Shaw well knew, a taboo subject, one of the "three great taboos on the question of sex," he said—the other two being abortion and venereal disease (*The Nation*, 16 November 1907). Incest is in the play because Shaw wanted to show that it was one of the "inevitable" consequences of the kind of business and personal situations arranged by Mrs Warren, and he knew that the scenarios he was presenting were not farfetched. He told William Archer in a letter of 7 November 1905, for example, that he "knew of a case of a young man who, on being initiated by a modern Madame de Warens (observe the name), was rather taken aback by her reproaching him for being 'not half the man his father was'" (Laurence II, 574).[1] Shaw knew full well, however, that references to incest, even brief and guarded references, would be a further impediment to getting a licence for the play. This is perhaps why the discussion of the possibility of an incestuous relationship between Vivie and Crofts is more circumspect in the published text of the play than it was in the original manuscript text. Crofts' line "Maynt a man take an interest in a girl?" (115) originally read "Maynt a man take an interest in a girl?—a fatherly interest," and was followed by this:

---

1 Shaw also hints here at potential incest within his own family: "I also watched the case of a man who was a friend of my mother in her young days. When my sister grew up he became infatuated about her and wanted to marry her" (Laurence II, 574). Madame de Warens was the mistress of French philosopher Jean Jacques Rousseau (1712–78).

MRS WARREN (*lowering her voice*) How do you know that the
girl maynt be your own daughter, eh?
CROFTS How do you know that that maynt be one of the
fascinations of the thing? What harm if she is?

Shaw self-censored himself by cutting the lines before publication
and performance (Tyson 274). Even so, he declared, the "taboo
against incest ... is why *Mrs Warren's Profession* is forbidden" (*The
Nation*, 16 November 1907).[1]

Grein's Independent Theatre Society closed down in December
1898, but was quickly succeeded by another organization—also
operated as a private theatre club beyond the jurisdiction of the
Lord Chamberlain—dedicated to producing controversial and
non-commercial plays. Founded by Fabian writer and lecturer
Frederick Whelen (1867-1955), the new organization was called
the Stage Society.[2] Unlike Grein, Whelen had no qualms
about the subject matter of *Mrs Warren's Profession*, and after the
Society's inaugural production of Shaw's *You Never Can Tell* on 26
November 1899 Whelen offered to produce the still-unlicensed
play. After considerable difficulty in locating a theatre willing to
rent its facilities (some managers being worried about possible
reprisals from the Lord Chamberlain for helping Shaw and
Whelen circumvent the ban), *Mrs Warren's Profession* opened for
two performances at the small New Lyric Club (on Coventry
Street, between Piccadilly Circus and Leicester Square) on 5 and
6 January 1902, the first full production of the play. Directed by
Shaw himself, with Fanny Brough (1854-1914) as Mrs Warren,
Madge McIntosh (1870-1950) as Vivie, and Harley Granville Barker
(1877-1946) as Frank, the production pleased Shaw (he praised the
actors—and himself—in a curtain speech on opening night) and

---

1 Another controversial play of the period, John Millington Synge's *Playboy of the
Western World* (1907), also contains references to incest. See Eugene Benson, *J.M.
Synge* (London: Macmillan, 1982) 116-17.

2 The Stage Society ran for forty years, mounting over 200 productions, including
several Shaw plays. See Allan Wade, "Shaw and the Stage Society," in Raymond
Mander and Joe Mitchenson, *Theatrical Companion to Shaw* (New York: Pitman, 1955)
285-87. Wade was an actor who eventually became secretary to the Stage Society. See
his *Memories of the London Theatre 1900-1914*, ed. Alan Andrews (London: The Society
for Theatre Research, 1983).

MRS. WARREN'S PROFESSION

A Play in Four Acts

BY

BERNARD SHAW.

Praed	JULIUS KNIGHT
Sir George Crofts	CHARLES GOODHART
Rev. Samuel Gardner	COSMO STUART
Frank	H. GRANVILLE BARKER
Vivie	Miss MADGE MCINTOSH
Mrs. Warren	Miss FANNY BROUGH

Program for the Stage Society production of *Mrs Warren's Profession*, New Lyric Club, London, 5 January 1902. Courtesy Dan H. Laurence Collection, L.W. Conolly Theatre Archives, University of Guelph.

ACT I.

The Garden of Vivie Warren's Holiday Cottage at Haslemere.

ACT II.

Inside the Cottage.

ACT III.

The Vicarage Garden.

ACT IV.

Honoria Fraser's Chambers in Chancery Lane.

The intervals will be as follows :—

Between Acts	I. and II.	15 minutes.
Do.	Acts II. and III.	20 minutes.
Do.	Acts III. and IV.	15 minutes.

Stage Manager ... ... GUY WALLER.

Fanny Brough as Mrs Warren, Stage Society, New Lyric Club, London, 5 January 1902. Courtesy Dan H. Laurence Collection, L.W. Conolly Theatre Archives, University of Guelph.

the select Stage Society audience, but did not impress some less partial observers. Given the low profile of the production, public and critical reaction was muted compared to that in New Haven and New York in 1905, but a taste of transatlantic things to come could be seen in the reaction of the *St James's Gazette* whose critic found the play's "unmentionable subject" handled "in a manner

Fanny Brough as Mrs Warren, Madge McIntosh as Vivie Warren, Stage Society, New Lyric Club, London, 5 January 1902. Courtesy Dan H. Laurence Collection, L.W. Conolly Theatre Archives, University of Guelph.

that even the least squeamish might find revoltingly offensive." Shaw's talent is wasted on this "dingy drama" the tendency of which is "wholly evil" (see Appendix C1).

Still, at least Shaw and a select number of friends and colleagues had had the satisfaction of seeing a professional production of *Mrs Warren's Profession*, an experience denied the wider British public for another twenty-three years. Between 1902 and the first public production of *Mrs Warren's Profession* in England at the Prince of Wales Theatre in Birmingham on 27 July 1925 several attempts were made by Shaw and various friends and supporters to persuade whoever was occupying the office of Lord Chamberlain to license the play, all to no avail (see Conolly 59-87). On one occasion, in 1917, a producer named Edwin Heys presented a petition to the Lord Chamberlain (Lord Sandhurst) to license the play; the petition was signed by many leading writers and critics as well as three bishops, twelve senior army officers, and forty-four privy councillors and Members of Parliament. In response to the petition, Lord Sandhurst met with Heys, told him that he was not willing to license the play, and "declared the matter over" (Conolly 74). The breakthrough finally came in August 1924 when the then Lord Chamberlain, Earl Cromer, recognising that *Mrs Warren's Profession* had been performed "all over Europe & America" and that it would be "absurd to go on refusing a Licence to this Play, ignoring the march of time and the change it brings about in public opinion over facing such questions [i.e. prostitution] openly," decided, "reluctantly," to grant the licence. The Lord Chamberlain's only condition was that the reference to the Duke of Beaufort in Act 2 be deleted. Shaw obliged by turning him into a Duke of nowhere (109).[1]

Reviews of the Birmingham production (and the subsequent London première at the Regent Theatre on 28 September 1925) mostly turned previous critical reaction upside down, the *Birmingham Gazette* (28 July 1925), for example, pronouncing *Mrs Warren's Profession* "the most truly moral play ever produced on the English stage" (see Appendix C7)—a far cry from the "wholly evil" judgement rendered by the *St James's Gazette*. The producer of the Birmingham production, Charles Macdona,[2] took the play to London after the Birmingham engagement. It opened

---

1 When Shaw first submitted *Mrs Warren's Profession* for licensing, the Duke of Beaufort (the 8th Duke) was Henry Charles Fitzroy Somerset (1824-99), noted sportsman and an early proponent of homeopathy. He was succeeded on his death by his son, Henry Adelbert Wellington Somerset (1847-1924).

2 Macdona (1860-1946) founded and managed a touring company, the Macdona Players, that performed Shaw's plays regularly throughout Great Britain and abroad.

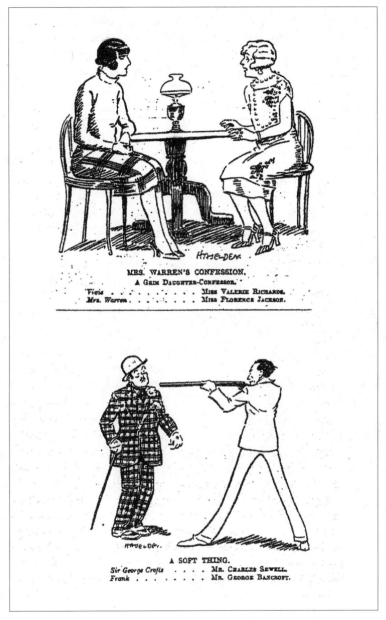

MRS. WARREN'S CONFESSION.
A GRIM DAUGHTER-CONFESSOR.

Vivie . . . . Miss VALERIE RICHARDS.
Mrs. Warren . . . . . . Miss FLORENCE JACKSON.

A SOFT THING.

Sir George Crofts . . . . Mr. CHARLES SEWELL.
Frank . . . . Mr. GEORGE BANCROFT.

Scenes from the Regent Theatre, London, production of *Mrs Warren's Profession*,
28 September 1925. *Punch*, 7 October 1925.

at the Regent Theatre, King's Cross, on 28 September 1925 and ran (in repertory) for twenty-one performances. Macdona then moved it to the West End, where it opened at the Strand Theatre on 3 March 1926. After the final dress rehearsal at the Strand on 2 March 1926 there was "persistent cheering" from the audience, prompting Shaw to bow an acknowledgement from his box and, with uncharacteristic brevity, to say simply, "Ladies and gentlemen, good-night. Come again" (*Daily News*, 3 March 1926). And come again they did—for sixty-eight performances at the Strand and regularly after that as *Mrs Warren's Profession* finally established itself in the mainstream of the British and international repertoire.

Shaw and Censorship

The ban imposed on *Mrs Warren's Profession* in 1898 signalled Shaw's first clash with the Lord Chamberlain; others were to follow. In February 1909 Shaw responded to a request from actor-manager Beerbohm Tree to write a short play for a benefit matinée at His Majesty's Theatre in aid of a children's charity. The play was *The Shewing-up of Blanco Posnet*. Set in a courtroom "in a Territory of the United States of America," this animated and amusing one-act "Sermon in Crude Melodrama," as Shaw puts it in the subtitle, recounts the activities of a God-defying horse-thief who gets caught only because he gives up a stolen horse to a woman who desperately needs it to get her sick child to a doctor. The trial is punctuated by Blanco Posnet's blasphemous curses against a "sly" and "mean" God, and a prayer for God to "keep me wicked till I die." There is also another prostitute in the play, the key witness against Blanco, said by Blanco to have had "immoral relations with every man in this town." The play was in rehearsal early in May 1909 when Shaw and Tree heard that the licence application had been refused because of alleged blasphemy. The play had to be withdrawn from His Majesty's, but Shaw soon arranged for it to be produced in Dublin, where it opened—amid great public interest, but no disquiet—at the Abbey Theatre on 25 August 1909. The Abbey Company then performed it in a private production for the

Stage Society at the Aldwych Theatre in London on 5 December 1909, but the first public production (duly licensed by then) had to wait until 10 April 1916 when another company from the Abbey (the Irish Players) performed it in Liverpool. West End audiences didn't get to see it until 1921 in a production that opened at the Queen's Theatre and ran for twenty-nine performances (Mander and Mitchenson 124).

Shortly after finishing *Blanco Posnet* in March 1909, Shaw left England for a holiday in North Africa. During the holiday he wrote another short play, a satiric farce called *Press Cuttings*, subtitled *A Topical Sketch Compiled from the Editorial and Correspondence Columns of the Daily Papers during the Woman's War in 1909*. The "Woman's War in 1909" was the suffragettes' struggle for the right to vote, supported by Shaw—he wrote *Press Cuttings* in aid of the London Society for Women's Suffrage—but opposed by the then Liberal Government led by Prime Minister Herbert Asquith (1852-1928). In *Press Cuttings* there is a prime minister named Balsquith (neatly incorporating former Conservative Prime Minister Arthur Balfour [1848-1930] into the equation) who enters dressed as a woman. Another character is named General Mitchener, too close a parallel in the Examiner of Play's mind to Boer War hero General Kitchener (1850-1916). Because of these personal allusions (more so than because of its attack on government policy) the play was denied a licence, causing the production at the Royal Court Theatre on 9 July 1909 (repeated on 12 July) to be given as a "private reception," by invitation only. When Shaw later agreed to drop the names of Balsquith and Mitchener (he changed them to Bones and Johnson), a licensed production of *Press Cuttings* was given in Manchester on 27 September 1909 (Mander and Mitchenson 128).

Neither of these two instances of censorship could (or should) have surprised Shaw. Blasphemy and ridicule of prominent establishment figures stood little or no chance of being approved, and it seems likely that Shaw was being deliberately provocative—looking for a fight with the Lord Chamberlain—with both plays. He had vigorously attacked Britain's stage censorship system after the ban on *Mrs Warren's Profession* in an article in a Boston periodical, the *North American Review.*[1] The Lord Chamberlain, he pointed out, was an unelected official, responsible to no-one but the Queen (or King). His Examiner of Plays, despite having immense responsibility and authority ("The President of the United States himself practically cannot see a new play without first getting the Examiner's leave"[67]) need have no particular literary or theatrical qualifications: "You are not allowed to sell stamps in an English post office without previously passing an examination; but you may become Examiner of Plays without necessarily knowing how to read or write" (67). The censorship, Shaw argued, inevitably restricted the ability of plays to present "new opinions on important subjects" (76), a restriction imposed only on playwrights—not, for example, on novelists or poets, whose work was not subject to any kind of licensing system. What should be done about it? "Nothing could be simpler. Abolish it, root and branch, throwing the whole legal responsibility for plays on the author and manager, precisely as the legal responsibility for a book is thrown on the author, the printer, and the publisher" (79).

A major problem, however, as Shaw acknowledged in his *North American Review* article, was that his own keen sense of the absurdities and injustices of theatre censorship was not widely shared. A Parliamentary review in 1892 had concluded that the system should continue (Johnston 34-35), and Shaw had to concede that for most people there simply wasn't a problem: "no complaints in Parliament, none in the Press, no petitions from the Society of Authors or from the managers." The public, Shaw concluded, "is either satisfied or indifferent" (79),[2] a situation that Shaw was determined to rectify.

---

1 "The Censorship of the Stage in England," *North American Review* 169 (August 1899): 251-62. Reprinted in E.J. West, ed., *Shaw on Theatre* (New York: Hill and Wang, 1958) 66-80, from which I quote.

2 Relatively few playwrights had their work banned. Johnston (278) presents data showing that between 1900 and 1968 (when theatre censorship in England was abolished) 411 plays were denied a licence—less than 1% of those submitted. Another 352, however, were effectively denied a licence because their authors refused to make the changes demanded by the Examiner. There is, of course, no way of calculating how many plays simply weren't submitted because of the censorship, or were self-censored, or, indeed, weren't written at all.

In the decade between the *North American Review* article and the suppression of *The Shewing-up of Blanco Posnet* and *Press Cuttings* Shaw continued to agitate against the censorship through articles, speeches, and letters to the press, gathering increasing support along the way. He was joined by seventy other writers, for example, in a protest letter to *The Times* on 29 October 1907 in which they asked "to be freed from the menace hanging over every dramatist of having his work and the proceeds of his work destroyed at a pen's stroke by the arbitrary action of a single official neither responsible to Parliament nor amenable to law" (see Appendix F3). Shaw was optimistic, he wrote to actor-manager Lena Ashwell (1872-1957) on 4 November 1907 (Laurence II, 718-19), that there would be some concessions from the government, optimism that increased when Prime Minister Henry Campbell-Bannerman (1836-1908) agreed to meet a deputation led by playwrights J.M. Barrie (1860-1937) and Arthur Wing Pinero (Shaw, probably wisely, deciding that his presence on the deputation would not necessarily be helpful).[1] A private member's bill (i.e. one not proposed by the government) to abolish the censorship powers of the Lord Chamberlain, introduced in December 1908 (Nicholson 45), continued the momentum, but the bill was dropped after the government announced that there would be another Parliamentary review of the licensing system of plays and theatres by a Joint Select Committee of the House of Lords and the House of Commons.

The Joint Committee met for the first time on 29 July 1909, and—working more expeditiously than has since become the norm for government enquiries—issued its final report and recommendations on 8 November 1909. There was widespread discussion (mostly generated by Shaw) in the columns of *The Times* and elsewhere throughout the summer of 1909 on the censorship of *The Shewing-up of Blanco Posnet* and *Press Cuttings*, and Shaw made sure that he was also one of the Joint Committee's key witnesses. He prepared an 11,000 word statement on censorship for the committee, and gave evidence in person on 30 July 1909. He was ques-

---

1   The deputation was, in the event, received by Home Secretary Herbert Gladstone (1854-1930).

tioned extensively on his statement, but his main point was clear, straightforward, and consistent: plays and playwrights should be treated in the same way as novels and novelists, poetry and poets, and any other kind of writing and writers—they should all be publicly accountable to the law (e.g. on obscenity, blasphemy, or libel), not to a royal official and his bureaucrats who had absolute authority over the drama and whose decisions were not subject to public scrutiny. Should there be "some form of control" of drama "in the social interest" the chair of the committee asked Shaw. Yes, Shaw replied, "the law of the land." (See Appendix F4 for extracts from Shaw's evidence to the committee.)[1]

Shaw's view was supported by many of the witnesses who appeared before the committee, though most theatre managers expressed the view that the Lord Chamberlain's licence was a welcome protection against just what Shaw was willing to face—possible legal action against a play, with all the cost and adverse publicity that might generate. And even some playwrights believed that some form of censorship was needed. W.S. Gilbert (1836-1911), famous for his collaborations on comic operas with Arthur Sullivan (1842-1900), told the committee that he didn't believe the theatre to be "a proper pulpit from which to disseminate doctrines possibly of Anarchism, Socialism, and Agnosticism," nor was it "a proper platform upon which to discuss questions of adultery and free love before a mixed audience" (qtd. in Nicholson 48).[2] So much for the Shaws and Ibsens of the world.

To its credit, the Joint Committee emerged from their intensive consultations with a series of innovative proposals, confirming the Lord Chamberlain's censorship role, but making him responsible to Parliament, defining the criteria by which a play could be banned, creating an advisory committee for controversial cases, and, most important, making a licence application

---

1   Committee members read Shaw's statement, but, much to Shaw's distress, would not allow it to be entered as a formal part of the record. He published it in *The Doctor's Dilemma, Getting Married, & The Shewing-up of Blanco Posnet* (London: Constable, 1911). See Holroyd II, 224-38 for a more detailed account of Shaw's engagements with the censorship issue.

2   Gilbert had, however, signed the 29 October 1907 protest letter in *The Times* (see Appendix F3).

optional—that is, managers who were willing to submit to the authority of the Lord Chamberlain could seek the licensing of a play in the normal way, confident that if it were licensed they would not have to worry about possible legal challenges later on, while those managers who objected to the Lord Chamberlain's interference could go ahead and produce an unlicensed play and take their chances with the law. To its discredit, the government ignored all but one of the recommendations—that setting up an advisory committee. Everything else about the system continued just as before.[1]

By the time of the report of the Joint Committee, *Press Cuttings* had been licensed, but *The Shewing-up of Blanco Posnet* and *Mrs Warren's Profession* remained banned from the public stage in England; the ban on *Mrs Warren's Profession* lasted another fifteen years. No other plays by Shaw were ever banned in England, but he never gave up his campaign against censorship. In the year before his death he wrote yet another letter to *The Times* on the subject (7 April 1949), pointing out once more the absurdity of charging "a staff of clerks at schoolmasters' salaries" with the responsibility of determining what was fit or not fit to be seen and heard on the English stage. The absurdity continued until 1968 when a new Theatres Act finally abolished censorship and did exactly what Shaw had argued in 1909 should be done—subjected plays and playwrights to the law on the same footing as all other literature and all other writers.[2]

Shaw's Later Career

Because of the ban, *Mrs Warren's Profession* was a recurring factor in Shaw's life for over thirty years, from its composition in 1893, through its tumultuous reception in the United States in 1905 and the controversies about its suppression in England, to its first public performances in England in Birmingham in 1925 and London in 1926—a recurring factor, but not, except occasionally, a dominant

---

1   There is a thorough discussion of the work of the 1909 Joint Committee in Nicholson 46-70.
2   See Johnston 225-46 for an account of the 1968 legislation.

factor. Shaw had too rich and varied a life for any one facet of it to be dominant.

Many more plays were to be written, including some for which Shaw is most famous: *Pygmalion* (first performed—in German—in 1913), *Heartbreak House* (1920), the mammoth five-part *Back to Methuselah* (1922), *Saint Joan* (1923), *The Apple Cart* (1929, in Polish), *Too True to be Good* (1932), *The Millionairess* (1936, in German). In 1929 a Festival (at Malvern in Worcestershire) was founded by Barry Jackson (1879-1961) to celebrate Shaw's plays, an honour that Shaw welcomed and nurtured.[1] Other honours were declined—a knighthood in 1926 (his seventieth birthday), for example—but Shaw did agree later that year to accept the 1925 Nobel Prize for Literature, stipulating that the prize money be used to establish a foundation to encourage and support the translation of Swedish literature into English. And he remained controversial. The disputes about *Mrs Warren's Profession* and censorship were small potatoes compared to the reaction to his iconoclastic and courageous criticism of Britain's involvement in World War I (1914-18), expressed in his book *Common Sense about the War* (1914). His sympathetic attitude towards Germany generated "a fury of outrage and splenetic derogation from the press," as Dan H. Laurence has put it (Laurence III, 239), friends shunning him and booksellers and librarians removing his books from their shelves (the ultimate form of censorship). His respect for Hitler and Stalin (whom he met in Moscow in 1931), qualified and ultimately repudiated in both cases, caused more fury, though those who bellowed their hostility might have put their energy to better use, as Shaw did, in exploring alternatives to the palpable failings of democratic government and democratic leaders—widespread unemployment, poverty, massive social and economic inequality.

Other Shavian forays into political commentary were greeted with praise, not calumny. *The Intelligent Woman's Guide to*

---

1 See L.W. Conolly, ed., *Bernard Shaw and Barry Jackson* (Toronto: U of Toronto P, 2002). The Malvern Festival continued until 1949 and has been held intermittently since then (with or without a Shaw presence). The Shaw Festival, founded at Niagara-on-the-Lake, Ontario, in 1962 has been held annually since then, always with two or three Shaw plays in the repertoire.

Socialism and Capitalism (1928) was lauded by Labour Prime Minister Ramsay MacDonald (1866-1937) as "after the Bible ... the most important book that humanity possesses"—a remark that revealed MacDonald to be "more of a wit than I suspected," Shaw said (qtd. in Holroyd III, 133). Winston Churchill (1874-1965), no political ally of Shaw, yet considered Shaw (writing in 1937) "the greatest living master of letters in the English-speaking world" (qtd. in Holroyd III, 226). Shaw's opinions on matters great and small were sought wherever he travelled—and he travelled almost everywhere, by ship, train, bicycle, car, balloon, and plane, embracing new technology and adventure whenever the opportunity arose. Abroad and at home he was greeted, befriended, and sought after by politicians, sportsmen, artists, writers, musicians, scientists, photographers, and film stars—Gandhi, Nehru, Gorky, Gene Tunney, Rodin, Mark Twain, H.G. Wells, Lawrence of Arabia, Edward Elgar, Einstein, Karsh, Chaplin, Garbo, and many more. He quickly recognized the potential of the new media of radio, television, and film, broadcasting his talks and plays on radio stations around the world, and filming adaptations of his plays.[1] Bernard Shaw remains the only person to have received both a Nobel Prize and an Oscar, which he won for the screenplay of *Pygmalion* in 1938.

Vegetarian, teetotaller, spelling and alphabet reformer, antivivisectionist as well as playwright and social activist *par excellence*; there was hardly an aspect of human activity during a life

---

1   Films made in Shaw's lifetime include *How He Lied to Her Husband* (1931, with Robert Harris, Edmund Gwenn, and Vera Lennox), *Arms and the Man* (1932, with Maurice Colbourne and Barry Jones), *Pygmalion* (1938, with Leslie Howard and Wendy Hiller), *Major Barbara* (1941, with Rex Harrison and Wendy Hiller), and *Caesar and Cleopatra* (1945, with Claude Rains and Vivien Leigh). Later films include *Androcles and the Lion* (1953, with Maurice Evans, Victor Mature, and Jean Simmons), *Saint Joan* (1957, with Jean Seberg, Richard Widmark, John Gielgud, and Richard Todd), *The Devil's Disciple* (1959, with Burt Lancaster, Kirk Douglas, Laurence Olivier, and Janette Scott), and *The Millionairess* (1961, with Sophia Loren and Peter Sellers). Several foreign film adaptations have also been made. See Donald P. Costello, *The Serpent's Eye. Shaw and the Cinema* (Notre Dame and London: U of Notre Dame P, 1965) and Bernard F. Dukore, ed., *The Collected Screenplays of Bernard Shaw* (Athens, Georgia: U of Georgia P, 1980). For Shaw's early experiences with radio broadcasting, see L.W. Conolly, "GBS and the BBC: In the Beginning (1923-1928)," *SHAW: The Annual of Bernard Shaw Studies* 23 (2003): 75-116.

that lasted nearly a century that Shaw did not participate in or comment on. He probably wrote more letters and postcards (estimated, conservatively, to be at least a quarter of a million) than any one in history. The estimate was made by Dan H. Laurence, editor of Shaw's *Collected Letters* (I, xi); Laurence (IV, 3) has also suggested—plausibly—that by his seventieth birthday Shaw was "probably the most famous person in the world." His death (from complications following a fall in his garden while pruning a shrub) in his home in the isolated village of Ayot St Lawrence in Hertfordshire on 2 November 1950 was front-page headline news in practically every newspaper in the world, and the lights of Times Square and Broadway theatre marquees were blacked out in respect.

But rich and varied though Shaw's life and work were, he always remained engaged with the central concerns of *Mrs Warren's Profession* and his early plays—injustice, poverty, the status of women. Shaw's last recorded conversation, on 25 October 1950, was with Judy Musters, his secretary from 1907 to 1912. She encouraged him to remember "the enjoyment you've given ... and the stimulus." Shaw, apparently, chuckled at this: "you might say the same of any Mrs Warren" (Laurence IV, 882).

Sources for the Introduction

Baker, Stuart E. *Bernard Shaw's Remarkable Religion. A Faith that Fits the Facts.* Gainesville: U of Florida P, 2002.

Bartley, Paula. *Prostitution. Prevention and Reform in England, 1860-1914.* London and New York: Routledge, 2000.

Berst, Charles A. *Bernard Shaw and the Art of Drama.* Urbana: U of Illinois P, 1973.

Bullough, Geoffrey. "Literary Relations of Shaw's Mrs Warren." *Philological Quarterly* 41.1 (1962): 339-58.

Carpenter, Charles. *Bernard Shaw & the Art of Destroying Ideals. The Early Plays.* Madison: U of Wisconsin P, 1969.

Chothia, Jean, ed. *The New Woman and Other Emancipated Woman Plays.* Oxford: Oxford UP, 1998.

Conolly, L.W. "*Mrs Warren's Profession* and the Lord Chamberlain." *SHAW: The Annual of Bernard Shaw Studies* 24 (2004): 46-95.

—— and Ellen M. Pearson, eds. *Bernard Shaw on Stage. Papers from the 1989 International Shaw Conference.* Guelph: University of Guelph, 1991.

Crompton, Louis. *Shaw the Dramatist.* London: George Allen & Unwin, 1971.

Egan, Michael, ed. *Ibsen: The Critical Heritage.* London: Routledge, 1972.

Evans, T.F., ed. *Shaw: The Critical Heritage.* London: Routledge, 1976.

Fisher, Trevor. *Prostitution and the Victorians.* New York: St Martin's Press, 1997.

Gainor, J. Ellen. *Shaw's Daughters: Dramatic and Narrative Constructions of Gender.* Ann Arbor: U of Michigan P, 1991.

Gibbs, A.M. *A Bernard Shaw Chronology.* London: Palgrave, 2001.

Greer, Germaine. "A Whore in Every Home." *Fabian Feminist. Bernard Shaw and Woman.* Ed. Rodelle Weintraub. University Park, PA: Pennsylvania State UP, 1977. 163–66.

Haney, Robert W. *Comstockery in America: Patterns of Censorship and Control.* Boston: Beacon Press, 1960.

Holroyd, Michael. *Bernard Shaw.* 5 vols. London: Chatto & Windus, 1988–92.

Innes, Christopher, ed. *A Sourcebook on Naturalist Theatre.* London and New York: Routledge, 2000.

Johnston, John. *The Lord Chamberlain's Blue Pencil.* London: Hodder & Stoughton, 1990.

Laurence, Dan H. "Victorians Unveiled: Some Thoughts on *Mrs Warren's Profession.*" *SHAW: The Annual of Bernard Shaw Studies* 24 (2004): 38–45.

——, ed. *Bernard Shaw: Collected Letters.* 4 vols. New York: Viking Penguin, 1985–88.

Mander, Raymond, and Joe Mitchenson. *Theatrical Companion to Shaw.* New York: Pitman, 1955.

Morgan, Margery. *The Shavian Playground: An Exploration of the Art of Bernard Shaw.* London: Methuen, 1972.

Nelson, Raymond S. "*Mrs Warren's Profession* and English Prostitution." *Journal of Modern Literature* 2.3 (1971–72): 357–66.

Nicholson, Steve. *The Censorship of British Drama 1900-1968.* Volume 1: 1900-1932. Exeter: U of Exeter P, 2003.

Nield, Keith, ed. *Prostitution in the Victorian Age. Debates on the Issue from 19th Century Critical Journals*. Farnborough, Hants.: Gregg International, 1973.

Pearl, Cyril. *The Girl with the Swansdown Seat*. Indianapolis: Bobbs-Merrill, 1955.

Shaw, Bernard. "Author's Apology," *Mrs Warren's Profession*. London: Grant Richards, 1902.

———. *The Bodley Head Bernard Shaw. Collected Plays with Their Prefaces*. Volume 1. London: Max Reinhardt, The Bodley Head, 1970.

Shaw, Mary. "My 'Immoral' Play." *McClure's Magazine* 38 (April 1912): 684-94.

Turco, Alfred. *Shaw's Moral Vision. The Self and Salvation*. Ithaca: Cornell UP, 1976.

Tyson, Brian F. "Shaw Among the Actors: Theatrical Additions to *Plays Unpleasant*." *Modern Drama* 14 (1971-72): 264-75.

Valency, Maurice. *The Cart and the Trumpet. The Plays of George Bernard Shaw*. New York: Oxford UP, 1973.

Whitman, Robert F. *Shaw and the Play of Ideas*. Ithaca: Cornell UP, 1977.

Wiley, Catherine. "The Matter with Manners: the New Woman and the Problem Play." *Women in Theatre*. Ed. James Redmond. Cambridge: Cambridge UP, 1989. 109-27.

Bernard Shaw: A Brief Chronology

[For a comprehensive and detailed chronology of Shaw's life, see A.M. Gibbs, *A Bernard Shaw Chronology* (Basingstoke: Palgrave, 2001). Early American and British productions (public and private) of *Mrs Warren's Profession* are discussed in L.W. Conolly, "*Mrs Warren's Profession* and the Lord Chamberlain," *SHAW: The Annual of Bernard Shaw Studies* 24 (2004): 46-95. Dates of British and foreign productions of Shaw's plays are given in Raymond Mander and Joe Mitchenson, *Theatrical Companion to Shaw* (New York: Pitman, 1955), and definitive bibliographical information on Shaw can be found in Dan H. Laurence, *Bernard Shaw: A Bibliography*, 2 vols. (Oxford: Clarendon Press, 1983).]

1856 Born in Dublin, 26 July, to George Carr Shaw and Lucinda Elizabeth Shaw.

1871 Leaves school and takes an office job with a Dublin property agency.

1876 Moves from Dublin to London.

1879 Completes his first novel, *Immaturity* (published 1930).

1880 Completes his second novel, *The Irrational Knot* (published in serial form in *Our Corner*, 1885-87).

1881 Completes his third novel, *Love Among the Artists* (published 1900).

1883 Completes his fourth and fifth (his last) novels, *Cashel Byron's Profession* (published 1886) and *An Unsocial Socialist* (published in serial form in *To-Day*, 1884).

1884 Joins the Fabian Society.

1885 Publishes first music and drama criticism in the *Dramatic Review*.

1891 Publishes *The Quintessence of Ibsenism*.

1892 *Widowers' Houses* performed by the Independent Theatre Society, London.

1893 Completes *The Philanderer* and *Mrs Warren's Profession*.

1894 *Arms and the Man* performed at the Avenue Theatre,

London, and the Herald Square Theatre, New York; completes *Candida*.

1895 Begins writing theatre criticism for the *Saturday Review*. Meets H.G. Wells.

1896 Meets Charlotte Payne-Townshend, his future wife. Completes *You Never Can Tell* and *The Devil's Disciple*.

1897 *Candida* performed by the Independent Theatre Company, Aberdeen. *The Man of Destiny* performed at the Grand Theatre, Croydon. American actor Richard Mansfield produces *The Devil's Disciple* in Albany and New York.

1898 Marries Charlotte Payne-Townshend. Publishes *Plays Pleasant* [*Arms and the Man, Candida, The Man of Destiny, You Never Can Tell*] and *Unpleasant* [*Widowers' Houses, The Philanderer, Mrs Warren's Profession*]. Completes *Caesar and Cleopatra*.

1899 *You Never Can Tell* performed by the Stage Society.

1901 Publishes *Three Plays for Puritans* [*The Devil's Disciple, Caesar and Cleopatra, Captain Brassbound's Conversion*].

1902 *Mrs Warren's Profession* performed by the Stage Society. Completes *Man and Superman*.

1903 Publishes *Man and Superman*.

1904 Begins his partnership with Harley Granville Barker and J.E. Vedrenne at the Court Theatre (until 1907). *John Bull's Other Island* performed there.

1905 *Mrs Warren's Profession* performed (then banned) in New Haven and New York. *Man and Superman* and *Major Barbara* performed at the Court Theatre, London. *The Philanderer* performed by the New Stage Club, London.

1906 *The Doctor's Dilemma* performed at the Court Theatre; *Caesar and Cleopatra* performed (in German) in Berlin.

1909 *The Shewing-up of Blanco Posnet* banned in England, but performed in Dublin. *Press Cuttings* banned in England. Completes *Misalliance*.

1911 *Fanny's First Play* performed at the Little Theatre, London. Runs for 622 performances (a record for a Shaw première).

1912 Private production of *Mrs Warren's Profession* by the

Pioneer Players, King's Hall, Covent Garden. Completes *Pygmalion*.

1913 Private production of *Mrs Warren's Profession* by the Glasgow Players, Royalty Theatre, Glasgow. *Pygmalion* performed (in German) in Vienna.

1914 *Mrs Warren's Profession* performed by the Dublin Repertory Theatre, Little Theatre, Dublin. *Pygmalion* performed at His Majesty's Theatre, London. Outbreak of World War One. Publishes *Common Sense about the War*.

1917 Visits front line sites in France. Completes *Heartbreak House*.

1918 End of World War One.

1920 *Heartbreak House* performed by the Theatre Guild, New York. Completes *Back to Methuselah*.

1922 *Back to Methuselah* performed by the Theatre Guild, New York. Meets T.E. Lawrence (Lawrence of Arabia).

1923 Completes *Saint Joan*. It is performed in New York by the Theatre Guild.

1924 First British production of *Saint Joan*, New Theatre, London, with Sybil Thorndike as Joan. The Lord Chamberlain's ban on *Mrs Warren's Profession* is removed.

1925 First public performances in England of *Mrs Warren's Profession* (in Birmingham and London).

1926 Awarded the 1925 Nobel Prize for Literature.

1928 Publishes *The Intelligent Woman's Guide to Socialism and Capitalism*.

1929 *The Apple Cart* performed (in Polish) in Warsaw.

1931 Visits Russia; meets Gorky and Stalin.

1932 Begins world cruise.

1934 Visits New Zealand.

1936 *The Millionairess* performed (in German) in Vienna.

1938 *Pygmalion* is filmed, starring Leslie Howard and Wendy Hiller.

1939 Outbreak of World War Two. Wins an Oscar for the screenplay of *Pygmalion*.

1940 *Major Barbara* is filmed, starring Rex Harrison and Wendy Hiller.

1943 Charlotte Shaw dies.

1944 Publishes *Everybody's Political What's What?*

1945 *Caesar and Cleopatra* is filmed, starring Claude Rains and Vivien Leigh. End of World War Two.

1950 Dies, 2 November, aged 94, from complications after a fall while pruning a shrub in his garden.

A Note on British Currency

Prior to decimalization in 1971, which divided the pound into one hundred pence, British currency consisted of three basic units: pounds, shillings, and pence. There were twenty shillings to a pound, and twelve pence to a shilling. Thus the amount of fifty pounds (£50) won by Vivie Warren for doing well at Cambridge (90-91) amounts to more than two years' income for one of Mrs Warren's half-sisters who works in a factory for nine shillings a week (122), and more than a year's income for the government-employed husband (eighteen shillings a week) of her other half-sister (122). Mrs Warren herself earns four shillings a week and board working in a bar (123). Appendices D1 and D8 document actual cases of incomes for working-class women. Examples of the purchasing power of these amounts are given in the note (90) on Vivie's £50, and in Appendix D8.

The notation for the pound was (and remains) "£"; the notations for shillings and pence were "s." and "d." Thus three shillings and sixpence appears as 3s. 6d. The shillings notation might also appear as "/-"; thus three shillings is 3/- .

A Note on the Text

Mrs Warren's Profession was first published in 1898 in volume 1 (*Plays Unpleasant*) of *Plays Pleasant and Unpleasant*, in London by Grant Richards, and in Chicago and New York by Herbert S. Stone. The other plays in *Plays Unpleasant* were *Widowers' Houses* and *The Philanderer*. The first separate edition of *Mrs Warren's Profession* was published in London by Grant Richards in 1902 in an identical text, but with a new preface by Shaw and photographs of the Stage Society production of 5-6 January 1902. Shaw revised *Mrs Warren's Profession* for the *Plays Unpleasant* volume (1930) of *The Works of Bernard Shaw: Collected Edition*, published in London by Constable between 1930 and 1938. This was the text of *Mrs Warren's Profession* used for *Bernard Shaw: Collected Plays with Their Prefaces* published in seven volumes by Max Reinhardt between 1970 and 1974 under the editorial supervision of Dan H. Laurence, and subsequently by Penguin Books, again under the editorial supervision of Dan H. Laurence. The definitive Penguin text is the copytext for this Broadview edition.

Shaw made numerous revisions in the 1898 text for the 1930 edition. Many are relatively minor, but those that suggest significant changes in Shaw's thinking about a character or situation are recorded in footnotes in this edition.

Shaw had strong opinions on matters of spelling, punctuation, and typography. He retained some archaic spellings (e.g. *shew* for *show*), and dropped the "u" in "our" spellings of words such as *honor, labor,* and *neighbor.* He preferred to reserve the use of italics for stage directions and descriptions of settings and characters (which are detailed and elaborate for the benefit of readers who might never have the opportunity of seeing his plays), electing to indicate emphasis of a word by spacing the letters (e.g. d e a r for *dear*, v e r y for *very*). He had no choice but to use italics for stressing *I*, and he sometimes chose to use small capital letters for stressing some words (e.g. ME for *me*).

Shaw disliked the apostrophe, believing it to be redundant (and ugly) in most instances. He eliminated it whenever he could (e.g. in *Ive, youve, thats, werent, dont, wont*), though it was necessary to retain it where its omission might cause confusion (e.g. *I'll, it's, he'll*).

For some readers Shaw's rationale for these practices is unconvincing, and the idiosyncrasies are irritating. They are, however, Shaw's clear preferences, and serve if nothing else as a frequent reminder of his nonconformity—the essence of the man and his work—and have, therefore, been retained in this edition.

Mrs Warren's Profession: A Play in Four Acts. By Bernard Shaw.

The harlot's cry from street to street
Shall weave old England's winding-sheet.
          BLAKE'S AUGURIES OF INNOCENCE.

London: Grant Richards, 48 Leicester Square, W.C. 1902

Title-page of the first separate edition (1902) of *Mrs Warren's Profession*. Courtesy Dan H. Laurence Collection, L.W. Conolly Theatre Archives, University of Guelph.

MRS WARREN'S[1] PROFESSION

---

1   In July 1950 Shaw received a letter from a Mr Holden asking if there was any connection between his Mrs Warren and a Mrs Warren who had been fined in April 1868 for "harbouring prostitutes knowingly" in a "refreshment-house" on Jermyn St in London (as reported in *The Times*, 25 April 1868). Shaw replied that he was only twelve years old at the time, and explained that the name Warren "was suggested by a famous case (Virginia Crawford v. Sir Charles Dilke), the most scandalous incident of which took place in Warren St, close to my door in Fitzroy Square." A prominent politician, Dilke conducted an adulterous relationship with Mrs Crawford at 65 Warren St. (See Roy Jenkins, *Dilke: A Victorian Tragedy* [London: Macmillan, 1996].) A copy of the Holden/Shaw exchange is in the Dan H. Laurence file on *Mrs Warren's Profession*, Archival and Special Collections, University of Guelph Library. The Commissioner of the Metropolitan Police who gave the order to attack demonstrators (including Shaw) against the British government's Irish policy in Trafalgar Square on 13 November 1887 ("Bloody Sunday") was named Sir Charles Warren.

ACT I

Summer afternoon in a cottage garden on the eastern slope of a hill a little south of Haslemere[1] in Surrey. Looking up the hill, the cottage is seen in the left hand corner of the garden, with its thatched roof and porch, and a large latticed[2] window to the left of the porch. A paling completely shuts in the garden, except for a gate on the right. The common rises uphill beyond the paling to the sky line. Some folded canvas garden chairs are leaning against the side bench in the porch. A lady's bicycle is propped against the wall, under the window. A little to the right of the porch a hammock is slung from two posts. A big canvas umbrella, stuck in the ground, keeps the sun off the hammock, in which a young lady lies reading and making notes, her head towards the cottage and her feet towards the gate. In front of the hammock, and within reach of her hand, is a common kitchen chair, with a pile of serious-looking books and a supply of writing paper on it.

A gentleman walking on the common comes into sight from behind the cottage. He is hardly past middle age, with something of the artist about him, unconventionally but carefully dressed and clean-shaven except for a moustache, with an eager susceptible face and very amiable and considerate manners. He has silky black hair, with waves of grey and white in it. His eyebrows are white, his moustache black. He seems not certain of his way. He looks over the paling; takes stock of the place; and sees the young lady.

THE GENTLEMAN [*taking off his hat*]. I beg your pardon. Can you direct me to Hindhead View—Mrs Alison's?

THE YOUNG LADY [*glancing up from her book*]. This is Mrs Alison's. [*She resumes her work.*]

THE GENTLEMAN. Indeed! Perhaps—may I ask are you Miss Vivie Warren?

THE YOUNG LADY [*sharply, as she turns on her elbow to get a good look at him*]. Yes.

---

1 A market town about 40 miles southwest of London, with a population (1901) of 2,614. "The invigorating air has combined with scenic attraction to make the district a favourite place of residence" (*Encyclopaedia Britannica*, 11th ed.). Shaw lived briefly in Haslemere during the early years of his marriage.
2 Divided by strips into square or diamond-shaped sections.

THE GENTLEMAN [*daunted and conciliatory*]. I'm afraid I appear intrusive. My name is Praed.[1] [*Vivie at once throws her books upon the chair, and gets out of the hammock.*] Oh, pray dont[2] let me disturb you.

VIVIE [*striding to the gate and opening it for him*]. Come in, Mr. Praed. [*He comes in.*] Glad to see you. [*She proffers her hand and takes his with a resolute and hearty grip. She is an attractive specimen of the sensible, able, highly-educated young middle-class Englishwoman. Age 22. Prompt, strong, confident, self-possessed. Plain business-like dress, but not dowdy. She wears a chatelaine[3] at her belt, with a fountain pen and a paper knife among its pendants.*]

PRAED. Very kind of you indeed, Miss Warren. [*She shuts the gate with a vigorous slam. He passes in to the middle of the garden, exercising his fingers, which are slightly numbed by her greeting.*] Has your mother arrived?

VIVIE [*quickly, evidently scenting aggression*]. Is she coming?

PRAED [*surprised*]. Didnt you expect us?

VIVIE. No.

PRAED. Now, goodness me, I hope Ive not mistaken the day. That would be just like me, you know. Your mother arranged that she was to come down from London and that I was to come over from Horsham[4] to be introduced to you.

VIVIE [*not at all pleased*]. Did she? Hm! My mother has rather a trick of taking me by surprise—to see how I behave myself when she's away, I suppose. I fancy I shall take my mother very much by surprise one of these days, if she makes arrangements that concern me without consulting me beforehand. She hasnt come.

PRAED [*embarrassed*]. I'm really very sorry.

---

1 Praed's name is perhaps an allusion to Winthrop Mackworth Praed (1802-39), a Cambridge-educated politician and poet. Shaw could have seen his portrait (by Irish painter Daniel Maclise) in the National Gallery in London. Praed St is just north of Hyde Park in west central London.

2 Shaw deliberately omits the apostrophe. See A Note on the Text, above, p. 80.

3 A set of short chains attached to a woman's belt used for carrying small items (such as Vivie's fountain pen and paper knife).

4 A market town about 38 miles southwest of London (about 15 miles east of Haslemere), with a population (1901) of 9,446. "The town has industries of tanning, founding, carriage-building and flour milling" (*Encyclopaedia Britannica*, 11th ed.).

VIVIE [*throwing off her displeasure*]. It's not your fault, Mr Praed, is it? And I'm very glad youve come. You are the only one of my mother's friends I have ever asked her to bring to see me.

PRAED [*relieved and delighted*]. Oh, now this is really very good of you, Miss Warren!

VIVIE. Will you come indoors; or would you rather sit out here and talk?

PRAED. It will be nicer out here, dont you think?

VIVIE. Then I'll go and get you a chair. [*She goes to the porch for a garden chair.*]

PRAED [*following her*]. Oh, pray, pray! Allow me. [*He lays hands on the chair.*]

VIVIE [*letting him take it*]. Take care of your fingers, theyre rather dodgy things, those chairs. [*She goes across to the chair with the books on it; pitches them into the hammock; and brings the chair forward with one swing.*]

PRAED [*who has just unfolded his chair*]. Oh, now do let me take that hard chair. I like hard chairs.

VIVIE. So do I. Sit down, Mr Praed. [*This invitation she gives with genial peremptoriness, his anxiety to please her clearly striking her as a sign of weakness of character on his part. But he does not immediately obey.*]

PRAED. By the way, though, hadnt we better go to the station to meet your mother?

VIVIE [*coolly*]. Why? She knows the way.

PRAED [*disconcerted*]. Er—I suppose she does [*he sits down*].

VIVIE. Do you know, you are just like what I expected. I hope you are disposed to be friends with me.

PRAED [*again beaming*]. Thank you, my d e a r[1] Miss Warren: thank you. Dear me! I'm so glad your mother hasnt spoilt you!

VIVIE. How?

PRAED. Well, in making you too conventional. You know, my dear Miss Warren, I am a born anarchist. I hate authority. It spoils the relations between parent and child: even between mother

---

1 The spacing between the letters is Shaw's way of giving emphasis to the word. See A Note on the Text, above, p. 80.

and daughter. Now I was always afraid that your mother would strain her authority to make you very conventional. It's such a relief to find that she hasnt.

VIVIE. Oh! have I been behaving unconventionally?

PRAED. Oh no: oh dear no. At least not conventionally unconventionally, you understand. [*She nods and sits down. He goes on, with a cordial outburst.*] But it was so charming of you to say that you were disposed to be friends with me! You modern young ladies are splendid: perfectly splendid!

VIVIE [*dubiously*]. Eh? [*watching him with dawning disappointment as to the quality of his brains and character*].

PRAED. When I was your age, young men and women were afraid of each other: there was no good fellowship. Nothing real. Only gallantry copied out of novels, and as vulgar and affected as it could be. Maidenly reserve! gentlemanly chivalry! always saying no when you meant yes! simple purgatory[1] for shy and sincere souls.

VIVIE. Yes, I imagine there must have been a frightful waste of time. Especially women's time.

PRAED. Oh, waste of life, waste of everything. But things are improving. Do you know, I have been in a positive state of excitement about meeting you ever since your magnificent achievements at Cambridge: a thing unheard of in my day. It was perfectly splendid, your tieing with the third wrangler.[2] Just the right place, you know. The first wrangler is always a dreamy, morbid fellow, in whom the thing is pushed to the length of a disease.

VIVIE. It doesnt pay. I wouldnt do it again for the same money!

PRAED [*aghast*]. The same money!

VIVIE. I did it for £50.[3]

---

1 A place in Catholic doctrine for spiritual cleansing of the dead before entry to heaven.

2 Wranglers were those who achieved a first-class honours degree in mathematics at Cambridge. Vivie had placed equal third among the wranglers in her year. The top student was designated senior wrangler.

3 £50 was a considerable sum. Vivie could have used it, for example, to buy 25 gold watches, 500 restaurant dinners, 25 good coats, 600 bottles of claret, or five bicycles. She could also have rented a three-bedroom house for a year or stayed in a hotel for 150 nights. (Prices as advertised in issues of the *Cambridge Evening News*, 1889-90.) It

PRAED. Fifty pounds!

VIVIE. Yes. Fifty pounds. Perhaps you dont know how it was. Mrs Latham, my tutor at Newnham,[1] told my mother that I could distinguish myself in the mathematical tripos[2] if I went in for it in earnest. The papers were full just then of Phillipa Summers[3] beating the senior wrangler.[4] You remember about it, of course.

PRAED [*shakes his head energetically*] ! ! !

VIVIE. Well anyhow she did: and nothing would please my mother but that I should do the same thing. I said flatly it was not worth my while to face the grind since I was not going in for teaching; but I offered to try for fourth wrangler or thereabouts for £50. She closed with me at that, after a little grumbling; and I was better than my bargain. But I wouldnt do it again for that. £200 would have been nearer the mark.

PRAED [*much damped*]. Lord bless me! Thats a very practical way of looking at it.

VIVIE. Did you expect to find me an unpractical person?

PRAED. But surely its practical to consider not only the work these honors cost, but also the culture they bring.

VIVIE. Culture! My dear Mr Praed: do you know what the mathematical tripos means? It means grind, grind, grind for six to eight hours a day at mathematics, and nothing but mathematics. I'm supposed to know something about science; but I know nothing except the mathematics it involves. I can make calculations for engineers, electricians, insurance companies, and so on; but I know next to nothing about engineering or

---

would have taken most working-class women two years to earn £50. See A Note on British Currency, above, p. 79.

1 Newnham College was founded as a women's college of Cambridge University in 1871. The first Cambridge college for women, Girton, was founded in 1869. All other colleges of the University admitted men only.

2 The Tripos was (and is) the honours course at Cambridge, so-called because of the medieval tradition of the examiner sitting on a three-legged stool.

3 An allusion to Philippa Fawcett, daughter of Henry Fawcett (1833-84), Professor of Political Economy at Cambridge and Liberal Member of Parliament, and Millicent Fawcett (1847-1929), leader of the women's suffrage movement and strong proponent of women's education at Cambridge. Philippa Fawcett gained the highest mark in the mathematical tripos in June 1890 (*The Times*, 9 June 1890), the first woman to do so.

4 See p. 90, note 2.

electricity or insurance. I dont even know arithmetic well. Outside mathematics, lawn-tennis, eating, sleeping, cycling, and walking, I'm a more ignorant barbarian than any woman could possibly be who hadnt gone in for the tripos.

PRAED [*revolted*]. What a monstrous, wicked, rascally system! I knew it! I felt at once that it meant destroying all that makes womanhood beautiful.

VIVIE. I dont object to it on that score in the least. I shall turn it to very good account, I assure you.

PRAED. Pooh! in what way?

VIVIE. I shall set up chambers[1] in the City, and work at actuarial calculations and conveyancing.[2] Under cover of that I shall do some law, with one eye on the Stock Exchange all the time. Ive come down here by myself to read law: not for a holiday, as my mother imagines. I hate holidays.

PRAED. You make my blood run cold. Are you to have no romance, no beauty in your life?

VIVIE. I dont care for either, I assure you.

PRAED. You cant mean that.

VIVIE. Oh yes I do. I like working and getting paid for it. When I'm tired of working, I like a comfortable chair, a cigar, a little whisky, and a novel with a good detective story in it.

PRAED [*rising in a frenzy of repudiation*]. I dont believe it. I am an artist; and I cant believe it: I refuse to believe it. It's only that you havnt discovered yet what a wonderful world art can open up to you.

VIVIE. Yes I have. Last May I spent six weeks in London with Honoria Fraser. Mamma thought we were doing a round of sightseeing together; but I was really at Honoria's chambers in Chancery Lane[3] every day, working away at actuarial calculations for her, and helping her as well as a greenhorn could. In the evenings we smoked and talked, and never dreamt of going out except for exercise. And I never enjoyed myself more in

---

1   The term used in England for law offices.

2   Vivie will specialize as an actuary (compiling and analyzing statistics to calculate insurance risks and premiums) and a conveyancer (transferring ownership of property).

3   A street in west central London; the location of many legal offices and related businesses.

my life. I cleared all my expenses, and got initiated into the business without a fee into the bargain.

PRAED. But bless my heart and soul, Miss Warren, do you call that discovering art?

VIVIE. Wait a bit. That wasnt the beginning. I went up to town on an invitation from some artistic people in Fitzjohn's Avenue:[1] one of the girls was a Newnham chum. They took me to the National Gallery—[2]

PRAED [approving]. Ah ! ! [He sits down, much relieved.]

VIVIE [continuing]—to the Opera—

PRAED [still more pleased]. Good!

VIVIE.—and to a concert where the band played all the evening: Beethoven and Wagner[3] and so on. I wouldnt go through that experience again for anything you could offer me. I held out for civility's sake until the third day; and then I said, plump out, that I couldnt stand anymore of it, and went off to Chancery Lane. Now you know the sort of perfectly splendid modern young lady I am. How do you think I shall get on with my mother?

PRAED [startled]. Well, I hope—er—

VIVIE. It's not so much what you hope as what you believe, that I want to know.

PRAED. Well, frankly, I am afraid your mother will be a little disappointed. Not from any shortcoming on your part, you know: I dont mean that. But you are so different from her ideal.

VIVIE. Her what?!

PRAED. Her ideal.

VIVIE. Do you mean her ideal of ME?

PRAED. Yes.

VIVIE. What on Earth is it like?

PRAED. Well, you must have observed, Miss Warren, that people who are dissatisfied with their own bringing-up generally

---

1   A street in the fashionable district of Hampstead, northwest of central London.

2   Founded in 1824, the National Gallery moved to its current location on the north side of Trafalgar Square in 1838. The Gallery holds one of the world's finest collections of European paintings. Shaw was a frequent visitor.

3   German composers Ludwig van Beethoven (1770-1827) and Wilhelm Richard Wagner (1813-83).

think that the world would be all right if everybody were to be brought up quite differently. Now your mother's life has been—er—I suppose you know—

VIVIE. Dont suppose anything, Mr Praed. I hardly know my mother. Since I was a child I have lived in England, at school or college, or with people paid to take charge of me. I have been boarded out all my life. My mother has lived in Brussels or Vienna and never let me go to her. I only see her when she visits England for a few days. I dont complain: it's been very pleasant; for people have been very good to me; and there has always been plenty of money to make things smooth. But dont imagine I know anything about my mother. I know far less than you do.

PRAED [*very ill at ease*]. In that case—[*He stops, quite at a loss. Then, with a forced attempt at gaiety.*] But what nonsense we are talking! Of course you and your mother will get on capitally. [*He rises, and looks abroad at the view.*] What a charming little place you have here!

VIVIE [*unmoved*]. Rather a violent change of subject, Mr Praed. Why wont my mother's life bear being talked about?

PRAED. Oh, you really musnt say that. Isnt it natural that I should have a certain delicacy in talking to my old friend's daughter about her behind her back? You and she will have plenty of opportunity of talking about it when she comes.

VIVIE. No: s h e wont talk about it either. [*Rising.*] However, I daresay you have good reasons for telling me nothing. Only, mind this, Mr Praed. I expect there will be a battle royal when my mother hears of my Chancery Lane project.

PRAED [*ruefully*]. I'm afraid there will.

VIVIE. Well, I shall win because I want nothing but my fare to London to start there to-morrow earning my own living by devilling[1] for Honoria. Besides, I have no mysteries to keep up; and it seems she has. I shall use that advantage over her if necessary.

PRAED [*greatly shocked*]. Oh no! No, pray. Youd not do such a thing.

---

1   To devil is to serve as a barrister's (i.e. lawyer's) junior assistant.

VIVIE. Then tell me why not.

PRAED. I really cannot. I appeal to your good feeling. [*She smiles at his sentimentality.*] Besides, you may be too bold. Your mother is not to be trifled with when she's angry.

VIVIE. You can't frighten me, Mr Praed. In that month at Chancery Lane I had opportunities of taking the measure of one or two women v e r y like my mother. You may back me to win. But if I hit harder in my ignorance than I need, remember that it is you who refuse to enlighten me. Now, let us drop the subject. [*She takes her chair and replaces it near the hammock with the same vigorous swing as before.*]

PRAED [*taking a desperate resolution*]. One word, Miss Warren. I had better tell you. It's very difficult; but—

Mrs Warren and Sir George Crofts arrive at the gate. Mrs Warren is between 40 and 50, formerly pretty, showily dressed in a brilliant hat and a gay blouse fitting tightly over her bust and flanked by fashionable sleeves. Rather spoilt and domineering, and decidedly vulgar, but, on the whole, a genial and fairly presentable old blackguard[1] of a woman.

Crofts is a tall powerfully-built man of about 50, fashionably dressed in the style of a young man. Nasal voice, reedier than might be expected from his strong frame. Clean-shaven bulldog jaws, large flat ears, and thick neck: gentlemanly combination of the most brutal types of city man, sporting man, and man about town.

VIVIE. Here they are. [*Coming to them as they enter the garden.*] How do, mater? Mr Praed's been here this half hour waiting for you.

MRS WARREN. Well, if youve been waiting, Praddy, it's your own fault: I thought youd have had the gumption[2] to know I was coming by the 3:10 train. Vivie: put your hat on, dear: youll get sunburnt. Oh, I forgot to introduce you. Sir George Crofts: my little Vivie.

---

1   A person characterized by dishonourable behaviour; here used by Shaw more as a term of endearment. In the 1898 text Mrs Warren is still "good-looking" (not just "formerly pretty"), and she is not described as "decidedly vulgar."

2   Common sense.

Crofts advances to Vivie with his most courtly manner. She nods, but makes no motion to shake hands.

CROFTS. May I shake hands with a young lady whom I have known by reputation very long as the daughter of one of my oldest friends?

VIVIE [*who has been looking him up and down sharply*]. If you like. [*She takes his tenderly proffered hand and gives it a squeeze that makes him open his eyes; then turns away and says to her mother.*] Will you come in, or shall I get a couple more chairs? [*She goes into the porch for the chairs.*]

MRS WARREN. Well, George, what do you think of her?

CROFTS [*ruefully*]. She has a powerful fist. Did you shake hands with her, Praed?

PRAED. Yes: it will pass off presently.

CROFTS. I hope so. [*Vivie reappears with two more chairs. He hurries to her assistance.*] Allow me.

MRS WARREN [*patronizingly*]. Let Sir George help you with the chairs, dear.

VIVIE [*pitching them into his arms*]. Here you are. [*She dusts her hands and turns to Mrs Warren.*] Youd like some tea, wouldnt you?

MRS WARREN [*sitting in Praed's chair and fanning herself*]. I'm dying for a drop to drink.

VIVIE. I'll see about it. [*She goes into the cottage.*]

Sir George has by this time managed to unfold a chair and plant it beside Mrs Warren, on her left. He throws the other on the grass and sits down, looking dejected and rather foolish, with the handle of his stick in his mouth. Praed, still very uneasy, fidgets about the garden on their right.

MRS WARREN [*to Praed, looking at Crofts*]. Just look at him, Praddy: he looks cheerful, dont he? He's been worrying my life out these three years to have that little girl of mine shewn to him; and now that Ive done it, he's quite out of countenance. [*Briskly.*] Come! sit up, George; and take your stick out of your mouth. [*Crofts sulkily obeys.*]

PRAED. I think, you know—if you dont mind my saying so—that

we had better get out of the habit of thinking of her as a little girl. You see she has really distinguished herself; and I'm not sure, from what I have seen of her, that she is not older than any of us.

MRS WARREN [*greatly amused*]. Only listen to him, George! Older than any of us! Well, she h a s been stuffing you nicely with her importance.

PRAED. But young people are particularly sensitive about being treated in that way.

MRS WARREN. Yes; and young people have to get all that nonsense taken out of them, and a good deal more besides. Dont you interfere, Praddy: I know how to treat my own child as well as you do. [*Praed, with a grave shake of his head, walks up the garden with his hands behind his back. Mrs Warren pretends to laugh, but looks after him with perceptible concern. Then she whispers to Crofts.*] Whats the matter with him? What does he take it like that for?

CROFTS [*morosely*]. Youre afraid of Praed.

MRS WARREN. What! Me! Afraid of dear old Praddy! Why, a fly wouldnt be afraid of him.

CROFTS. Y o u r e afraid of him.

MRS WARREN [*angry*]. I'll trouble you to mind your own business, and not try any of your sulks on me. I'm not afraid of y o u , anyhow. If you cant make yourself agreeable, youd better go home. [*She gets up, and, turning her back on him, finds herself face to face with Praed.*] Come, Praddy, I know it was only your tender-heartedness. Youre afraid I'll bully her.

PRAED. My dear Kitty: you think I'm offended. Dont imagine that: pray dont. But you know I often notice things that escape you; and though you never take my advice, you sometimes admit afterwards that you ought to have taken it.

MRS WARREN. Well, what do you notice now?

PRAED. Only that Vivie is a grown woman. Pray, Kitty, treat her with every respect.

MRS WARREN [*with genuine amazement*]. Respect! Treat my own daughter with respect! What next, pray!

VIVIE [*appearing at the cottage door and calling to Mrs Warren*]. Mother: will you come to my room before tea?

MRS WARREN. Yes, dearie. [*She laughs indulgently at Praed's gravity, and pats him on the cheek as she passes him on her way to the porch.*] Dont be cross, Praddy. [*She follows Vivie in to the cottage.*]

CROFTS [*furtively*]. I say, Praed.

PRAED. Yes.

CROFTS. I want to ask you a rather particular question.

PRAED. Certainly. [*He takes Mrs Warren's chair and sits close to Crofts.*]

CROFTS. Thats right: they might hear us from the window. Look here: did Kitty ever tell you who that girl's father is?

PRAED. Never.

CROFTS. Have you any suspicion of who it might be?

PRAED. None.

CROFTS [*not believing him*]. I know, of course, that you perhaps might feel bound not to tell if she had said anything to you. But it's very awkward to be uncertain about it now that we shall be meeting the girl every day. We wont exactly know how we ought to feel towards her.

PRAED. What difference can that make? We take her on her own merits. What does it matter who her father was?

CROFTS [*suspiciously*]. Then you know who he was?

PRAED [*with a touch of temper*]. I said no just now. Did you not hear me?

CROFTS. Look here, Praed. I ask you as a particular favor. If you d o know [*movement of protest from Praed*]—I only say, if you know, you might at least set my mind at rest about her. The fact is, I feel attracted.

PRAED [*sternly*]. What do you mean?

CROFTS. Oh, dont be alarmed: it's quite an innocent feeling. Thats what puzzles me about it. Why, for all I know *I* might be her father.

PRAED. You! Impossible!

CROFTS [*catching him up cunningly*]. You know for certain that I'm not?

PRAED. I know nothing about it, I tell you, any more than you. But really, Crofts—oh no, it's out of the question. Theres not the least resemblance.

CROFTS. As to that, theres no resemblance between her and her mother that I can see. I suppose she's not y o u r daughter, is she?

PRAED [*rising indignantly*]. Really, Crofts—!

CROFTS. No offence, Praed. Quite allowable as between two men of the world.

PRAED [*recovering himself with an effort and speaking gently and gravely*]. Now listen to me, my dear Crofts. [*He sits down again.*] I have nothing to do with that side of Mrs Warren's life, and never had. She has never spoken to me about it; and of course I have never spoken to her about it. Your delicacy will tell you that a handsome woman needs some friends who are not—well, not on that footing with her. The effect of her own beauty would become a torment to her if she could not escape from it occasionally. You are probably on much more confidential terms with Kitty than I am. Surely you can ask her the question yourself.

CROFTS. I h a v e asked her, often enough. But she's so determined to keep the child all to herself that she would deny that it ever had a father if she could. [*Rising.*] I'm thoroughly uncomfortable about it, Praed.

PRAED [*rising also*]. Well, as you are, at all events, old enough to be her father, I dont mind agreeing that we both regard Miss Vivie in a parental way, as a young girl whom we are bound to protect and help. What do you say?

CROFTS [*aggressively*]. I'm no older than you, if you come to that.

PRAED. Yes you are, my dear fellow: you were born old. I was born a boy: Ive never been able to feel the assurance of a grown-up man in my life. [*He folds his chair and carries it to the porch.*]

MRS WARREN [*calling from within the cottage*]. Prad-dee! George! Tea-ea-ea-ea!

CROFTS [*hastily*]. She's calling us. [*He hurries in.*]

Praed shakes his head bodingly, and is following Crofts when he is hailed by a young gentleman who has just appeared on the common, and is making for the gate. He is pleasant, pretty, smartly dressed, cleverly good-for-nothing, not long turned 20, with a charming voice and agreeably disrespectful manners. He carries a light sporting magazine rifle.[1]

THE YOUNG GENTLEMAN. Hallo! Praed!

PRAED. Why, Frank Gardner! [*Frank comes in and shakes hands cordially.*] What on earth are you doing here?

FRANK. Staying with my father.

PRAED. The Roman father?[2]

FRANK. He's rector here. I'm living with my people this autumn for the sake of economy. Things came to a crisis in July: the Roman father had to pay my debts. He's stony broke in consequence; and so am I. What are you up to in these parts? Do you know the people here?

PRAED. Yes: I'm spending the day with a Miss Warren.

FRANK [*enthusiastically*]. What! Do you know Vivie? Isnt she a jolly girl? I'm teaching her to shoot with this [*putting down the rifle*]. I'm so glad she knows you: youre just the sort of fellow she ought to know. [*He smiles, and raises the charming voice almost to a singing tone as he exclaims.*] It's e v e r so jolly to find you here, Praed.

PRAED. I'm an old friend of her mother. Mrs Warren brought me over to make her daughter's acquaintance.

FRANK. The mother! Is s h e here?

PRAED. Yes: inside, at tea.

MRS WARREN [*calling from within*]. Prad-dee-ee-ee-eee! The tea-cake'll be cold.

PRAED [*calling*]. Yes, Mrs Warren. In a moment. Ive just met a friend here.

MRS WARREN. A what?

PRAED [*louder*]. A friend.

MRS WARREN. Bring him in.

---

1 i.e. an automatic rifle. In his description of Frank in the 1898 text Shaw makes him "entirely good-for-nothing" rather than "cleverly good-for-nothing."

2 This might be thought to suggest that Frank's father is a Catholic priest, but he is in fact a clergyman of the Church of England. It is more likely an ironic reference to supposed "Roman" qualities of strictness and integrity—hardly qualities that we recognize in the Reverend Samuel (or his son).

PRAED. All right. [to Frank.] Will you accept the invitation?

FRANK [incredulous, but immensely amused]. Is that Vivie's mother?

PRAED. Yes.

FRANK. By Jove! What a lark! Do you think she'll like me?

PRAED. Ive no doubt youll make yourself popular as usual. Come in and try [moving toward the house].

FRANK. Stop a bit. [Seriously.] I want to take you into my confidence.

PRAED. Pray dont. It's only some fresh folly, like the barmaid at Redhill.[1]

FRANK. Its ever so much more serious than that. You say youve only just met Vivie for the first time?

PRAED. Yes.

FRANK [rhapsodically]. Then you can have no idea what a girl she is. Such character! Such sense! And her cleverness! Oh, my eye, Praed, but I can tell you she is clever! And—need I add?—she loves me.

CROFTS [putting his head out of the window]. I say, Praed: what are you about? Do come along. [He disappears.]

FRANK. Hallo! Sort of chap that would take a prize at a dog show, aint he? Who's he?

PRAED. Sir George Crofts, an old friend of Mrs Warren's. I think we had better come in.

On their way to the porch they are interrupted by a call from the gate. Turning, they see an elderly clergyman looking over it.

THE CLERGYMAN [calling]. Frank!

FRANK. Hallo! [To Praed.] The Roman father. [To the clergyman.] Yes, gov'nor: all right: presently. [To Praed.] Look here, Praed: youd better go in to tea. I'll join you directly.

PRAED. Very good. [He goes into the cottage.]

---

1 A small town about 25 miles south of London, with a population (1901) of 25,993 (Encyclopaedia Britannica, 11th ed.). Frank's "folly" with the barmaid is not further explained, but it hints at the nature of his pre-Vivie relationships.

The clergyman remains outside the gate, with his hands on the top of it. The Rev. Samuel Gardner, a beneficed[1] clergyman of the Established Church,[2] is over 50. Externally he is pretentious, booming, noisy, important. Really he is that obsolescent social phenomenon the fool of the family dumped on the Church by his father the patron, clamorously asserting himself as father and clergyman without being able to command respect in either capacity.

REV. S. Well, sir. Who are your friends here, if I may ask?

FRANK. Oh, it's all right, gov'nor! Come in.

REV. S. No, sir; not until I know whose garden I am entering.

FRANK. It's all right. It's Miss Warren's.

REV. S. I have not seen her at church since she came.

FRANK. Of course not: she's a third wrangler. Ever so intellectual. Took a higher degree than you did; so why should she go to hear you preach?

REV. S. Dont be disrespectful, sir.

FRANK. Oh, it dont matter: nobody hears us. Come in. [*He opens the gate, unceremoniously pulling his father with it into the garden.*] I want to introduce you to her. Do you remember the advice you gave me last July, gov'nor?

REV. S. [*severely*]. Yes. I advised you to conquer your idleness and flippancy, and to work your way into an honorable profession and live on it and not upon me.

FRANK. No: thats what you thought of afterwards. What you actually said was that since I had neither brains nor money, I'd better turn my good looks to account by marrying somebody with both. Well, look here, Miss Warren has brains: you cant deny that.

REV. S. Brains are not everything.

FRANK. No, of course not: theres the money—

REV. S. [*interrupting him austerely*]. I was not thinking of money sir. I was speaking of higher things. Social position, for instance.

FRANK. I dont care a rap about that.

REV. S. But I do, sir.

---

1 Supported by the church (with house and salary).
2 Church of England.

FRANK. Well, nobody wants y o u to marry her. Anyhow, she has what amounts to a high Cambridge degree;[1] and she seems to have as much money as she wants.

REV. S. [*sinking into a feeble vein of humor*]. I greatly doubt whether she has as much money as y o u will want.

FRANK. Oh, come: I havnt been so very extravagant. I live ever so quietly; I dont drink; I dont bet much; and I never go regularly on the razzle-dazzle as you did when you were my age.

REV. S. [*booming hollowly*]. Silence, sir.

FRANK. Well, you told me yourself, when I was making ever such an ass of myself about the barmaid at Redhill, that you once offered a woman £50 for the letters you wrote to her when—

REV. S. [*terrified*]. Sh-sh-sh, Frank, for Heaven's sake! [*He looks around apprehensively. Seeing no one within earshot he plucks up courage to boom again, but more subduedly.*] You are taking an ungentlemanly advantage of what I confided to you for your own good, to save you from an error you would have repented all your life long. Take warning by your father's follies, sir; and dont make them an excuse for your own.

FRANK. Did you ever hear the story of the Duke of Wellington and his letters?

REV. S. No, sir; and I dont want to hear it.

FRANK. The old Iron Duke didnt throw away £50: not he. He just wrote: 'Dear Jenny: publish and be damned! Yours affectionately, Wellington.' Thats what you should have done.[2]

REV. S. [*piteously*]. Frank, my boy: when I wrote those letters I put myself into that woman's power. When I told you about them I put myself, to some extent, I am sorry to say, in your power. She refused my money with these words, which I shall never

---

1 Vivie has not actually been awarded a degree by Cambridge, only, as Frank says, "what amounts to one." See Introduction, 49.

2 Arthur Wellesley, 1st Duke of Wellington (1769-1852), defeated Napoleon at Waterloo in 1815. He later served as Prime Minister, 1828-30. His comment "Publish and be damned" was in response to a blackmail letter from Joseph Stockdale, publisher of the *Memoirs* (1825) of Harriette Wilson, a London courtesan well-known to Wellington. See Elizabeth Longford, *Wellington* (London: Weidenfeld and Nicolson, 1992) 109-10. Frank's account differs somewhat, but it fits more neatly with his father's situation. Wellington's iron-fisted discipline in military matters caused him to be known as the Iron Duke.

forget. 'Knowledge is power,' she said; 'and I never sell power'. Thats more than twenty years ago; and she has never made use of her power or caused me a moment's uneasiness. You are behaving worse to me than she did, Frank.

FRANK. Oh yes I dare say! Did you ever preach at her the way you preach at me every day?

REV. S. [*wounded almost to tears*]. I leave you, sir. You are incorrigible. [*He turns toward the gate.*]

FRANK. [*utterly unmoved*]. Tell them I shant be home to tea, will you, gov'nor, like a good fellow? [*He moves towards the cottage door and is met by Praed and Vivie coming out.*]

VIVIE [*to Frank*]. Is that your father, Frank? I do so want to meet him.

FRANK. Certainly. [*Calling after his father.*] Gov'nor. Youre wanted. [*The parson turns at the gate, fumbling nervously at his hat. Praed crosses the garden to the opposite side, beaming in anticipation of civilities.*] My father: Miss Warren.

VIVIE [*going to the clergyman and shaking his hand*]. Very glad to see you here, Mr Gardner. [*Calling to the cottage.*] Mother: come along: youre wanted.

Mrs Warren appears on the threshold, and is immediately transfixed recognizing the clergyman.

VIVIE [*continuing*]. Let me introduce—

MRS WARREN [*swooping on the Reverend Samuel*]. Why, it's Sam Gardner, gone into the church! Well, I never! Dont you know us, Sam? This is George Crofts, as large as life and twice as natural. Dont you remember me?

REV. S. [*very red*]. I really—er—

MRS WARREN. Of course you do. Why, I have a whole album of your letters still: I came across them only the other day.

REV. S. [*miserably confused*]. Miss Vavasour,[1] I believe.

---

1   The name used by Mrs Warren at the time the Reverend Samuel knew her. A vavasour was a medieval vassal owing allegiance to a great lord. Mrs Warren now owes allegiance to no-one. There have been other explanations of the name, including the Ann Vavasour who had an affair with the Earl of Oxford, one of the maids of honour

MRS WARREN [*correcting him quickly in a loud whisper*]. Tch! Nonsense!
Mrs Warren: dont you see my daughter there?

---

of Elizabeth I, and Lilian Vavasour, heroine of Tom Taylor's and Augustus Dubourg's play *New Men and Old Acres* (1869). Shaw saw Ellen Terry play the role in 1876. See letters from Irving McKee and Sidney P. Albert, *The Shavian* 3:6 (Winter 1966-67) and 3:7 (Spring-Summer 1967).

ACT II

Inside the cottage after nightfall. Looking eastward from within instead of westward from without, the latticed window, with its curtains drawn, is now seen in the middle of the front wall of the cottage, with the porch door to the left of it. In the left-hand side wall is the door leading to the kitchen. Farther back against the same wall is a dresser with a candle and matches on it, and Frank's rifle standing beside them, with the barrel resting in the plate-rack. In the centre a table stands with a lighted lamp on it. Vivie's books and writing materials are on a table to the right of the window, against the wall. The fireplace is on the right, with a settle:[1] there is no fire. Two of the chairs are set right and left of the table.

The cottage door opens, shewing a fine starlit night without; and Mrs Warren, her shoulders wrapped in a shawl borrowed from Vivie, enters, followed by Frank, who throws his cap on the window seat. She has had enough of walking, and gives a gasp of relief as she unpins her hat; takes it off; sticks the pin through the crown; and puts it on the table.

MRS WARREN. O Lord! I dont know which is the worst of the country, the walking or the sitting at home with nothing to do. I could do with a whisky and soda now very well, if only they had such a thing in this place.

FRANK. Perhaps Vivie's got some.

MRS WARREN. Nonsense! What would a young girl like her be doing with such things! Never mind: it dont matter. I wonder how she passes her time here! I'd a good deal rather be in Vienna.

FRANK. Let me take you there. [*He helps her to take off her shawl, gallantly giving her shoulders a very perceptible squeeze[2] as he does so.*]

MRS WARREN. Ah! would you? I'm beginning to think youre a chip of the old block.[3]

FRANK. Like the gov'nor, eh? [*He hangs the shawl on the nearest chair and sits down.*]

---

1   A wooden bench with high back and arms, and a box or draw under the seat.

2   In the 1898 text Frank's "*very perceptible squeeze*" is "*the most delicate possible little caress.*"

3   "Chip *off* the old block" is relatively recent usage. "Chip *of* the old block" was standard in Shaw's time.

MRS WARREN. Never you mind. What do you know about such things? Youre only a boy. [*She goes to the hearth, to be farther from temptation.*]

FRANK. Do come to Vienna with me. It'd be ever such larks.

MRS WARREN. No, thank you. Vienna is no place for you—at least not until youre a little older. [*She nods at him to emphasize this piece of advice. He makes a mock-piteous face, belied by his laughing eyes. She looks at him; then comes back to him.*] Now, look here, little boy [*taking his face in her hands and turning it up to her*]: I know you through and through by your likeness to your father, better than you know yourself. Dont you go taking any silly ideas into your head about me. Do you hear?

FRANK [*gallantly wooing her with his voice*]. Cant help it, my dear Mrs Warren: it runs in the family.

She pretends to box his ears; then looks at the pretty laughing upturned face for a moment, tempted. At last she kisses him, and immediately turns away, out of patience with herself.

MRS WARREN. There! I shouldnt have done that. I a m wicked. Never mind, my dear: it's only a motherly kiss. Go and make love to Vivie.

FRANK. So I have.

MRS WARREN [*turning on him with a sharp note of alarm in her voice*]. What!

FRANK. Vivie and I are ever such chums.

MRS WARREN. What do you mean? Now see here: I wont have any young scamp tampering with my little girl. Do you hear? I wont have it.

FRANK [*quite unabashed*]. My dear Mrs Warren: dont you be alarmed. My intentions are honorable: ever so honorable; and your little girl is jolly well able to take care of herself. She dont need looking after half so much as her mother. She aint so handsome, you know.

MRS WARREN [*taken aback by his assurance*]. Well, you have got a nice healthy two inches thick of cheek all over you. I dont know where you got it. Not from your father, anyhow.

CROFTS [in the garden]. The gipsies, I suppose?

REV. S. [replying]. The broomsquires[1] are far worse.

MRS WARREN [to Frank]. Sh-sh! Remember! youve had your warning.

Crofts and the Reverend Samuel come in from the garden, the clergy-man continuing his conversation as he enters.

REV. S. The perjury at the Winchester assizes is deplorable.[2]

MRS WARREN. Well? what became of you two? And wheres Praddy and Vivie?

CROFTS [putting his hat on the settle and his stick in the chimney cor-ner]. They went up the hill. We went to the village. I wanted a drink. [He sits down on the settle, putting his legs up along the seat.]

MRS WARREN. Well, she oughtnt go off like that without tell-ing me. [To Frank.] Get your father a chair, Frank: where are your manners? [Frank springs up and gracefully offers his father his chair; then takes another from the wall and sits down at the table, in the middle, with his father on his right and Mrs Warren on his left.] George: where are you going to stay tonight? You cant stay here. And whats Praddy going to do?

CROFTS. Gardner'll put me up.

MRS WARREN. Oh, no doubt youve taken care of yourself! But what about Praddy?

CROFTS. Dont know. I suppose he can sleep at the inn.

MRS WARREN. Havnt you room for him, Sam?

REV. S. Well—er—you see, as rector here, I am not free to do as I like. Er—what is Mr Praed's social position?

MRS WARREN. Oh, he's all right: he's an architect. What an old stick-in-the-mud you are, Sam!

FRANK. Yes, it's all right, gov'nor. He built that place down in

---

1 Itinerant makers and vendors of brooms made from a bunch of heather or twigs. Crofts and the Reverend Samuel appear to have been chatting about some of the nuisances (from their point of view) of English country life.

2 Shaw may have had a particular case in mind, but it has not been traced. The line does not appear in the 1898 text.

Wales for the Duke. Caernarvon Castle[1] they call it. You must have heard of it. [*He winks with lightning smartness at Mrs Warren, and regards his father blandly.*]

REV. S. Oh, in that case, of course we shall only be too happy. I suppose he knows the Duke personally.

FRANK. Oh, ever so intimately! We can stick him in Georgina's[2] old room.

MRS WARREN. Well, thats settled. Now if those two would only come in and let us have supper. Theyve no right to stay out after dark like this.

CROFTS [*aggressively*]. What harm are they doing you?

MRS WARREN. Well, harm or not, I dont like it.

FRANK. Better not wait for them, Mrs Warren. Praed will stay out as long as possible. He has never known before what it is to stray over the heath on a summer night with my Vivie.

CROFTS [*sitting up in some consternation*]. I say, you know! Come!

REV. S. [*rising, startled out of his professional manner into real force and sincerity*]. Frank, once for all, it's out of the question. Mrs Warren will tell you that it's not to be thought of.

CROFTS. Of course not.

FRANK [*with enchanting placidity*]. Is that so, Mrs Warren?

MRS WARREN [*reflectively*]. Well, Sam, I dont know. If the girl wants to get married, no good can come of keeping her unmarried.

REV. S. [*astounded*]. But married to h i m! —your daughter to my son! Only think: it's impossible.

CROFTS. Of course it's impossible. Dont be a fool, Kitty.

MRS WARREN [*nettled*]. Why not? Isnt my daughter good enough for your son?

REV. S. But surely, my dear Mrs Warren, you know the reasons—

---

1 A castle at Caernarvon in northwest Wales was built by the Romans in about 75 CE, but the present castle (the one referred to by Frank) was built for Edward I in the thirteenth century. In the 1898 text Frank makes the equally preposterous claim that Praed has built Tintern Abbey for the Duke of Beaufort. Frank's father doesn't know any better in either case. The deletion of the reference to the Duke of Beaufort was the only change required by the Lord Chamberlain when the play was licensed in 1924. (See Introduction, p. 62.)

2 One of Frank's sisters. The other is Bessie. See p. 152, note 2.

MRS WARREN [*defiantly*]. I know no reasons. If you know any, you can tell them to the lad, or to the girl, or to your congregation, if you like.

REV. S. [*collapsing helplessly into his chair*]. You know very well that I couldnt tell anyone the reasons. But my boy will believe me when I tell him there a r e reasons.

FRANK. Quite right, Dad: he will. But has your boy's conduct ever been influenced by your reasons?

CROFTS. You cant marry her; and thats all about it. [*He gets up and stands on the hearth, with his back to the fireplace, frowning determinedly.*]

MRS WARREN [*turning on him sharply*]. What have you got to do with it, pray?

FRANK [*with his prettiest lyrical cadence*]. Precisely what I was going to ask myself, in my own graceful fashion.

CROFTS [*to Mrs Warren*]. I suppose you dont want to marry the girl to a man younger than herself and without either a profession or twopence to keep her on. Ask Sam, if you dont believe me. [*To the parson.*] How much more money are you going to give him?

REV. S. Not another penny. He has had his patrimony and he spent the last of it in July. [*Mrs Warren's face falls.*]

CROFTS [*watching her*]. There! I told you. [*He resumes his place on the settle and puts his legs on the seat again, as if the matter were finally disposed of.*]

FRANK [*plaintively*]. This is ever so mercenary. Do you suppose Miss Warren's going to marry for money? If we love one another—

MRS WARREN. Thank you. Your love's a pretty cheap commodity, my lad. If you have no means of keeping a wife, that settles it: you cant have Vivie.

FRANK [*much amused*]. What do you say, gov'nor, eh?

REV. S. I agree with Mrs Warren.

FRANK. And good old Crofts has already expressed his opinion.

CROFTS [*turning angrily on his elbow*]. Look here: I want none of y o u r cheek.

FRANK [*pointedly*]. I'm e v e r so sorry to surprise you, Crofts, but you allowed yourself the liberty of speaking to me like a father a moment ago. One father is enough, thank you.

CROFTS [*contemptuously*]. Yah! [*He turns away again.*]

FRANK [*rising*]. Mrs Warren: I cannot give my Vivie up, even for your sake.

MRS WARREN [*muttering*]. Young scamp!

FRANK [*continuing*]. And as you no doubt intend to hold out other prospects to her, I shall lose no time in placing my case before her. [*They stare at him, and he begins to declaim gracefully*]

> He either fears his fate too much,
> Or his deserts are small,
> That dares not put it to the touch
> To gain or lose it all.[1]

The cottage door opens whilst he is reciting; and Vivie and Praed come in. He breaks off. Praed puts his hat on the dresser. There is an immediate improvement in the company's behavior. Crofts takes down his legs from the settle and pulls himself together as Praed joins him at the fireplace. Mrs Warren loses her ease of manner and takes refuge in querulousness.[2]

MRS WARREN. Wherever have you been, Vivie?

VIVIE [*taking off her hat and throwing it carelessly on the table*]. On the hill.

MRS WARREN. Well, you shouldnt go off like that without letting me know. How could I tell what had become of you? And night coming on too!

VIVIE [*going to the door of the kitchen and opening it, ignoring her mother*]. Now, about supper? [*All rise except Mrs Warren.*] We shall be rather crowded in here, I'm afraid.

MRS WARREN. Did you hear what I said, Vivie?

VIVIE [*quietly*]. Yes, mother. [*Reverting to the supper difficulty.*] How many are we? [*Counting.*] One, two, three, four, five, six. Well,

---

1 From "My Dear and Only Love," a poem by the Scottish soldier and writer James Graham, Marquess of Montrose (1612-50). Frank slightly misquotes. "He either fears his fate too much,/Or his deserts are small,/That puts it not unto the touch/To win or lose it all."

2 Petulance.

two will have to wait until the rest are done: Mrs Alison has only plates and knives for four.

PRAED. Oh, it doesnt matter about me. I—

VIVIE. You have had a long walk and are hungry, Mr Praed: you shall have your supper at once. I can wait myself. I want one person to wait with me. Frank: are you hungry?

FRANK. Not the least in the world. Completely off my peck,[1] in fact.

MRS WARREN [*to Crofts*]. Neither are you, George. You can wait.

CROFTS. Oh, hang it, Ive eaten nothing since tea-time. Cant Sam do it?

FRANK. Would you starve my poor father?

REV. S. [*testily*]. Allow me to speak for myself, sir. I am perfectly willing to wait.

VIVIE [*decisively*]. Theres no need. Only two are wanted. [*She opens the door of the kitchen.*] Will you take my mother in, Mr Gardner. [*The parson takes Mrs Warren; and they pass into the kitchen. Praed and Crofts follow. All except Praed clearly disapprove of the arrangement, but do not know how to resist it. Vivie stands at the door looking in at them.*] Can you squeeze past to that corner, Mr Praed: it's a rather tight fit. Take care of your coat against the white-wash: thats right. Now, are you all comfortable?

PRAED [*within*]. Quite, thank you.

MRS WARREN [*within*]. Leave the door open, dearie. [*Vivie frowns; but Frank checks her with a gesture, and steals to the cottage door, which he softly sets wide open.*] Oh Lor, what a draught! Youd better shut it, dear.

Vivie shuts it with a slam,[2] and then, noting with disgust that her mother's hat and shawl are lying about, takes them tidily to the window seat, whilst Frank noiselessly shuts the cottage door.

FRANK [*exulting*]. Aha! Got rid of em. Well, Vivvums: what do you think of my governor?

VIVIE [*preoccupied and serious*]. Ive hardly spoken to him. He doesnt

---

1   Not hungry.

2   In the 1898 text Vivie merely shuts the door "*promptly.*"

strike me as being a particularly able person.

FRANK. Well, you know, the old man is not altogether such a fool as he looks. You see, he was shoved into the church rather; and in trying to live up to it he makes a much bigger ass of himself than he really is. I dont dislike him as much as you might expect. He means well. How do you think youll get on with him?

VIVIE [*rather grimly*]. I dont think my future life will be much concerned with him, or with any of that old circle of my mother's, except perhaps Praed. [*She sits down on the settle.*] What do you think of my mother?

FRANK. Really and truly?

VIVIE. Yes, really and truly.

FRANK. Well, she's ever so jolly. But she's rather a caution,[1] isnt she? And Crofts! oh, my eye, Crofts! [*He sits beside her.*]

VIVIE. What a lot, Frank!

FRANK. What a crew!

VIVIE [*with intense contempt for them*]. If I thought that *I* was like that—that I was going to be a waster, shifting along from one meal to another with no purpose, and no character, and no grit in me, I'd open an artery and bleed to death without one moment's hesitation.

FRANK. Oh no, you wouldnt. Why should they take any grind when they can afford not to? I wish I had their luck. No: what I object to is their form. It isnt the thing: it's slovenly, ever so slovenly.

VIVIE. Do you think your form will be any better when youre as old as Crofts, if you dont work?

FRANK. Of course I do. Ever so much better. Vivvums musnt lecture: her little boy's incorrigible. [*He attempts to take her face caressingly in his hands.*]

VIVIE [*striking his hands down sharply*]. Off with you: Vivvums is not in a humor for petting her little boy this evening. [*She rises and comes forward to the other side of the room.*]

FRANK [*following her*]. How unkind!

---

1   An eccentric person; a "bit of a character."

VIVIE [*stamping at him*]. Be serious. I'm serious.

FRANK. Good. Let us talk learnedly. Miss Warren: do you know that all the most advanced thinkers are agreed that half the diseases of modern civilization are due to starvation of the affections in the young. Now, *I*—

VIVIE [*cutting him short*]. You are very tiresome. [*She opens the inner door.*] Have you room for Frank there? He's complaining of starvation.

MRS WARREN [*within*]. Of course there is [*clatter of knives and glasses as she moves the things on the table*]. Here! theres room now beside me. Come along, Mr Frank.

FRANK. Her little boy will be ever so even with his Vivvums for this. [*He passes into the kitchen.*]

MRS WARREN [*within*]. Here, Vivie: come on you too, child. You must be famished. [*She enters, followed by Crofts, who holds the door open for Vivie with marked deference. She goes out without looking at him; and shuts the door after her.*] Why, George, you cant be done: youve eaten nothing. Is there anything wrong with you?

CROFTS. Oh, all I wanted was a drink. [*He thrusts his hands in his pockets, and begins prowling around the room, restless and sulky.*]

MRS WARREN. Well, I like enough to eat. But a little of that cold beef and cheese and lettuce goes a long way. [*With a sigh of only half repletion she sits down lazily on the settle.*]

CROFTS. What do you go encouraging that young pup for?

MRS WARREN [*on the alert at once*]. Now see here, George: what are you up to about that girl? Ive been watching your way of looking at her. Remember: I know you and what your looks mean.

CROFTS. Theres no harm in looking at her, is there?

MRS WARREN. I'd put you out and pack you back to London pretty soon if I saw any of your nonsense. My girl's little finger is more to me than any of your body and soul. [*Crofts receives this with a sneering grin. Mrs Warren, flushing a little at her failure to impose on him in the character of a theatrically devoted mother, adds in a lower key.*] Make your mind easy: the young pup has no more chance than you have.

CROFTS. Maynt a man take an interest in a girl?

MRS WARREN. Not a man like you.

CROFTS. How old is she?

MRS WARREN. Never you mind how old she is.

CROFTS. Why do you make such a secret of it?

MRS WARREN. Because I choose.

CROFTS. Well, I'm not fifty yet; and my property is as good as ever it was —

MRS WARREN [*interrupting him*]. Yes, because youre as stingy as youre vicious.

CROFTS [*continuing*]. And a baronet[1] isnt to be picked up every day. No other man in my position would put up with you for a mother-in-law. Why shouldnt she marry me?

MRS WARREN. You!

CROFTS. We three could live together quite comfortably: I'd die before her and leave her a bouncing widow with plenty of money. Why not? It's been growing in my mind all the time Ive been walking with that fool inside there.

MRS WARREN [*revolted*]. Yes: it's the sort of thing that w o u l d grow in your mind.

He halts in his prowling; and the two look at one another, she stead-fastly, with a sort of awe behind her contemptuous disgust: he stealthily, with a carnal gleam in his eye and a loose grin.

CROFTS [*suddenly becoming anxious and urgent as he sees no sign of sympathy in her*]. Look here, Kitty: youre a sensible woman: you neednt put on any moral airs. I'll ask no more questions; and you need answer none. I'll settle the whole property on her; and if you want a cheque for yourself on the wedding day, you can name any figure you like — in reason.

MRS WARREN. So it's come to that with you, George, like all the other worn-out old creatures!

CROFTS [*savagely*]. Damn you!

---

1   The lowest of Britain's hereditary titles, established in 1611. It confers a knighthood, however: hence, *Sir* George Crofts. His wife would be titled *Lady* Crofts.

Before she can retort[1] the door of the kitchen is opened; and the voices of the others are heard returning. Crofts, unable to recover his presence of mind, hurries out of the cottage. The clergyman appears at the kitchen door.

REV. S. [*looking around*]. Where is Sir George?

MRS WARREN. Gone out to have a pipe. [*The clergyman takes his hat from the table, and joins Mrs Warren at the fireside. Meanwhile Vivie comes in, followed by Frank, who collapses into the nearest chair with an air of extreme exhaustion. Mrs Warren looks round at Vivie and says, with her affectation of maternal patronage even more forced than usual.*] Well, dearie, have you had a good supper?

VIVIE. You know what Mrs Alison's suppers are. [*She turns to Frank and pets him.*] Poor Frank! was all the beef gone? did it get nothing but bread and cheese and ginger beer? [*Seriously, as if she had done quite enough trifling for one evening.*] Her butter is really awful. I must get some down from the stores.

FRANK. Do, in Heaven's name!

Vivie goes to the writing-table and makes a memorandum to order the butter. Praed comes in from the kitchen, putting up his handkerchief, which he has been using as a napkin.

REV. S. Frank, my boy: it is time for us to be thinking of home. Your mother does not know yet that we have visitors.

PRAED. I'm afraid we're giving trouble.

FRANK [*rising*]. Not the least in the world: my mother will be delighted to see you. She's a genuinely intellectual artistic woman; and she sees nobody here from one year's end to another except the gov'nor; so you can imagine how jolly dull it pans out for her. [*To his father.*] Y o u r e not intellectual or artistic: are you pater? So take Praed home at once; and I'll stay here and entertain Mrs Warren. Youll pick up Crofts in the garden. He'll be excellent company for the bull-pup.[2]

PRAED [*taking his hat from the dresser, and coming close to Frank*].

---

1 In the 1898 text Mrs Warren is given more time: "*She rises and turns fiercely on him.*"
2 Presumably a sarcastic reference to Praed. He's not a bull-*dog*.

Come with us, Frank. Mrs Warren has not seen Miss Vivie for a long time; and we have prevented them from having a moment together yet.

FRANK [*quite softened and looking at Praed with romantic admiration*]. Of course. I forgot. Ever so thanks for reminding me. Perfect gentleman, Praddy. Always were. My ideal through life. [*He rises to go, but pauses a moment between the two older men, and puts his hand on Praed's shoulder.*] Ah, if you had only been my father instead of this unworthy old man! [*He puts his other hand on his father's shoulder.*]

REV. S. [*blustering*]. Silence, sir, silence: you are profane.

MRS WARREN [*laughing heartily*]. You should keep him in better order, Sam. Goodnight. Here: take George his hat and stick with my compliments.

REV. S. [*taking them*]. Goodnight. [*They shake hands. As he passes Vivie he shakes hands with her also and bids her goodnight. Then, in booming command, to Frank.*] Come along, sir, at once. [*He goes out.*]

MRS WARREN. Byebye, Praddy.

PRAED. Byebye, Kitty.

They shake hands affectionately and go out together, she accompanying him to the garden gate.

FRANK [*to Vivie*]. Kissums?

VIVIE [*fiercely*]. No. I hate you.[1] [*She takes a couple of books and some paper from the writing-table, and sits down with them at the middle table, at the end next the fireplace.*]

FRANK [*grimacing*]. Sorry. [*He goes for his cap and rifle. Mrs Warren returns. He takes her hand.*] Goodnight, d e a r Mrs Warren. [*He kisses her hand.[2] She snatches it away, her lips tightening, and looks more than half disposed to box his ears. He laughs mischievously and runs off, clapping-to[3] the door behind him.*]

---

1   In the 1898 text Frank "*silently begs a kiss*," and receives in return from Vivie "*a stern glance*," rather than her fierce comment.

2   In the 1898 text Frank "*squeezes*" Mrs Warren's hand.

3   Slamming.

MRS WARREN [*resigning herself to an evening of boredom now that the men are gone*]. Did you ever in your life hear anyone rattle on so? Isnt he a tease? [*She sits at the table.*] Now that I think of it, dearie, dont you go encouraging him. I'm sure he's a regular good-for-nothing.

VIVIE [*rising to fetch more books*]. I'm afraid so. Poor Frank! I shall have to get rid of him; but I shall feel sorry for him, though he's not worth it. That man Crofts does not seem to me to be good for much either: is he? [*She throws the books on the table rather roughly.*]

MRS WARREN [*galled by Vivie's indifference[1]*]. What do you know of men, child, to talk that way about them? Youll have to make up your mind to see a good deal of Sir George Crofts, as he's a friend of mine.

VIVIE [*quite unmoved*]. Why? [*She sits down and opens a book.*] Do you expect that we shall be much together? You and I, I mean?

MRS WARREN [*staring at her*]. Of course: until youre married. Youre not going back to college again.

VIVIE. Do you think my way of life would suit you? I doubt it.

MRS WARREN. Y o u r way of life! What do you mean?

VIVIE [*cutting a page of her book with the paper knife on her chatelaine*]. Has it really never occurred to you, mother, that I have a way of life like other people?

MRS WARREN. What nonsense is this youre trying to talk? Do you want to shew your independence, now that youre a great little person at school? Dont be a fool, child.

VIVIE [*indulgently*]. Thats all you have to say on the subject, is it, mother?

MRS WARREN [*puzzled, then angry*]. Dont you keep on asking me questions like that. [*Violently.*] Hold your tongue. [*Vivie works on, losing no time, and saying nothing.*] You and your way of life, indeed! What next? [*She looks at Vivie again. No reply.*] Your way of life will be what I please, so it will. [*Another pause.*] Ive been noticing these airs in you ever since you got that tripos or whatever you call it. If you think I'm going to put up with

---

1   In the 1898 text Mrs Warren is galled by Vivie's "*cool tone,*" rather than her indifference.

them youre mistaken; and the sooner you find it out, the better. [*Muttering.*] All I have to say on the subject, indeed! [*Again raising her voice angrily.*] Do you know who youre speaking to, Miss?

VIVIE [*looking across at her without raising her head from her book*]. No. Who are you? What are you?

MRS WARREN [*rising breathless*]. You young imp!

VIVIE. Everybody knows my reputation, my social standing, and the profession I intend to pursue. I know nothing about you. What is that way of life which you invite me to share with you and Sir George Crofts, pray?

MRS WARREN. Take care. I shall do something I'll be sorry for after, and you too.

VIVIE [*putting aside her books with cool decision*]. Well, let us drop the subject until you are better able to face it. [*Looking critically at her mother.*] You want some good walks and a little lawn tennis to set you up. You are shockingly out of condition: you were not able to manage twenty yards uphill today without stopping to pant; and your wrists are mere rolls of fat. Look at mine [*she holds out her wrists*].

MRS WARREN [*after looking at her helplessly, begins to whimper*]. Vivie—

VIVIE [*springing up sharply*]. Now pray dont begin to cry. Anything but that. I really cannot stand whimpering. I will go out of the room if you do.

MRS WARREN [*piteously*]. Oh, my darling, how can you be so hard on me? Have I no rights over you as your mother?

VIVIE. A r e you my mother?

MRS WARREN [*appalled*]. A m I your mother! Oh, Vivie!

VIVIE. Then where are our relatives? my father? our family friends? You claim the rights of a mother: the right to call me fool and child; to speak to me as no woman in authority over me at college dare speak to me; to dictate my way of life; and to force on me the acquaintance of a brute whom any one can see to be the most vicious sort of London man about town. Before I give myself the trouble to resist such claims, I may as well find out whether they have any real existence.

MRS WARREN [*distracted, throwing herself on her knees*]. Oh no, no.

Stop, stop. I a m your mother, I swear it. Oh, you cant mean to turn on me—my own child! it's not natural. You believe me, dont you? Say you believe me.

VIVIE. Who was my father?

MRS WARREN. You dont know what youre asking. I cant tell you.

VIVIE [*determinedly*]. Oh yes you can, if you like. I have a right to know; and you know very well that I have that right. You can refuse to tell me, if you please; but if you do you will see the last of me tomorrow morning.

MRS WARREN. Oh, it's too horrible to hear you talk like that. You wouldnt—you c o u l d n t leave me.

VIVIE [*ruthlessly*]. Yes, without a moment's hesitation, if you trifle with me about this. [*Shivering with disgust.*] How can I feel sure that I may not have the contaminated blood of that brutal waster in my veins?

MRS WARREN. No, no. On my oath it's not he, nor any of the rest that you have ever met. I'm certain of that, at least.

Vivie's eyes fasten sternly on her mother as the significance of this flashes on her.

VIVIE [*slowly*]. You are certain of that, at l e a s t. Ah! You mean that that is all you are certain of. [*Thoughtfully.*] I see. [*Mrs Warren buries her face in her hands.*] Dont do that, mother: you know you dont feel it a bit. [*Mrs Warren takes down her hands and looks up deplorably at Vivie, who takes out her watch and says*] Well, that is enough for tonight. At what hour would you like breakfast? Is half-past eight too early for you?

MRS WARREN [*wildly*]. My God, what sort of woman are you?

VIVIE [*coolly*].The sort the world is mostly made of, I should hope. Otherwise I dont understand how it gets its business done. Come [*taking her mother by the wrist, and pulling her up pretty resolutely*]: pull yourself together. Thats right.

MRS WARREN [*querulously*].Youre very rough with me, Vivie.

VIVIE. Nonsense. What about bed? It's past ten.

MRS WARREN [*passionately*]. Whats the use of my going to bed? Do you think I could sleep?

VIVIE. Why not? I shall.

MRS WARREN. You! youve no heart. [*She suddenly breaks out ve-hemently in her natural tongue—the dialect of a woman of the peo-ple—with all her affectations of maternal authority and conventional manners gone, and an overwhelming inspiration of true conviction and scorn in her.*] Oh, I wont bear it: I wont put up with the injustice of it. What right have you to set yourself up above m e like this? You boast of what you are to me—to me, who gave who you the chance of being what you are. What chance had I? Shame on you for a bad daughter and a stuck-up prude!

VIVIE [*sitting down with a shrug,*[1] *no longer confident; for her replies, which have sounded sensible and strong to her so far, now begin to ring rather woodenly and even priggishly against the new tone of her mother*]. Dont think for a moment I set myself up against you in any way. You attacked me with the conventional authority of a mother: I defended myself with the conventional superiority of a respectable woman. Frankly, I am not going to stand any of your nonsense; and when you drop it I shall not expect you to stand any of mine. I shall always respect your right to your own opinions and your own way of life.

MRS WARREN. My own opinions and my own way of life! Listen to her talking! Do you think I was brought up like you? able to pick and choose my own way of life? Do you think I did what I did because I liked it, or thought it right, or wouldnt rather have gone to college and been a lady if I'd had the chance?

VIVIE. Everybody has some choice, mother. The poorest girl alive may not be able to choose between being Queen of England or Principal of Newnham; but she can choose between ragpick-ing and flowerselling, according to her taste. People are always blaming their circumstances for what they are. I dont believe in circumstances. The people who get on in this world are the people who get up and look for the circumstances they want, and, if they cant find them, make them.

MRS WARREN. Oh, it's easy to talk, very easy, isnt it? Here! would you like to know what m y circumstances were?

VIVIE. Yes: you had better tell me. Wont you sit down?

---

1   In the 1898 text Vivie is still "*cool and determined*" at this point.

MRS WARREN. Oh, I'll sit down: dont you be afraid. [*She plants her chair farther forward with brazen energy, and sits down. Vivie is impressed in spite of herself.*] D'you know what your gran'mother was?

VIVIE. No.

MRS WARREN. No, you dont. I do. She called herself a widow and had a fried-fish shop down by the Mint,[1] and kept herself and four daughters out of it. Two of us were sisters: that was me and Liz; and we were both good-looking and well made. I suppose our father was a well-fed man: mother pretended he was a gentleman; but I dont know. The other two were only half sisters: undersized, ugly, starved looking, hard working, honest poor creatures: Liz and I would have half-murdered them if mother hadnt half-murdered u s to keep our hands off them. They were the respectable ones. Well, what did they get by their respectability? I'll tell you. One of them worked in a whitelead factory[2] twelve hours a day for nine shillings a week until she died of lead poisoning. She only expected to get her hands a little paralyzed; but she died. The other was always held up to us as a model because she married a Government laborer in the Deptford victualling yard,[3] and kept his room and the three children neat and tidy on eighteen shillings a week—until he took to drink. That was worth being respectable for, wasnt it?

VIVIE [*now thoughtfully attentive*]. Did you and your sister think so?

MRS WARREN. Liz didnt, I can tell you: she had more spirit. We both went to a church school—that was part of the ladylike airs we gave ourselves to be superior to the children that knew nothing and went nowhere—and we stayed there until Liz went out one night and never came back. I know the schoolmistress

---

1 The Royal Mint is the official manufacturer of British coinage. In Shaw's time it was located in working-class East End London. It moved in 1968 to its present location in Llantrisant, South Wales.

2 Whitelead is a mixture of lead carbonate and hydrated lead oxide used as a white pigment in paint.

3 The Royal Victualling Yard—for providing supplies and provisions for the Royal Navy—was established at Deptford (on the River Thames) in 1742.

thought I'd soon follow her example; for the clergyman was always warning me that Lizzie'd end by jumping off Waterloo Bridge.[1] Poor fool: that was all he knew about it! But I was more afraid of the whitelead factory than I was of the river; and so would you have been in my place. That clergyman got me a situation as scullery[2] maid in a temperance restaurant[3] where they sent out for anything you liked. Then I was waitress; and then I went to the bar at Waterloo station:[4] fourteen hours a day serving drinks and washing glasses for four shillings a week and my board. That was considered a great promotion for me. Well, one cold, wretched night, when I was so tired I could hardly keep myself awake, who should come up for a half of scotch[5] but Lizzie, in a long fur cloak, elegant and comfortable, with a lot of sovereigns[6] in her purse.

VIVIE [*grimly*]. My aunt Lizzie!

MRS WARREN. Yes; and a very good aunt to have, too. She's living down at Winchester[7] now, close to the cathedral, one of the most respectable ladies there. Chaperones girls at the county ball, if you please. No river for Liz, thank you! You remind me of Liz a little: she was a first-rate business woman — saved money from the beginning — never let herself look too like what she was — never lost her head or threw away a chance. When she saw I'd grown up good-looking she said to me across the bar 'What are you doing there, you little fool? wearing out your health and your appearance for other people's profit!' Liz was saving money then to take a house for herself in Brussels; and she thought we two could save faster than one. So she lent

---

1 Waterloo Bridge connects Victoria Embankment with Waterloo on the south bank of the Thames. The original bridge (built in 1817) was demolished in 1936 and replaced with the present structure.

2 The scullery is a small room adjacent to the kitchen used mainly for washing dishes.

3 A restaurant that does not serve alcohol.

4 Then and now, one of London's principal railway stations. By the end of the nineteenth century it was handling about 700 trains a day.

5 A large glass of Scotch whisky.

6 A gold coin nominally worth £1.

7 A city about 65 miles southwest of London, with a population (1901) of 20,929. The origins of its famous cathedral date to the second half of the seventh century (*Encyclopaedia Britannica*, 11th ed.).

me some money and gave me a start; and I saved steadily and first paid her back, and then went into business with her as her partner. Why shouldnt I have done it? The house in Brussels was real high class: a much better place for a woman to be in than the factory where Anne Jane got poisoned. None of our girls were ever treated as I was treated in the scullery of that temperance place, or at the Waterloo bar, or at home. Would you have had me stay in them and become a worn-out old drudge before I was forty?

VIVIE [*intensely interested by this time*]. No, but why did you choose that business? Saving money and good management will succeed in any business.

MRS WARREN. Yes, saving money. But where can a woman get the money to save in any other business? Could you save out of four shillings a week and keep yourself dressed as well? Not you. Of course, if youre a plain woman and cant earn anything more; or if you have a turn for music, or the stage, or newspaper-writing: thats different. But neither Liz nor I had any turn for such things: all we had was our appearance and our turn for pleasing men. Do you think we were such fools as to let other people trade in our good looks by employing us as shopgirls, or barmaids, or waitresses, when we could trade in them ourselves and get all the profits instead of starvation wages? Not likely.

VIVIE. You were certainly quite justified—from the business point of view.

MRS WARREN. Yes; or any other point of view. What is any respectable girl brought up to do but to catch some rich man's fancy and get the benefit of his money by marrying him?—as if a marriage ceremony could make any difference in the right or wrong of the thing! Oh, the hypocrisy of the world makes me sick! Liz and I had to work and save and calculate just like other people; elseways[1] we should be as poor as any good-for-nothing drunken waster of a woman that thinks her luck will last forever. [*With great energy.*] I despise such people: theyve no character; and if theres a thing I hate in a woman, it's want of character.

---

1 Otherwise.

VIVIE. Come now, mother: frankly! Isn't it part of what you call character in a woman that she should greatly dislike such a way of making money?

MRS WARREN. Why, of course. Everybody dislikes having to work and make money; but they have to do it all the same. I'm sure Ive often pitied a poor girl, tired out and in low spirits, having to try to please some man that she doesnt care two straws for—some half-drunken fool that thinks he's making himself agreeable when he's teasing and worrying and disgusting a woman so that hardly any money could pay her for putting up with it. But she has to bear with disagreeables and take the rough with the smooth, just like a nurse in a hospital or anyone else. It's not work that any woman would do for pleasure, goodness knows; though to hear the pious people talk you would suppose it was a bed of roses.

VIVIE. Still, you consider it worth while. It pays.

MRS WARREN. Of course it's worth while to a poor girl, if she can resist temptation and is good-looking and well conducted and sensible. It's far better than any other employment open to her. I always thought that oughtnt to be. It c a n t be right, Vivie, that there shouldnt be better opportunities for women. I stick to that: it's wrong. But it's so, right or wrong; and a girl must make the best of it. But of course it's not worth while for a lady. If you took to it youd be a fool; but I should have been a fool if I'd taken to anything else.

VIVIE [more and more deeply moved]. Mother: suppose we were both as poor as you were in those wretched old days, are you quite sure that you wouldnt advise me to try the Waterloo bar, or marry a laborer, or even go into the factory?

MRS WARREN [indignantly]. Of course not. What sort of mother do you take me for! How could you keep your self-respect in such starvation and slavery? And whats a woman worth? whats life worth? without self-respect! Why am I independent and able to give my daughter a first-rate education, when other women that had just as good opportunities are in the gutter? Because I always knew how to respect myself and control myself. Why is Liz looked up to in a cathedral town? The same reason. Where would we be now if we'd minded the clergyman's foolishness?

Scrubbing floors for one and sixpence a day and nothing to look forward to but the workhouse infirmary.[1] Dont you be led astray by people who dont know the world, my girl. The only way for a woman to provide for herself decently is for her to be good to some man that can afford to be good to her. If she's in his own station of life, let her make him marry her; but if she's far beneath him she cant expect it: why should she? it wouldnt be for her own happiness. Ask any lady in London society that has daughters; and she'll tell you the same, except that I tell you straight and she'll tell you crooked. Thats all the difference.

VIVIE [*fascinated, gazing at her*]. My dear mother: you are a wonderful woman: you are stronger than all England. And are you really and truly not one wee bit doubtful—or —or—ashamed?

MRS WARREN. Well, of course, dearie, it's only good manners to be ashamed of it: it's expected from a woman. Women have to pretend to feel a great deal that they dont feel. Liz used to be angry with me for plumping out the truth about it. She used to say that when every woman could learn enough from what was going on in the world before her eyes, there was no need to talk about it to her. But then Liz was such a perfect lady! She had the true instinct of it; while I was always a bit of a vulgarian. I used to be so pleased when you sent me your photos to see that you were growing up like Liz: youve just her ladylike, determined way. But I cant stand saying one thing when everyone knows I mean another. Whats the use in such hypocrisy? If people arrange the world that way for women, there's no good pretending it's arranged the other way. No: I never was a bit ashamed really. I consider I had a right to be proud of how we managed everything so respectably, and never had a word against us, and how the girls were so well taken care of. Some of them did very well: one of them married an ambassador. But of course now I darent talk about such things: whatever would they think of us! [*She yawns.*] Oh dear! I do believe I'm getting

---

1 Workhouses, which supported the sick and the indigent, had existed in England since the early seventeenth century. The Poor Law Amendment Act of 1834 limited assistance to the able-bodied poor and made conditions as uncomfortable as possible. Most workhouses had their own infirmaries where rudimentary medical help was provided. Workhouses were phased out in England by about 1930.

sleepy after all. [*She stretches herself lazily, thoroughly relieved by her explosion, and placidly ready for her night's rest.*]

VIVIE. I believe it is I who will not be able to sleep now. [*She goes to the dresser and lights the candle. Then she extinguishes the lamp, darkening the room a good deal.*]Better let in some fresh air before locking up. [*She opens the cottage door, and finds that it is broad moonlight.*] What a beautiful night! Look! [*She draws aside the curtains of the window. The landscape is seen bathed in the radiance of the harvest moon rising over Blackdown.[1]*]

MRS WARREN [*with a perfunctory glance of the scene*]. Yes, dear; but take care you dont catch your death of cold from the night air.

VIVIE [*contemptuously*]. Nonsense.

MRS WARREN [*querulously*]. Oh yes: everything I say is nonsense, according to you.

VIVIE [*turning to her quickly*]. No: really that is not so, mother. You have got completely the better of me tonight, though I intended it to be the other way. Let us be good friends now.

MRS WARREN [*shaking her head a little ruefully*]. So it h a s been the other way. But I suppose I must give in to it. I always got the worst of it from Liz; and now I suppose it'll be the same with you.

VIVIE. Well, never mind. Come: goodnight, dear old mother. [*She takes her mother in her arms.*]

MRS WARREN [*fondly*]. I brought you up well, didnt I, dearie?

VIVIE. You did.

MRS WARREN. And youll be good to your poor old mother for it, wont you?

VIVIE. I will, dear. [*Kissing her.*] Goodnight.

MRS WARREN [*with unction*]. Blessings on my own dearie darling! a mother's blessing!

She embraces her daughter protectingly, instinctively looking upward for divine sanction.

---

1   A prominent hill about three miles south of Haslemere.

ACT III

In the Rectory garden next morning, with the sun shining from a cloudless sky. The garden wall has a five-barred wooden gate, wide enough to admit a carriage, in the middle. Beside the gate hangs a bell on a coiled spring, communicating with a pull outside. The carriage drive comes down the middle of the garden and then swerves to its left, where it ends in a little gravelled circus[1] opposite the Rectory porch. Beyond the gate is seen the dusty high road, parallel with the wall, bounded on the farther side by a strip of turf and an unfenced pine wood. On the lawn, between the house and the drive, is a clipped yew tree, with a garden bench in its shade. On the opposite side the garden is shut in by a box hedge; and there is a sundial on the turf, with an iron chair near it. A little path leads off through the box hedge, behind the sundial.

Frank, seated on the chair near the sundial, on which he has placed the morning papers, is reading The Standard.[2] His father comes from the house, red-eyed and shivery, and meets Frank's eye with misgiving.

FRANK [*looking at his watch*]. Half-past eleven. Nice hour for a rector to come down to breakfast!

REV. S. Dont mock, Frank: dont mock. I am a little—er— [*Shivering*]—

FRANK. Off color?

REV. S. [*repudiating the expression*]. No, sir: u n w e l l this morning. Wheres your mother?

FRANK. Dont be alarmed: she's not here. Gone to town by the 11.13 with Bessie.[3] She left several messages for you. Do you feel equal to receiving them now, or shall I wait til you have breakfasted?

REV. S. I h a v e breakfasted, sir. I am surprised at your mother going to town when we have people staying with us. Theyll think it very strange.

FRANK. Possibly she has considered that. At all events, if Crofts is going to stay here, and you are going to sit up every night with

---

1 The driveway is circular.
2 A leading London daily newspaper, first published in 1827.
3 Frank's sister. See p. 109, note 2.

him until four, recalling the incidents of your fiery youth, it is clearly my mother's duty, as a prudent housekeeper, to go up to the stores and order a barrel of whisky and a few hundred siphons.[1]

REV. S. I did not observe that Sir George drank excessively.

FRANK. You were not in a condition to, gov'nor.

REV. S. Do you mean to say that I—?

FRANK [calmly]. I never saw a beneficed clergyman less sober. The anecdotes you told about your past career were so awful that I really dont think Praed would have passed the night under your roof if it hadnt been for the way my mother and he took to one another.

REV. S. Nonsense, sir. I am Sir George Crofts' host. I must talk to him about something; and he has only one subject. Where is Mr Praed now?

FRANK. He is driving my mother and Bessie to the station.

REV. S. Is Crofts up yet?

FRANK. Oh, long ago. He hasnt turned a hair: he's in much better practice than you. He has kept it up ever since, probably. He's taken himself off somewhere to smoke.

Frank resumes his paper. The parson turns disconsolately towards the gate; then comes back irresolutely.

REV. S. Er—Frank.

FRANK. Yes.

REV. S. Do you think the Warrens will expect to be asked here after yesterday afternoon?

FRANK. Theyve been asked already.

REV. S. [appalled]. What! ! !

FRANK. Crofts informed us at breakfast that you told him to bring Mrs Warren and Vivie over here today, and to invite them to make this house their home. My mother then found she must go to town by the 11.13 train.

REV. S. [with despairing vehemence]. I never gave any such invitation. I never thought of such a thing.

---

1 The siphons (pressurized bottles) contain soda to mix with the whisky.

FRANK [*compassionately*]. How do you know, gov'nor, what you said and thought last night?

PRAED [*coming in through the hedge*]. Good morning.

REV. S. Good morning. I must apologize for not having met you at breakfast. I have a touch of—of—

FRANK. Clergyman's sore throat, Praed. Fortunately not chronic.

PRAED [*changing the subject*]. Well, I must say your house is in a charming spot here. Really most charming.

REV. S. Yes: it is indeed. Frank will take you for a walk, Mr Praed, if you like. I'll ask you to excuse me: I must take the opportunity to write my sermon while Mrs Gardner is away and you are all amusing yourselves. You wont mind, will you?

PRAED. Certainly not. Dont stand on the slightest ceremony with me.

REV. S. Thank you. I'll—er—er—[*He stammers his way to the porch and vanishes into the house.*]

PRAED. Curious thing it must be writing a sermon every week.

FRANK. Ever so curious, if h e did it. He buys em. He's gone for some soda water.

PRAED. My dear boy: I wish you would be more respectful to your father. You know you can be so nice when you like.

FRANK. My dear Praddy: you forget that I have to live with the governor. When two people live together—it dont matter whether theyre father and son or husband and wife or brother and sister—they cant keep up the polite humbug thats so easy for ten minutes on an afternoon call. Now the governor, who unites to many admirable domestic qualities the irresoluteness of a sheep and the pompousness and aggressiveness of a jackass—

PRAED. No, pray, pray, my dear Frank, remember! He is your father.

FRANK. I give him due credit for that. [*Rising and flinging down his paper.*] But just imagine his telling Crofts to bring the Warrens over here! He must have been ever so drunk. You know, my dear Praddy, my mother wouldnt stand Mrs Warren for a moment. Vivie mustnt come here until she has gone back to town.

PRAED. But your mother doesnt know anything about Mrs

Warren, does she? [*He picks up the paper and sits down to read it.*]

FRANK. I dont know. Her journey to town looks as if she did. Not that my mother would mind in the ordinary way: she has stuck like a brick to lots of women who had got into trouble. But they were all nice women. Thats what makes the real difference. Mrs Warren, no doubt, has her merits; but she's ever so rowdy; and my mother simply wouldnt put up with her. So—hallo! [*This exclamation is provoked by the reappearance of the clergyman, who comes out of the house in haste and dismay.*]

REV. S. Frank: Mrs Warren and her daughter are coming across the heath with Crofts: I saw them from the study windows. What a m I to say about your mother?

FRANK. Stick on your hat and go out and say how delighted you are to see them; and that Frank's in the garden; and that mother and Bessie have been called to the bedside of a sick relative, and were ever so sorry that they couldnt stop; and that you hope Mrs Warren slept well; and—and—say any blessed thing except the truth, and leave the rest to Providence.

REV. S. But how are we to get rid of them afterwards?

FRANK. Theres no time to think of that now. Here! [*He bounds into the house.*]

REV. S. He's so impetuous. I dont know what to do with him, Mr Praed.

FRANK [*returning with a clerical felt hat, which he claps on his father's head*]. Now: off with you. [*Rushing him through the gate.*] Praed and I'll wait here, to give the thing an unpremeditated air. [*The clergyman, dazed but obedient, hurries off.*]

FRANK. We must get the old girl back to town somehow, Praed. Come! Honestly, dear Praddy, do you like seeing them together?

PRAED. Oh, why not?

FRANK [*his teeth on edge*]. Dont it make your flesh creep ever so little? that wicked old devil, up to every villainy under the sun, I'll swear, and Vivie—ugh!

PRAED. Hush, pray. Theyre coming.

The clergyman and Crofts are seen coming along the road, followed by Mrs Warren and Vivie walking affectionately together.

FRANK. Look: she actually has her arm round the old woman's waist. It's her right arm: she began it. She's gone sentimental, by God! Ugh! ugh! Now do you feel the creeps? [*The clergyman opens the gate; and Mrs Warren and Vivie pass him and stand in the middle of the garden looking at the house. Frank, in an ecstasy of dissimulation, turns gaily to Mrs Warren, exclaiming*] Ever so delighted to see you, Mrs Warren. This quiet old rectory garden becomes you perfectly.

MRS WARREN. Well, I never! Did you hear that, George? He says I look well in a quiet old rectory garden.

REV. S. [*still holding the gate for Crofts, who loafs through it, heavily bored*]. You look well everywhere, Mrs Warren.

FRANK. Bravo, gov'nor! Now look here: lets have a treat before lunch. First lets see the church. Everyone has to do that. It's a regular old thirteenth century church, you know: the gov'nor's ever so fond of it, because he got up a restoration fund and had it completely rebuilt six years ago. Praed will be able to shew its points.

PRAED [*rising*]. Certainly, if the restoration has left any to shew.

REV. S. [*mooning[1] hospitably at them*]. I shall be pleased, I'm sure, if Sir George and Mrs Warren really care about it.

MRS WARREN. Oh, come along and get it over.

CROFTS [*turning back towards the gate*]. Ive no objection.

REV. S. Not that way. We go through the fields, if you dont mind. Round here. [*He leads the way by the little path through the box hedge.*]

CROFTS. Oh, all right. [*He goes with the parson.*]

Praed follows with Mrs Warren. Vivie does not stir: she watches them until they have gone, with all the lines of purpose in her face marking it strongly.

FRANK. Aint you coming?

VIVIE. No. I want to give you a warning, Frank. You were making fun of my mother just now when you said that about the rectory garden. That is barred in the future. Please treat my

---

1 Listlessly, without energy (he has a hangover).

mother with as much respect as you treat your own.

FRANK. My dear Viv: she wouldnt appreciate it: the two cases require different treatment. But what on earth has happened to you? Last night we were perfectly agreed as to your mother and her set. This morning I find you attitudinizing sentimentally with your arm round your parent's waist.

VIVIE [*flushing*]. Attitudinizing!

FRANK. That was how it struck me. First time I ever saw you do a second-rate thing.

VIVIE [*controlling herself*]. Yes, Frank: there has been a change; but I dont think it a change for the worse. Yesterday I was a little prig.

FRANK. And today?

VIVIE [*wincing; then looking at him steadily*]. Today I know my mother better than you do.

FRANK. Heaven forbid!

VIVIE. What do you mean?

FRANK. Viv: theres a freemasonry among thoroughly immoral people that you know nothing of. Youve too much character. T h a t s the bond between your mother and me: thats why I know her better than youll ever know her.

VIVIE. You are wrong: you know nothing about her. If you knew the circumstances against which my mother had to struggle—

FRANK [*adroitly finishing the sentence for her*]. I should know why she is what she is, shouldnt I? What difference would that make? Circumstances or no circumstances, Viv, you wont be able to stand your mother.

VIVIE [*very angrily*]. Why not?

FRANK. Because she's an old wretch, Viv. If you ever put your arm round her waist in my presence again, I'll shoot myself there and then as a protest against an exhibition which revolts me.

VIVIE. Must I choose between dropping your acquaintance and dropping my mother's?

FRANK [*gracefully*]. That would put the old lady at ever such a disadvantage. No, Viv; your infatuated little boy will have to stick to you in any case. But he's all the more anxious that you shouldnt make mistakes. It's no use, Viv: your mother's impossible. She may be a good sort; but she's a bad lot, a very bad lot.

VIVIE [*hotly*]. Frank—! [*He stands his ground. She turns away and sits down on the bench under the yew tree, struggling to recover her self-command. Then she says*] Is she to be deserted by all the world because she's what you call a bad lot? Has she no right to live?

FRANK. No fear of that, Viv: she wont ever be deserted. [*He sits on the bench beside her.*]

VIVIE. But I am to desert her, I suppose.

FRANK [*babyishly, lulling her and making love to her with his voice*]. Musnt go live with her. Little family group of mother and daughter wouldnt be a success. Spoil o u r little group.

VIVIE [*falling under the spell*]. What little group?

FRANK. The babes in the wood: Vivie and little Frank. [*He nestles against her like a weary child.*] Lets go and get covered up with leaves.

VIVIE [*rhythmically, rocking him like a nurse*]. Fast asleep, hand in hand, under the trees.

FRANK. The wise little girl with her silly little boy.

VIVIE. The dear little boy with his dowdy little girl.

FRANK. Ever so peaceful, and relieved from the imbecility of the little boy's father and the questionableness of the little girl's—

VIVIE [*smothering the word against her breast*]. Sh-sh-sh-sh! little girl wants to forget all about her mother. [*They are silent for some moments, rocking one another. Then Vivie wakes up with a shock, exclaiming*] What a pair of fools we are! Come: sit up. Gracious! your hair. [*She smooths it.*] I wonder do all grown up people play in that childish way when nobody is looking. I never did it when I was a child.

FRANK. Neither did I. You are my first playmate. [*He catches her hand to kiss it, but checks himself to look round first. Very unexpectedly, he sees Crofts emerging from the box hedge.*] Oh damn!

VIVIE. Why damn, dear?

FRANK [*whispering*]. Sh! Heres this brute Crofts. [*He sits farther away from her with an unconcerned air.*][1]

---

1 At this point in the 1898 text Vivie says: "Dont be rude to him, Frank. I particularly want to be polite to him. It will please my mother."

CROFTS. Could I have a few words with you, Miss Vivie?

VIVIE. Certainly.

CROFTS [to Frank]. Youll excuse me, Gardner. Theyre waiting for you in the church, if you dont mind.

FRANK [rising]. Anything to oblige you, Crofts—except church. If you should happen to want me, Vivvums, ring the gate bell. [He goes into the house with unruffled suavity.]

CROFTS [watching him with a crafty air as he disappears, and speaking to Vivie with an assumption of being on privileged terms with her]. Pleasant young fellow that, Miss Vivie. Pity he has no money, isnt it?

VIVIE. Do you think so?

CROFTS. Well, whats he to do? No profession. No property. Whats he good for?

VIVIE. I realize his disadvantages, Sir George.

CROFTS [a little taken aback at being so precisely interpreted]. Oh, it's not that. But while we're in this world, we're in it; and money's money. [Vivie does not answer.] Nice day, isnt it?

VIVIE [with scarcely veiled contempt for this effort at conversation]. Very.

CROFTS [with brutal good humor, as if he liked her pluck]. Well, thats not what I came to say. [Sitting down beside her.] Now listen, Miss Vivie. I'm quite aware that I'm not a young lady's man.

VIVIE. Indeed, Sir George?

CROFTS. No; and to tell you the honest truth I dont want to be either. But when I say a thing I mean it; when I feel a sentiment I feel it in earnest; and what I value I pay hard money for. Thats the sort of man I am.

VIVIE. It does you great credit, I'm sure.

CROFTS. Oh, I dont mean to praise myself. I have my faults, Heaven knows: no man is more sensible of[1] that than I am. I know I'm not perfect; thats one of the advantages of being a middle-aged man; for I'm not a young man, and I know it. But my code is a simple one, and, I think, a good one. Honor between man and man; fidelity between man and woman; and

---

1   Aware of.

no cant about this religion or that religion, but an honest belief that things are making for good on the whole.

VIVIE [*with biting irony*]. 'A power, not ourselves, that makes for righteousness', eh?[1]

CROFTS [*taking her seriously*]. Oh certainly. Not ourselves, of course. You understand what I mean. Well, now as to practical matters. You may have an idea that I have flung my money about; but I havnt: I'm richer today than when I first came into the property. Ive used my knowledge of the world to invest my money in ways that other men have overlooked; and whatever else I may be, I'm a safe man from the money point of view.

VIVIE. It's very kind of you to tell me all this.

CROFTS. Oh well, come, Miss Vivie: you neednt pretend you dont see what I'm driving at. I want to settle down with a Lady Crofts. I suppose you think me very blunt, eh?

VIVIE. Not at all: I am much obliged to you for being so definite and business-like. I quite appreciate the offer: the money, the position, L a d y C r o f t s and so on. But I think I will say no, if you dont mind. I'd rather not. [*She rises, and strolls across to the sundial to get out of his immediate neighborhood.*]

CROFTS [*not at all discouraged, and taking advantage of the additional room left him on the seat to spread himself comfortably, as if a few preliminary refusals were part of the inevitable routine of courtship*]. I'm in no hurry. It was only just to let you know in case young Gardner should try to trap you. Leave the question open.

VIVIE [*sharply*]. My no is final. I wont go back from it.

Crofts is not impressed. He grins; leans forward with his elbows on his knees to prod with his stick at some unfortunate insect in the grass; and looks cunningly at her. She turns away impatiently.

CROFTS. I'm a good deal older than you. Twenty-five years: quarter of a century. I shant live forever; and I'll take care that you shall be well off when I'm gone.

---

1   Matthew Arnold, *Literature and Dogma* (1873), chapter 8: "The eternal *not ourselves* that makes for righteousness." It is interesting that Vivie—consumed by mathematics and a self-declared "ignorant barbarian" (92)—can quote Arnold.

VIVIE. I am proof against even that inducement, Sir George. Dont you think youd better take your answer? There is not the slightest chance of my altering it.

CROFTS [rising, after a final slash at a daisy, and coming nearer to her]. Well, no matter. I could tell you some things that would change your mind fast enough; but I wont, because I'd rather win you by honest affection. I was a good friend to your mother: ask her whether I wasnt. She'd never have made the money that paid for your education if it hadnt been for my advice and help, not to mention the money I advanced her. There are not many men who would have stood by her as I have. I put not less than £40,000 into it, from first to last.

VIVIE [staring at him]. Do you mean to say you were my mother's business partner?

CROFTS. Yes. Now just think of all the trouble and the explanations it would save if we were to keep the whole thing in the family, so to speak. Ask your mother whether she'd like to have to explain all her affairs to a perfect stranger.

VIVIE. I see no difficulty, since I understand that the business is wound up, and the money invested.

CROFTS [stopping short, amazed]. Wound up! Wind up a business thats paying 35 per cent in the worst years! Not likely. Who told you that?

VIVIE [her color quite gone]. Do you mean that it is still—? [She stops abruptly, and puts her hand on the sundial to support herself. Then she gets quickly to the iron chair and sits down.] What business are you talking about?

CROFTS. Well, the fact is it's not what would be considered exactly a high-class business in my set—the county set, you know— o u r set it will be if you think better of my offer. Not that theres any mystery about it: dont think that. Of course you know by your mother's being in it that it's perfectly straight and honest. Ive known her for many years; and I can say of her that she'd cut off her hands sooner than touch anything that was not what it ought to be. I'll tell you all about it if you like. I dont know whether youve found in travelling how hard it is to find a really comfortable private hotel.

VIVIE [sickened, averting her face]. Yes: go on.

CROFTS. Well, thats all it is. Your mother has a genius for managing such things. Weve got two in Brussels, one in Ostend, one
in Vienna and two in Budapest.[1] Of course there are others
besides ourselves in it: but we hold most of the capital; and your
mother's indispensable as managing director. Youve noticed,
I dare say, that she travels a good deal. But you see you cant
mention such things in society. Once let out the word hotel
and everybody says you keep a public-house. You wouldnt like
people to say that of your mother, would you? Thats why we're
so reserved about it. By the way, youll keep it to yourself, wont
you? Since its been a secret so long, it had better remain so.

VIVIE. And this is the business you invite me to join you in?

CROFTS. Oh, no. My wife shant be troubled with business. Youll
not be in it more than youve always been.

VIVIE. *I* always been! What do you mean?

CROFTS. Only that youve always lived on it. It paid for your education and the dress you have on your back. Dont turn up your
nose at business, Miss Vivie; where would your Newnhams
and Girtons[2] be without it?

VIVIE [*rising, almost beside herself*]. Take care. I know what this
business is.

CROFTS [*starting, with a suppressed oath*]. Who told you?

VIVIE. Your partner. My mother.

CROFTS [*black with rage*]. The old—

VIVIE. Just so.

*He swallows the epithet and stands for a moment swearing and raging
foully to himself. But he knows that his cue is to be sympathetic. He
takes refuge in generous indignation.*

CROFTS. She ought to have had more consideration for you. *I'*d
never have told you.

VIVIE. I think you would probably have told me when we were
married: it would have been a convenient weapon to break me
in with.

---

1   In the 1898 text the count of brothels is slightly different: two in Brussels, one in
    Berlin, one in Vienna, and two in Budapest.
2   Girton and Newnham Colleges. See p. 91, note 1.

CROFTS [*quite sincerely*]. I never intended that. On my word as a gentleman I didnt.

Vivie wonders at him. Her sense of the irony of his protest cools and braces her. She replies with contemptuous self-possession.

VIVIE. It does not matter. I suppose you understand that when we leave here today our acquaintance ceases.

CROFTS. Why? Is it for helping your mother?

VIVIE. My mother was a very poor woman who had no reasonable choice but to do as she did. You were a rich gentleman; and you did the same for the sake of 35 per cent. You are a pretty common sort of scoundrel, I think. That is my opinion of you.

CROFTS [*after a stare: not at all displeased, and much more at his ease on these frank terms than on their former ceremonious ones*]. Ha! ha! ha! ha! Go it, little missie, go it; it doesnt hurt me and it amuses you. Why the devil shouldnt I invest my money that way? I take the interest on my capital like other people: I hope you dont think I dirty my own hands with the work. Come! you wouldnt refuse the acquaintance of my mother's cousin the Duke of Belgravia[1] because some of the rents he gets are earned in queer ways. You wouldnt cut the Archbishop of Canterbury,[2] I suppose, because the Ecclesiastical Commissioners[3] have a few publicans and sinners among their tenants. Do you remember your Crofts scholarship at Newnham? Well, that was founded by my brother the M.P. He gets his 22 per cent out of a factory with 600 girls in it, and not one of them getting wages enough to live on. How d'ye suppose they manage when they

---

1 Belgravia was (and is) a fashionable and expensive residential area of London. The title "Duke of Belgravia" is fictitious, though Shaw might well have had in mind the Duke of Westminster (Hugh Lupus Grosvenor, 1825-99), one of London's biggest landlords, some of whose rents, as Crofts puts it, were "earned in queer ways" —i.e. through ownership of slum properties.

2 The Archbishop of Canterbury in office at the time that Shaw was writing *Mrs Warren's Profession* was Edward White Benson (1829-96), Archbishop from 1882 to his death.

3 A body established in 1836 to buy, sell, and manage land and property and oversee other business operations for the Church of England. It consisted of leading ecclesiastics, politicians, and judges.

have no family to fall back on? Ask your mother. And do you expect me to turn my back on 35 per cent when all the rest are pocketing what they can, like sensible men? No such fool! If youre going to pick and choose your acquaintances on moral principles, youd better clear out of this country, unless you want to cut yourself out of all decent society.

VIVIE [*conscience stricken*]. You might go on to point out that I myself never asked where the money I spent came from. I believe I am just as bad as you.

CROFTS [*greatly reassured*]. Of course you are; and a very good thing too! What harm does it do after all? [*Rallying her jocularly.*] So you dont think me such a scoundrel now you come to think it over. Eh?

VIVIE. I have shared profits with you; and I admitted you just now to the familiarity of knowing what I think of you.

CROFTS [*with serious friendliness*]. To be sure you did. You wont find me a bad sort: I dont go in for being superfine intellectually: but Ive plenty of honest human feeling; and the old Crofts breed comes out in a sort of instinctive hatred of anything low, in which I'm sure youll sympathize with me. Believe me, Miss Vivie, the world isnt such a bad place as the croakers[1] make out. As long as you dont fly openly in the face of society, society doesnt ask any inconvenient questions; and it makes precious short work of the cads who do. There are no secrets better kept than the secrets everybody guesses. In the class of people I can introduce you to, no lady or gentleman would so far forget themselves as to discuss my business affairs or your mother's. No man can offer you a safer position.

VIVIE [*studying him curiously*]. I suppose you really think youre getting on famously with me.

CROFTS. Well, I hope I may flatter myself that you think better of me than you did at first.

VIVIE [*quietly*]. I hardly find you worth thinking about at all now.[2] When I think of the society that tolerates you, and the laws that protect you! when I think of how helpless nine out of ten

---

1 Congenital pessimists.

2 The 1898 text specifies that Vivie speaks to Crofts "*almost gently, but with intense conviction.*"

young girls would be in the hands of you and my mother! the unmentionable woman and her capitalist bully—

CROFTS [livid]. Damn you!

VIVIE. You need not. I feel among the damned already.

She raises the latch of the gate to open it and go out. He follows her and puts his hand heavily on the top bar to prevent its opening.

CROFTS [panting with fury]. Do you think I'll put up with this from you, you young devil?

VIVIE [unmoved]. Be quiet. Some one will answer the bell. [*Without flinching a step she strikes the bell with the back of her hand. It clangs harshly; and he starts back involuntarily. Almost immediately Frank appears at the porch with his rifle.*]

FRANK [with cheerful politeness]. Will you have the rifle, Viv; or shall I operate?

VIVIE. Frank: have you been listening?

FRANK [coming down into the garden]. Only for the bell, I assure you; so that you shouldnt have to wait. I think I shewed great insight into your character, Crofts.

CROFTS. For two pins I'd take that gun from you and break it across your head.

FRANK [stalking him cautiously]. Pray dont. I'm ever so careless in handling firearms. Sure to be a fatal accident, with a reprimand from the coroner's jury for my negligence.

VIVIE. Put the rifle away, Frank; it's quite unnecessary.

FRANK. Quite right, Viv. Much more sportsmanlike to catch him in a trap. [*Crofts, understanding the insult, makes a threatening movement.*] Crofts: there are fifteen cartridges in the magazine here; and I am a dead shot at the present distance and at an object of your size.

CROFTS. Oh, you neednt be afraid. I'm not going to touch you.

FRANK. Ever so magnanimous of you under the circumstances! Thank you!

CROFTS. I'll just tell you this before I go. It may interest you, since youre so fond of one another. Allow me, Mr Frank, to introduce you to your half-sister, the eldest daughter of the Reverend Samuel Gardner. Miss Vivie: your half-brother.

Good morning. [*He goes out through the gate along the road.*]

FRANK [*after a pause of stupefaction, raising the rifle*]. Youll testify before the coroner that its an accident, Viv. [*He takes aim at the retreating figure of Crofts. Vivie seizes the muzzle and pulls it round against her breast.*]

VIVIE. Fire now. You may.

FRANK [*dropping his end of the rifle hastily*]. Stop! take care. [*She lets it go. It falls on the turf.*] Oh, youve given your little boy such a turn. Suppose it had gone off! ugh! [*He sinks on the garden seat overcome.*]

VIVIE. Suppose it had: do you think it would not have been a relief to have some sharp physical pain tearing through me?

FRANK [*coaxingly*]. Take it ever so easy, dear Viv. Remember: even if the rifle scared that fellow into telling the truth for the first time in his life, that only makes us the babes in the wood in earnest. [*He holds out his arms to her.*] Come and be covered up with leaves again.

VIVIE [*with a cry of disgust*]. Ah, not that, not that. You make all my flesh creep.

FRANK. Why, whats the matter?

VIVIE. Goodbye. [*She makes for the gate.*]

FRANK [*jumping up*]. Hallo! Stop! Viv! Viv! [*She turns in the gateway.*] Where are you going to? Where shall we find you?

VIVIE. At Honoria Fraser's chambers, 67 Chancery Lane, for the rest of my life. [*She goes off quickly in the opposite direction to that taken by Crofts.*]

FRANK. But I say—wait—dash it! [*He runs after her.*]

ACT IV

Honoria Fraser's chambers in Chancery Lane. An office at the top of New Stone Buildings, with a plate-glass window, distempered[1] walls, electric light, and a patent stove.[2] Saturday afternoon. The chimneys of Lincoln's Inn[3] and the western sky beyond are seen through the window. There is a double writing table in the middle of the room, with a cigar box, ash pans, and a portable electric reading lamp almost snowed up in heaps of papers and books. This table has knee holes and chairs right and left and is very untidy. The clerk's desk, closed and tidy, with its high stool, is against the wall, near a door communicating with the inner rooms. In the opposite wall is the door leading to the public corridor. Its upper panel is of opaque glass, lettered in black on the outside, FRASER AND WARREN. *A baize screen hides the corner between this door and the window.*

Frank, in a fashionable light-colored coaching suit, with his stick, gloves, and white hat in his hands, is pacing up and down the office. Somebody tries the door with a key.

FRANK [*calling*]. Come in. It's not locked.

Vivie comes in, in her hat and jacket. She stops and stares at him.

VIVIE [*sternly*]. What are you doing here?
FRANK. Waiting to see you. Ive been here for hours. Is this the way you attend to your business? [*He puts his hat and stick on the table, and perches himself with a vault on the clerk's stool looking at her with every appearance of being in a specially restless, teasing, flippant mood.*]
VIVIE. Ive been away exactly twenty minutes for a cup of tea. [*She takes off her hat and jacket and hangs them up behind the screen.*] How did you get in?

---

1 Painted.
2 An open stove.
3 One of four institutions (Lincoln's Inn, Gray's Inn, Inner Temple, Middle Temple), all located in London, that have exercised the exclusive right since the Middle Ages of admitting barristers (lawyers) to the bar (i.e. to practise law). Lincoln's Inn is located just off Chancery Lane, near to Honoria Fraser's chambers.

FRANK. The staff had not left when I arrived. He's gone to play cricket on Primrose Hill.[1] Why dont you employ a woman, and give your sex a chance?

VIVIE. What have you come for?

FRANK [*springing off the stool and coming close to her*]. Viv: lets go and enjoy the Saturday half-holiday somewhere, like the staff. What do you say to Richmond,[2] and then a music hall,[3] and a jolly supper?

VIVIE. Cant afford it. I shall put in another six hours work before I go to bed.

FRANK. Cant afford it, cant we? Aha! Look here. [*He takes out a handful of sovereigns and makes them chink.*] Gold, Viv: gold!

VIVIE. Where did you get it?

FRANK. Gambling, Viv: gambling. Poker.

VIVIE. Pah! It's meaner than stealing it. No: I'm not coming. [*She sits down to work at the table, with her back to the glass door, and begins turning over the papers.*]

FRANK [*remonstrating piteously*]. But, my dear Viv, I want to talk to you ever so seriously.

VIVIE. Very well: sit down in Honoria's chair and talk here. I like ten minutes chat after tea. [*He murmurs.*] No use groaning: I'm inexorable. [*He takes the opposite seat disconsolately.*] Pass that cigar box, will you?

FRANK [*pushing the cigar box across*]. Nasty womanly habit. Nice men dont do it any longer.

VIVIE. Yes: they object to the smell in the office; and weve had to take to cigarets. See! [*She opens the box and takes out a cigaret, which she lights. She offers him one; but he shakes his head with a wry face. She settles herself comfortably in her chair, smoking.*] Go ahead.

FRANK. Well, I want to know what youve done—what arrangements youve made.

VIVIE. Everything was settled twenty minutes after I arrived here. Honoria has found the business too much for her this year; and

---

1　A parkland area northwest of central London, frequently visited by Shaw.

2　A town on the Thames, a few miles southwest of central London, with a population (1901) of 31,672 (*Encyclopaedia Britannica*, 11th ed.).

3　Music halls were popular places of entertainment in Victorian England, featuring songs, comedy, dances, and novelty acts.

she was on the point of sending for me and proposing partnership when I walked in and told her I hadnt a farthing[1] in the world. So I installed myself and packed her off for a fortnight's holiday. What happened at Haslemere when I left?

FRANK. Nothing at all. I said you had gone to town on particular business.

VIVIE. Well?

FRANK. Well, either they were too flabbergasted to say anything, or else Crofts had prepared your mother. Anyhow, she didnt say anything; and Crofts didnt say anything; and Praddy only stared. After tea they got up and went; and Ive not seen them since.

VIVIE [*nodding placidly with one eye on a wreath of smoke*]. Thats all right.

FRANK [*looking round disparagingly*]. Do you intend to stick in this confounded place?

VIVIE [*blowing the wreath decisively away, and sitting straight up*]. Yes. These two days have given me back all my strength and self-possession. I will never take a holiday again as long as I live.

FRANK [*with a very wry face*]. Mps! You look quite happy. And as hard as nails.

VIVIE [*grimly*]. Well for me that I am!

FRANK [*rising*]. Look here, Viv: we must have an explanation. We parted the other day under a complete misunderstanding. [*He sits on the table, close to her.*]

VIVIE [*putting away the cigaret*]. Well: clear it up.

FRANK. You remember what Crofts said?

VIVIE. Yes.

FRANK. That revelation was supposed to bring about a complete change in the nature of our feeling for one another. It placed us on the footing of brother and sister.

VIVIE. Yes.

FRANK. Have you ever had a brother?

VIVIE. No.

FRANK. Then you dont know what being brother and sister feels

---

1   A bronze coin, the smallest denomination of British currency (one quarter of a penny). The farthing was withdrawn from circulation in 1961.

like? Now I have lots of sisters; and the fraternal feeling is quite familiar to me. I assure you my feeling for you is not the least in the world like it. The girls will go their way; I will go mine; and we shant care if we never see one another again. Thats brother and sister. But as to you, I cant be easy if I have to pass a week without seeing you. Thats not brother and sister. It's exactly what I felt an hour before Crofts made his revelation. In short, dear Viv, it's love's young dream.

VIVIE [*bitingly*]. The same feeling, Frank, that brought your father to my mother's feet. Is that it?

FRANK [*so revolted that he slips off the table for a moment*]. I very strongly object, Viv, to have my feelings compared to any which the Reverend Samuel is capable of harboring; and I object still more to a comparison of you to your mother. [*Resuming his perch.*] Besides, I dont believe the story. I have taxed my father with it, and obtained from him what I consider tantamount to a denial.

VIVIE. What did he say?

FRANK. He said he was sure there must be some mistake.

VIVIE. Do you believe him?

FRANK. I am prepared to take his word as against Crofts'.

VIVIE. Does it make any difference? I mean in your imagination or conscience; for of course it makes no real difference.

FRANK [*shaking his head*]. None whatever to m e.

VIVIE. Nor to me.

FRANK [*staring*]. But this is ever so surprising! [*He goes back to his chair.*] I thought our whole relations were altered in your imagination and conscience, as you put it, the moment those words were out of that brute's muzzle.

VIVIE. No: it was not that. I didnt believe him. I only wish I could.

FRANK. Eh?

VIVIE. I think brother and sister would be a very suitable relation for us.

FRANK. You really mean that?

VIVIE. Yes. It's the only relation I care for, even if we could afford any other. I mean that.

FRANK [*raising his eyebrows like one on whom a new light has dawned, and rising with quite an effusion of chivalrous sentiment].* My dear Viv: why didnt you say so before? I am ever so sorry for persecuting you. I understand, of course.

VIVIE *[puzzled].* Understand what?

FRANK. Oh, I'm not a fool in the ordinary sense: only in the Scriptural sense of doing all the things the wise man declared to be folly, after trying them himself on the most extensive scale.[1] I see I am no longer Vivvum's little boy. Dont be alarmed: I shall never call you Vivvums again—at least unless you get tired of your new little boy, whoever he may be.

VIVIE. My new little boy!

FRANK *[with conviction].* Must be a new little boy. Always happens that way. No other way, in fact.

VIVIE. None that you know of, fortunately for you.

Someone knocks at the door.

FRANK. My curse upon yon caller, whoe'er he be!

VIVIE. It's Praed. He's going to Italy and wants to say goodbye. I asked him to call this afternoon. Go and let him in.

FRANK. We can continue our conversation after his departure for Italy. I'll stay him out. *[He goes to the door and opens it.]* How are you, Praddy? Delighted to see you. Come in.

Praed, dressed for travelling, comes in, in high spirits.

PRAED. How do you do, Miss Warren? *[She presses his hand cordially, though a certain sentimentality in his high spirits jars on her.]* I start in an hour from the Holborn Viaduct.[2] I wish I could persuade you to try Italy.

VIVIE. What for?

PRAED. Why, to saturate yourself with beauty and romance, of course.

---

1 Perhaps a reference to Solomon's comments on folly throughout the Book of Proverbs.

2 The Holborn Viaduct opened in London in 1869 as a route for trains over the valley of the Fleet River (which had been covered over since the middle of the eighteenth century).

Vivie, with a shudder, turns her chair to the table, as if the work waiting for her there were a support to her. Praed sits opposite to her. Frank places a chair near Vivie, and drops lazily and carelessly into it, talking at her over his shoulder.

FRANK. No use, Praddy. Viv is a little Philistine.[1] She is indifferent to my romance, and insensible to my beauty.

VIVIE. Mr Praed: once for all, there is no beauty and no romance in life for me. Life is what it is; and I am prepared to take it as it is.

PRAED [*enthusiastically*]. You will not say that if you come with me to Verona and on to Venice. You will cry with delight at living in such a beautiful world.

FRANK. This is most eloquent, Praddy. Keep it up.

PRAED. Oh, I assure you *I* have cried—I shall cry again, I hope —at fifty! At your age, Miss Warren, you would not need to go so far as Verona. Your spirits would absolutely fly up at the mere sight of Ostend. You would be charmed with the gaiety, the vivacity, the happy air of Brussels.

VIVIE [*springing up with an exclamation of loathing*]. Agh!

PRAED [*rising*]. Whats the matter?

FRANK [*rising*]. Hallo, Viv!

VIVIE [*to Praed, with deep reproach*]. Can you find no better example of your beauty and romance than Brussels to talk to me about?

PRAED [*puzzled*]. Of course it's very different from Verona. I dont suggest for a moment that—

VIVIE [*bitterly*]. Probably the beauty and romance come to much the same in both places.

PRAED [*completely sobered and much concerned*]. My dear Miss Warren: I—[*looking inquiringly at Frank*] Is anything the matter?

FRANK. She thinks your enthusiasm frivolous, Praddy. She's had ever such a serious call.

VIVIE [*sharply*]. Hold your tongue, Frank. Dont be silly.

---

1   Someone hostile or indifferent to culture and the arts. Enemies of the Israelites—and eventually defeated by David (2 Samuel 8:1)—the Philistines were reputed to be culturally ignorant.

FRANK [*sitting down*]. Do you call this good manners, Praed?

PRAED [*anxious and considerate*]. Shall I take him away, Miss Warren? I feel sure we have disturbed you at your work.

VIVIE. Sit down: I'm not ready to go back to work yet. [*Praed sits.*] You both think I have an attack of nerves. Not a bit of it. But there are two subjects I want dropped, if you dont mind. One of them [*to Frank*] is love's young dream in any shape or form: the other [*to Praed*] is the romance and beauty of life, especially Ostend and the gaiety of Brussels. You are welcome to any illusions you have left on these subjects: I have none. If we three are to remain friends, I must be treated as a woman of business, permanently single [*to Frank*] and permanently unromantic [*to Praed*].

FRANK. I shall also remain permanently single until you change your mind. Praddy: change the subject. Be eloquent about something else.

PRAED [*diffidently*]. I'm afraid theres nothing else in the world I c a n talk about. The Gospel of Art is the only one I can preach. I know Miss Warren is a great devotee of the Gospel of Getting On; but we cant discuss that without hurting your feelings, Frank, since you are determined not to get on.

FRANK. Oh, dont mind my feelings. Give me some improving advice by all means: it does me ever so much good. Have another try to make a successful man of me, Viv. Come: lets have it all: energy, thrift, foresight, self-respect, character. Dont you hate people who have no character, Viv?

VIVIE [*wincing*]. Oh, stop, stop: let us have no more of that horrible cant. Mr Praed: if there are really only those two gospels in the world, we had better all kill ourselves; for the same taint is in both, through and through.

FRANK [*looking critically at her*]. There is a touch of poetry about you today, Viv, which has hitherto been lacking.

PRAED [*remonstrating*]. My dear Frank: arnt you a little unsympathetic?

VIVIE [*merciless to herself*]. No: it's good for me. It keeps me from being sentimental.

FRANK [*bantering her*]. Checks your strong natural propensity that way, dont it?

VIVIE [*almost hysterically*]. Oh yes: go on: dont spare me. I was sentimental for one moment in my life—beautifully sentimental —by moonlight; and now—

FRANK [*quickly*]. I say, Viv: take care. Dont give yourself away.

VIVIE. Oh, do you think Mr Praed does not know all about my mother? [*Turning on Praed.*] You had better have told me that morning, Mr Praed. You are very old fashioned in your delicacies, after all.

PRAED. Surely it is you who are a little old fashioned in your prejudices, Miss Warren. I feel bound to tell you, speaking as an artist, and believing that the most intimate human relationships are far beyond and above the scope of the law, that though I know that your mother is an unmarried woman, I do not respect her the less on that account. I respect her more.

FRANK [*airily*]. Hear! Hear!

VIVIE [*staring at him*]. Is that all you know?

PRAED. Certainly that is all.

VIVIE. Then you neither of you know anything. Your guesses are innocence itself compared to the truth.

PRAED [*rising, startled and indignant, and preserving his politeness with an effort*]. I hope not. [*More emphatically.*] I hope not, Miss Warren.

FRANK [*whistles*]. Whew!

VIVIE. You are not making it easy for me to tell you, Mr Praed.

PRAED [*his chivalry drooping before their conviction*]. If there is anything worse—that is, anything else—are you sure you are right to tell us, Miss Warren?

VIVIE. I am sure that if I had the courage I should spend the rest of my life in telling everybody—stamping and branding it into them until they all felt their part in its abomination as I feel mine. There is nothing I despise more than the wicked convention that protects these things by forbidding a woman to mention them. And yet I cant tell you. The two infamous words[1] that describe what my mother is are ringing in my ears

---

1 Having read the page proofs of *Mrs Warren's Profession* in July 1897, actress Ellen Terry asked Shaw what the "two infamous words" were. Shaw replied, "Prostitute and Procuress." The page proofs and the slips of paper with question and response are in the Harry Ransom Humanities Research Center, University of Texas at

and struggling on my tongue; but I cant utter them: the shame of them is too horrible for me. [*She buries her face in her hands. The two men, astonished, stare at one another and then at her. She raises her head again desperately and snatches a sheet of paper and a pen.*] Here: let me draft you a prospectus.

FRANK. Oh, she's mad. Do you hear, Viv? mad. Come! pull yourself together.

VIVIE. You shall see. [*She writes.*] 'Paid up capital: not less than £40,000 standing in the name of Sir George Crofts, Baronet, the chief shareholder. Premises at Brussels, Ostend, Vienna and Budapest. Managing director: Mrs Warren'; and now dont let us forget her qualifications: the two words. [*She writes the words and pushes the paper to them.*] There! Oh no: dont read it: dont! [*She snatches it back and tears it to pieces; then seizes her head in her hands and hides her face on the table.*]

Frank, who has watched the writing over her shoulder, and opened his eyes very widely at it, takes a card from his pocket; scribbles the two words on it; and silently hands it to Praed, who reads it with amazement, and hides it hastily in his pocket.

FRANK [*whispering tenderly*]. Viv, dear: thats all right. I read what you wrote: so did Praddy. We understand. And we remain, as this leaves us at present, yours ever so devotedly.

PRAED. We do indeed, Miss Warren. I declare you are the most splendidly courageous woman I ever met.

This sentimental compliment braces Vivie. She throws it away from her with an impatient shake, and forces herself to stand up, though not without some support from the table.

FRANK. Dont stir, Viv, if you dont want to. Take it easy.

VIVIE. Thank you. You can always depend on me for two things: not to cry and not to faint. [*She moves a few steps towards the door*

Austin. See Dan H. Laurence, *Shaw: An Exhibit* [catalogue of an exhibit at the University of Texas at Austin, 11 September 1977-28 February 1978] (Austin: University of Texas, 1977), item 205.

of the inner room, and stops close to Praed to say] I shall need much more courage than that when I tell my mother that we have come to the parting of the ways. Now I must go into the next room for a moment to make myself neat again, if you dont mind.

PRAED. Shall we go away?

VIVIE. No: I'll be back presently. Only for a moment. [*She goes into the other room, Praed opening the door for her.*]

PRAED. What an amazing revelation! I'm extremely disappointed in Crofts: I am indeed.

FRANK. I'm not in the least. I feel he's perfectly accounted for at last. But what a facer[1] for me, Praddy! I cant marry her now.

PRAED [*sternly*]. Frank! [*The two look at one another, Frank unruffled, Praed deeply indignant.*] Let me tell you, Gardner, that if you desert her now you will behave very despicably.

FRANK. Good old Praddy! Ever chivalrous! But you mistake: it's not the moral aspect of the case: it's the money aspect. I really cant bring myself to touch the old woman's money now.

PRAED. And was that what you were going to marry on?

FRANK. What else? *I* havnt any money, nor the smallest turn for making it. If I married Viv now she would have to support me; and I should cost her more than I am worth.

PRAED. But surely a clever bright fellow like you can make something by your own brains.

FRANK. Oh yes, a little [*he takes out his money again*]. I made all that yesterday in an hour and a half. But I made it in a highly speculative business. No, dear Praddy: even if Bessie and Georgina[2] marry millionaires and the governor dies after cutting them off with a shilling,[3] I shall have only four hundred a year. And he wont die until he's three score and ten.[4] He hasnt originality enough. I shall be on short allowance for the next twenty years. No short allowance for Viv, if I can help it. I withdraw

---

1 A blow in the face (figuratively); a sudden difficulty.

2 Bessie and Georgina are Frank's sisters. In the 1898 text Bessie is Jessie, and Frank has other (unnamed) sisters.

3 A shilling was one-twentieth part of £1 in the British currency system prior to decimilization in 1971. See above, A Note on British Currency, p. 79.

4 Psalms 90:10: "The days of our years are three-score years and ten ...."

gracefully and leave the field to the gilded youth of England. So thats settled. I shant worry her about it: I'll just send her a little note after we're gone. She'll understand.

PRAED [*grasping his hand*]. Good fellow, Frank! I heartily beg your pardon. But must you never see her again?

FRANK. Never see her again! Hang it all, be reasonable. I shall come along as often as possible, and be her brother. I can n o t understand the absurd consequences you romantic people expect from the most ordinary transactions. [*A knock at the door.*] I wonder who this is. Would you mind opening the door? If it's a client it will look more respectable than if I appeared.

PRAED. Certainly. [*He goes to the door, and opens it. Frank sits down in Vivie's chair to scribble a note.*] My dear Kitty: come in: come in.

Mrs Warren comes in, looking apprehensively round for Vivie. She has done her best to make herself matronly and dignified. The brilliant hat is replaced by a sober bonnet, and the gay blouse covered by a costly black silk mantle. She is pitiably anxious and ill at ease: evidently panic-stricken.

MRS WARREN [*to Frank*]. What! Y o u r e here, are you?

FRANK [*turning in his chair from his writing, but not rising*]. Here, and charmed to see you. You come like a breath of spring.

MRS WARREN. Oh, get out with your nonsense. [*In a low voice.*] Wheres Vivie?

Frank points expressively to the door of the inner room, but says nothing.

MRS WARREN [*sitting down suddenly and almost beginning to cry*]. Praddy: wont she see me, dont you think?

PRAED. My dear Kitty: dont distress yourself. Why should she not?

MRS WARREN. Oh, you never can see why not: youre too innocent.[1] Mr Frank: did she say anything to you?

---

1 In the 1898 text Praed is "too amiable."

FRANK [*folding his note*]. She m u s t see you, if [*very expressively*] you wait til she comes in.

MRS WARREN [*frightened*]. Why shouldnt I wait?

Frank looks quizzically at her; puts his note carefully on the ink bottle, so that Vivie cannot fail to find it when next she dips her pen; then rises and devotes his attention to her.

FRANK. My dear Mrs Warren: suppose you were a sparrow—ever so tiny and pretty a sparrow hopping in the roadway—and you saw a steam roller coming in your direction, would you wait for it?

MRS WARREN. Oh, dont bother me with your sparrows. What did she run away from Haslemere like that for?

FRANK. I'm afraid she'll tell you if you rashly await her return.

MRS WARREN. Do you want me to go away?

FRANK. No: I always want you to stay. But I a d v i s e you to go away.

MRS WARREN. What! And never see her again!

FRANK. Precisely.

MRS WARREN [*crying again*]. Praddy: dont let him be cruel to me. [*She hastily checks her tears and wipes her eyes.*] She'll be so angry if she sees Ive been crying.

FRANK [*with a touch of real compassion in his airy tenderness*]. You know that Praddy is the soul of kindness, Mrs Warren. Praddy: what do y o u say? Go or stay?

PRAED [*to Mrs Warren*]. I really should be very sorry to cause you unnecessary pain; but I think perhaps you had better not wait. The fact is—[*Vivie is heard at the inner door.*]

FRANK. Sh! Too late. She's coming.

MRS WARREN. Dont tell her I was crying. [*Vivie comes in. She stops gravely on seeing Mrs Warren, who greets her with hysterical cheerfulness.*] Well, dearie. So here you are at last.

VIVIE. I am glad you have come. I want to speak to you. You said you were going, Frank, I think.

FRANK. Yes. Will you come with me, Mrs Warren? What do you say to a trip to Richmond, and the theatre in the evening? There is safety in Richmond. No steam roller there.

VIVIE. Nonsense, Frank. My mother will stay here.

MRS WARREN [*scared*]. I dont know: perhaps I'd better go. We're disturbing you at your work.

VIVIE [*with quiet decision*]. Mr Praed: please take Frank away. Sit down, mother. [*Mrs Warren obeys helplessly.*]

PRAED. Come, Frank. Goodbye, Miss Vivie.

VIVIE [*shaking hands*]. Goodbye. A pleasant trip.

PRAED. Thank you: thank you. I hope so.

FRANK [*to Mrs Warren*]. Goodbye: youd ever so much better have taken my advice. [*He shakes hands with her. Then airily to Vivie*] Byebye, Viv.

VIVIE. Goodbye. [*He goes out gaily without shaking hands with her.*]

PRAED [*sadly*]. Goodbye, Kitty.

MRS WARREN [*snivelling*]. —oobye!

Praed goes. Vivie, composed and extremely grave, sits down in Honoria's chair, and waits for her mother to speak. Mrs Warren, dreading a pause, loses no time in beginning.

MRS WARREN. Well, Vivie, what did you go away like that for without saying a word to me? How could you do such a thing! And what have you done to poor George? I wanted him to come with me; but he shuffled out of it. I could see that he was quite afraid of you. Only fancy: he wanted me not to come. As if [*trembling*] I should be afraid of you, dearie. [*Vivie's gravity deepens.*] But of course I told him it was all settled and comfortable between us, and that we were on the best of terms. [*She breaks down.*] Vivie: whats the meaning of this? [*She produces a commercial envelope, and fumbles at the enclosure with trembling fingers.*] I got it from the bank this morning.

VIVIE. It is my month's allowance. They sent it to me as usual the other day. I simply sent it back to be placed to your credit, and asked them to send you the lodgment receipt.[1] In future I shall support myself.

MRS WARREN [*not daring to understand*]. Wasnt it enough? Why didnt you tell me? [*With a cunning gleam in her eye.*] I'll double

---

1   Deposit receipt.

it: I was intending to double it. Only let me know how much you want.

VIVIE. You know very well that that has nothing to do with it. From this time I go my own way in my own business and among my own friends. And you will go yours. [*She rises.*] Goodbye.

MRS WARREN [*rising, appalled*]. Goodbye?

VIVIE. Yes: Goodbye. Come: dont let us make a useless scene: you understand perfectly well. Sir George Crofts has told me the whole business.

MRS WARREN [*angrily*]. Silly old— [*She swallows an epithet, and turns white at the narrowness of her escape from uttering it.*]

VIVIE. Just so.

MRS WARREN. He ought to have his tongue cut out. But I thought it was ended: you said you didnt mind.

VIVIE [*steadfastly*]. Excuse me: I d o mind.

MRS WARREN. But I explained—

VIVIE. You explained how it came about. You did not tell me that it is still going on. [*She sits.*]

Mrs Warren, silenced for a moment, looks forlornly at Vivie, who waits, secretly hoping that the combat is over. But the cunning expression comes back into Mrs Warren's face; and she bends across the table, sly and urgent, half whispering.

MRS WARREN. Vivie: do you know how rich I am?

VIVIE. I have no doubt you are very rich.

MRS WARREN. But you dont know all that that means: youre too young. It means a new dress every day; it means theatres and balls every night; it means having the pick of all the gentlemen in Europe at your feet; it means a lovely house and plenty of servants; it means the choicest of eating and drinking; it means everything you like, everything you want, everything you can think of. And what are you here? A mere drudge, toiling and moiling[1] early and late for your bare living and two

---

1 Working extremely hard. Vivie's "toiling and moiling" as an actuary would in fact have brought her a comfortable salary—probably about £350 a year. See Ellen J.

cheap dresses a year. Think over it. [*Soothingly.*] Youre shocked, I know. I can enter into your feelings; and I think they do you credit; but trust me, nobody will blame you: you may take my word for that. I know what young girls are; and I know youll think better of it when youve turned it over in your mind.

VIVIE. So thats how it's done, is it? You must have said all that to many a woman, mother, to have it so pat.

MRS WARREN [*passionately*]. What harm am I asking you to do? [*Vivie turns away contemptuously. Mrs Warren continues desperately.*] Vivie: listen to me: you dont understand: youve been taught wrong on purpose: you dont know what the world is really like.

VIVIE [*arrested*]. Taught wrong on purpose! What do you mean?

MRS WARREN. I mean that youre throwing away all your chances for nothing. You think that people are what they pretend to be: that the way you were taught at school and college to think right and proper is the way things really are. But it's not: it's all only a pretence, to keep the cowardly slavish common run of people quiet. Do you want to find that out, like other women, at forty when youve thrown yourself away and lost your chances; or wont you take it in good time now from your own mother, that loves you and swears to you that it's truth: gospel truth? [*Urgently.*] Vivie: the big people, the clever people, the managing people, all know it. They do as I do, and think what I think. I know plenty of them. I know them to speak to, to introduce you to, to make friends of for you. I dont mean anything wrong: thats what you dont understand: your head is full of ignorant ideas about me. What do the people that taught you know about life or about people like me? When did they ever meet me, or speak to me, or let anyone tell them about me? the fools! Would they ever have done anything for you if I hadnt paid them? Havnt I told you that I want you to be respectable? Havnt I brought you up to be respectable? And how can you keep it up without my money and my influence and Lizzie's friends? Cant you see that youre cutting your own throat as

Gainor, *Shaw's Daughters: Dramatic and Narrative Constructions of Gender* (Ann Arbor: U of Michigan P, 1991) 248, note 12.

well as breaking my heart in turning your back on me?

VIVIE. I recognize the Crofts philosophy of life, mother. I heard it all from him that day at the Gardners'.

MRS WARREN. You think I want to force that played-out old sot on you! I dont, Vivie: on my oath I dont.

VIVIE. It would not matter if you did: you would not succeed. [*Mrs Warren winces, deeply hurt by the implied indifference towards her affectionate intention. Vivie, neither understanding this nor concerning herself about it, goes on calmly.*] Mother: you dont at all know the sort of person I am. I dont object to Crofts more than to any other coarsely built man of his class. To tell you the truth, I rather admire him for being strongminded enough to enjoy himself in his own way and make plenty of money instead of living the usual shooting, hunting, dining-out, tailoring, loafing life of his set merely because all the rest do it. And I'm perfectly aware that if I'd been in the same circumstances as my aunt Liz, I'd have done exactly what she did. I dont think I'm more prejudiced or straitlaced than you: I think I'm less. I'm certain I'm less sentimental. I know very well that fashionable morality is all a pretence, and that if I took your money and devoted the rest of my life to spending it fashionably, I might be as worthless and vicious as the silliest woman could possibly want to be without having a word said to me about it. But I dont want to be worthless. I shouldnt enjoy trotting about the park to advertise my dressmaker and carriage builder, or being bored at the opera to shew off a shopwindowful of diamonds.

MRS WARREN [*bewildered*]. But—

VIVIE. Wait a moment. Ive not done. Tell me why you continue your business now that you are independent of it. Your sister, you told me, has left all that behind her. Why dont you do the same?

MRS WARREN. Oh, it's all very easy for Liz: she likes good society, and has the air of being a lady. Imagine me in a cathedral town! Why, the very rooks in the trees would find me out even if I could stand the dulness of it. I must have work and excitement, or I should go melancholy mad. And what else is there for me to do? The life suits me: I'm fit for it and not for anything else. If I didnt do it, somebody else would; so I dont do any real harm by it. And then it brings in money; and I like making money. No: it's no use: I cant it give up—not for anybody. But what need you know about it? I'll never mention it. I'll keep Crofts away. I'll not trouble you much: you see I have to be constantly running about from one place to another. Youll be quit of me altogether when I die.

VIVIE. No: I am my mother's daughter. I am like you: I must have work, and must make more money than I spend. But my work is not your work, and my way not your way. We must part. It will not make much difference to us: instead of meeting one another for perhaps a few months in twenty years, we shall never meet: thats all.

MRS WARREN [*her voice stifled in tears*]. Vivie: I meant to have been more with you: I did indeed.

VIVIE. It's no use, mother: I am not to be changed by a few cheap tears and entreaties any more than you are, I daresay.

MRS WARREN [*wildly*]. Oh, you call a mother's tears cheap.

VIVIE. They cost you nothing; and you ask me to give you the peace and quietness of my whole life in exchange for them. What use would my company be to you if you could get it? What have we two in common that could make either of us happy together?

MRS WARREN [*lapsing recklessly into her dialect*]. We're mother and daughter. I want my daughter. Ive a right to you. Who is to care for me when I'm old? Plenty of girls have taken to me like daughters and cried at leaving me; but I let them all go because I had you to look forward to. I kept myself lonely for you. Youve no right to turn on me now and refuse to do your duty as daughter.

VIVIE [*jarred and antagonized by the echo of the slums in her mother's voice*]. My duty as a daughter! I thought we should come to that presently. Now once for all, mother, you want a daughter and Frank wants a wife. I dont want a mother; and I dont want a husband. I have spared neither Frank nor myself in sending him about his business. Do you think I will spare y o u ?

MRS WARREN [*violently*]. Oh, I know the sort you are: no mercy for yourself or anyone else. *I* know. My experience has done that for me anyhow: I can tell the pious, canting, hard, selfish

woman when I meet her. Well, keep yourself to yourself: *I*
dont want you. But listen to this. Do you know what I would
do with you if you were a baby again? aye, as sure as theres a
Heaven above us.

VIVIE. Strangle me, perhaps.

MRS WARREN. No: I'd bring you up to be a real daughter to me,
and not what you are now, with your pride and your prejudices
and the college education you stole from me: yes, stole: deny
it if you can: what was it but stealing? I'd bring you up in my
own house, I would.

VIVIE [*quietly*]. In one of your own houses.

MRS WARREN [*screaming*]. Listen to her! listen to how she spits on
her mother's grey hairs! Oh, may you live to have your own
daughter tear and trample on you as you have trampled on
me. And you will: you will. No woman ever had luck with a
mother's curse on her.

VIVIE. I wish you wouldnt rant, mother. It only hardens me.
Come: I suppose I am the only young woman you ever had in
your power that you did good to. Dont spoil it all now.

MRS WARREN. Yes, Heaven forgive me, it's true; and you are the
only one that ever turned on me. Oh, the injustice of it! the
injustice! the injustice! I always wanted to be a good woman. I
tried honest work; and I was slave-driven until I cursed the day
I ever heard of honest work. I was a good mother; and because
I made my daughter a good woman she turns me out as if I was
a leper. Oh, if I only had my life to live over again! I'd talk to
that lying clergyman in the school. From this time forth, so
help me Heaven in my last hour, I'll do wrong and nothing but
wrong. And I'll prosper on it.

VIVIE. Yes: it's better to choose your line and go through with it.
If I had been you, mother, I might have done as you did: but I
should not have lived one life and believed in another. You are
a conventional woman at heart. That is why I am bidding you
goodbye now. I am right, am I not?

MRS WARREN [*taken aback*]. Right to throw away all my money?

VIVIE. No: right to get rid of you! I should be a fool not to. Isnt
that so?

MRS WARREN [*sulkily*]. Oh well, yes, if you come to that, I suppose you are. But Lord help the world if everybody took to doing the right thing! And now I'd better go than stay where I'm not wanted. [*She turns to the door.*]

VIVIE [*kindly*]. Wont you shake hands?

MRS WARREN [*after looking at her fiercely for a moment with a savage impulse to strike her*]. No, thank you. Goodbye.

VIVIE [*matter-of-factly*]. Goodbye. [*Mrs Warren goes out, slamming the door behind her. The strain on Vivie's face relaxes; her grave expression breaks up into one of joyous content; her breath goes out in a half sob, half laugh of intense relief. She goes buoyantly to her place at the writing-table; pushes the electric lamp out of the way; pulls over a great sheaf of papers; and is in the act of dipping her pen in the ink when she finds Frank's note. She opens it unconcernedly and reads it quickly, giving a little laugh at some quaint turn of expression in it.*] And goodbye, Frank. [*She tears the note up and tosses the pieces into the waste paper basket without a second thought. Then she goes at her work with a plunge, and soon becomes absorbed in its figures.*]

Appendix A: From Shaw's Prefaces to Plays Unpleasant *and* Mrs Warren's Profession

[Shaw wrote a preface for *Plays Pleasant and Unpleasant*. *The First Volume, Containing the Three Unpleasant Plays* (London: Grant Richards, 1898), in which *Mrs Warren's Profession* (together with *Widowers' Houses* and *The Philanderer*) was first published. He wrote a new preface, "The Author's Apology," for the first separate publication of *Mrs Warren's Profession* (London: Grant Richards, 1902). He revised both prefaces and added a "postscript" for *Plays Unpleasant*, published in 1930 as volume seven of the *Collected Edition* of his works (London: Constable, 1930-38). The revised prefaces and the "postscript" are collected in volume 1 of the definitive *Collected Plays with Their Prefaces* (London: Max Reinhardt, the Bodley Head, 1970-74, under the editorial supervision of Dan H. Laurence), from which the following extracts are taken.]

1. From the Preface to *Plays Unpleasant* (1930)

... Finally, a word as to why I have labelled the three plays in this volume Unpleasant. The reason is pretty obvious: their dramatic power is used to force the spectator to face unpleasant facts. No doubt all plays which deal sincerely with humanity must wound the monstrous conceit which it is the business of romance to flatter. But here we are confronted, not only with the comedy and tragedy of individual character and destiny, but with those social horrors which arise from the fact that the average homebred Englishman, however honorable and goodnatured he may be in his private capacity, is, as a citizen, a wretched creature who, whilst clamoring for a gratuitous millennium, will shut his eyes to the most villainous abuses if the remedy threatens to add another penny in the pound to the rates and taxes which he has to be half cheated, half coerced into paying. In *Widowers' Houses* I have shewn middle-class respectability and younger son gentility fattening on the poverty of the slum as flies fatten on filth. That is not a pleasant theme.[1]

In *The Philanderer* I have shewn the grotesque sexual compacts made between men and women under marriage laws which represent to some

---

1 *Widowers' Houses*, Shaw's first play, was first performed in a private production by the Independent Theatre Society in London on 9 December 1892. The first public performance was at the Midland Theatre, Manchester, on 7 October 1907. The play exposes the rapacity and hypocrisy of slum landlords in late-Victorian London.

of us a political necessity (especially for other people), to some a divine ordinance, to some a romantic ideal, to some a domestic profession for women, and to some that worst of blundering abominations, an institution which society has outgrown but not modified, and which "advanced" individuals are therefore forced to evade. The scene with which *The Philanderer* opens, the atmosphere in which it proceeds, and the marriage with which it ends, are, for the intellectually and artistically conscious classes in modern society, typical; and it will hardly be denied, I think, that they are unpleasant.[1]

In *Mrs Warren's Profession* I have gone straight at the fact that, as Mrs Warren puts it, "the only way for a woman to provide for herself decently is for her to be good to some man that can afford to be good to her" [Act 2, p. 126]. There are certain questions on which I am, like most Socialists, an extreme Individualist. I believe that any society which desires to found itself on a high standard of integrity of character in its units should organize itself in such a fashion as to make it possible for all men and all women to maintain themselves in reasonable comfort by their industry without selling their affections and convictions. At present we not only condemn women as a sex to attach themselves to breadwinners, licitly or illicitly, on pain of heavy privation and disadvantage; but we have great prostitute classes of men: for instance, the playwrights and journalists, to whom I myself belong, not to mention the legions of lawyers, doctors, clergymen, and platform politicians who are daily using their highest faculties to belie their real sentiments; a sin compared to which that of a woman who sells the use of her person for a few hours is too venial to be worth mentioning; for rich men without conviction are more dangerous in modern society than poor women without chastity. Hardly a pleasant subject, this!

I must, however, warn my readers that my attacks are directed against themselves, not against my stage figures. They cannot too thoroughly understand that the guilt of defective social organization does not lie alone on the people who actually work the commercial makeshifts which the defects make inevitable, and who often, like Sartorious[2] and Mrs Warren, display valuable executive capacities and even high

---

1   *The Philanderer* was first performed in a copyright production on 30 March 1898 at the Victoria Hall (Bijou Theatre), Bayswater (together with *Mrs Warren's Profession*). A private production was given by the New Stage Club, London, on 20 February 1905. The first public performance was at the Royal Court Theatre, London, on 5 February 1907. The opening scene of the play contains an argument between two women—demeaning to both—who want to marry the same man.

2   Sartorious is the slum landlord in *Widowers' Houses*.

moral virtues in their administration, but with the whole body of citizens whose public opinion, public action, and public contribution as ratepayers, alone can replace Sartorious's slums with decent dwellings, Charteris's[1] intrigues with reasonable marriage contracts, and Mrs Warren's profession with honorable industries guarded by a humane industrial code and a "moral minimum" wage.... [32–34]

2. From the Preface to *Mrs Warren's Profession* (1930)

... I am convinced that fine art is the subtlest, the most seductive, the most effective instrument of moral propaganda in the world, excepting only the example of personal conduct; and I waive even this exception in favor of the art of the stage, because it works by exhibiting examples of personal conduct made intelligible and moving to crowds of unobservant, unreflecting people to whom real life means nothing. I have pointed out again and again that the influence of the theatre in England is growing so great that private conduct, religion, law, science, politics, and morals are becoming more and more theatrical, whilst the theatre itself remains impervious to common sense, religion, science, politics, and morals. That is why I fight the theatre, not with pamphlets and sermons and treatises, but with plays; and so effective do I find the dramatic method that I have no doubt I shall at last persuade even London to take its conscience and its brains with it when it goes to the theatre, instead of leaving them at home with its prayer-book as it does at present. Consequently, I am the last man to deny that if the net effect of performing *Mrs Warren's Profession* were an increase in the number of persons entering that profession or employing it, its performance might well be made an indictable offence.... [236]

... I now come to those critics who, intellectually baffled by the problem in *Mrs Warren's Profession*, have made a virtue of running away from it on the gentlemanly ground that the theatre is frequented by women as well as men, and that such problems should not be discussed or even mentioned in the presence of women. With that sort of chivalry I cannot argue: I simply affirm that *Mrs Warren's Profession* is a play for women; that it was written for women; that it has been performed and produced mainly through the determination of women that it should be performed and produced; that the enthusiasm of women made its first performance excitingly successful; and that not one of these women had any inducement to support it except their belief in the timeliness and the power of the lesson the play teaches....

---

1   Leonard Charteris is the philanderer in *The Philanderer.*

My old Independent Theatre manager, Mr Grein, besides that re-proach to me for shattering his ideals, complains that Mrs Warren is not wicked enough, and names several romancers who would have clothed her black soul with all the terrors of tragedy.[1] I have no doubt they would; but that is just what I did not want to do. Nothing would please our sanctimonious British public more than to throw the whole guilt of Mrs Warren's profession on Mrs Warren herself. Now the whole aim of my play is to throw that guilt on the British public itself. Mr Grein may remember that when he produced my first play, *Widowers' Houses*, exactly the same misunderstanding arose. When the virtuous young gentleman rose up in wrath against the slum landlord,[2] the slum landlord very effectually showed him that slums are the product, not of individual Harpagons,[3] but of the indifference of virtuous young gentlemen to the condition of the city they live in, provided they live at the west end of it on money earned by somebody else's labor. The notion that prostitution is created by the wickedness of Mrs Warren is as silly as the notion—prevalent, nevertheless, to some extent in Temperance circles—that drunkenness is created by the wickedness of the publican. Mrs Warren is not a whit a worse woman than the repu-table daughter who cannot endure her. Her indifference to the ultimate social consequence of her means of making money, and her discovery of that means by the ordinary method of taking the line of least resistance to getting it, are too common in English society to call for any special remark. Her vitality, her thrift, her energy, her outspokenness, her wise care of her daughter, and the managing capacity which has enabled her and her sister to climb from the fried fish shop down by the Mint to the establishments of which she boasts, are all high English virtues. Her defence of herself is so overwhelming that it provokes the *St James's Gazette* to declare that "the tendency of the play is wholly evil" because "it contains one of the boldest and most specious defences of an immoral life for poor women that has ever been penned" [see Appendix C1]. Happily the *St James's Gazette* here speaks in its haste. Mrs Warren's

---

1   J.T. Grein (1862-1935) founded the Independent Theatre Society in 1891, where he produced *Widowers' Houses* on 9 December 1892. He rejected Shaw's offer of *Mrs Warren's Profession* for the Society. See Appendix C2 for extracts from Grein's sub-sequent review of the play. Among the "romancers" named by Grein (in the full review) are Alexandre Dumas *fils*, whose novel *La Dame aux Camélias* (1848) satisfied Grein's sense of just deserts for prostitutes. (See Introduction, above, p. 34-35.)

2   The "virtuous young gentleman" in *Widowers' Houses* is Harry Trench, whose ideal-ism concerning income from slum properties is transformed into self-interest as the play progresses.

3   Harpagon is the miser in Molière's *L'Avare*, first performed in 1668.

defence of herself is not only bold and specious, but valid and unanswerable. But it is no defence at all of the vice which she organizes. It is no defence of an immoral life to say that the alternative offered by society collectively to poor women is a miserable life, starved, overworked, fetid, ailing, ugly. Though it is quite natural and *right* for Mrs Warren to choose what is, according to her lights, the least immoral alternative, it is none the less infamous of society to offer such alternatives. For the alternatives offered are not morality and immorality, but two sorts of immorality. The man who cannot see that starvation, overwork, dirt, and disease are as anti-social as prostitution—that they are the vices and crimes of a nation, and not merely its misfortunes—is (to put it as politely as possible) a hopelessly Private Person.[1]

The notion that Mrs Warren must be a fiend is only an example of the violence and passion which the slightest reference to sex rouses in undisciplined minds, and which makes it seem natural to our lawgivers to punish silly and negligible indecencies with a ferocity unknown in dealing with, for example, ruinous financial swindling. Had my play been entitled *Mr Warren's Profession*, and Mr Warren been a bookmaker, nobody would have expected me to make him a villain as well. Yet gambling is a vice, and bookmaking an institution, for which there is absolutely nothing to be said. The moral and economic evil done by trying to get other people's money without working for it (and this is the essence of gambling) is not only enormous but uncompensated. There are no two sides to the question of gambling, no circumstances which force us to tolerate it lest its suppression lead to worse things, no consensus of opinion among responsible classes, such as magistrates and military commanders, that it is a necessity, no Athenian records of gambling made splendid by the talents of its professors, no contention that instead of violating morals it only violates a legal institution which is in many respects oppressive and unnatural, no possible plea that the instinct on which it is founded is a vital one. Prostitution can confuse the issue with all of these excuses: gambling has none of them. Consequently, if Mrs Warren must needs be a demon, a bookmaker must be a cacodemon.[2] Well, does anybody who knows the sporting world really believe that bookmakers are worse than their neighbors? On the contrary, they have to be a good deal better; for in that world nearly everybody whose social rank does not exclude such an occupation would be a bookmaker if he could; but the strength of character

---

1   i.e. an idiot; derived from the Greek for "private person", "layman" (*idiōtēs*).
2   Literally, "bad demon" (from the Greek, *kakos*, "bad"); malignant spirit.

required for handling large sums of money and for strict settlements and unflinching payment of losses is so rare that successful bookmakers are rare too. It may seem that at least public spirit cannot be one of a bookmaker's virtues; but I can testify from personal experience that excellent public work is done with money subscribed by bookmakers. It is true that there are abysses in bookmaking: for example, welshing.[1] Mr Grein hints that there are abysses in Mrs Warren's profession also. So there are in every profession: the error lies in supposing that every member of them sounds these depths. I sit on a public body which prosecutes Mrs Warren zealously;[2] and I can assure Mr Grein that she is often leniently dealt with because she has conducted her business "respectably" and held herself above its vilest branches. The degrees in infamy are as numerous and as scrupulously observed as the degrees in the peerage: the moralist's notion that there are depths at which the moral atmosphere ceases is as delusive as the rich man's notion that there are no social jealousies or snobberies among the very poor. No: had I drawn Mrs Warren as a fiend in human form, the very people who now rebuke me for flattering her would probably be the first to deride me for deducing character logically from occupation instead of observing it accurately in society.

One critic is so enslaved by this sort of logic that he calls my portraiture of the Reverend Samuel Gardner an attack on religion. According to this view Subaltern Iago is an attack on the army, Sir John Falstaff is an attack on knighthood, and King Claudius an attack on royalty.[3] Here again the clamor for naturalness and human feeling, raised by so many critics when they are confronted by the real thing on the stage, is really a clamor for the most mechanical and superficial sort of logic. The dramatic reason for making the clergyman what Mrs Warren calls "an old stick-in-the-mud," whose son, in spite of much capacity and charm, is a cynically worthless member of society, is to set up a mordant contrast between him and the woman of infamous profession, with her well brought-up, straightforward, hardworking daughter. The critics who have missed the contrast have doubtless observed often enough that many clergymen are in the church through no genuine calling,

---

1   i.e. defaulting on the payment of a debt.
2   From 1897 to 1903 Shaw served on the Vestry of the Parish of St Pancras (subsequently the St Pancras Metropolitan Borough Council), the body responsible for controlling prostitution in that area of London.
3   Characters in Shakespeare's *Othello* (Iago), *Henry IV* and *The Merry Wives of Windsor* (Falstaff), and *Hamlet* (Claudius).

but simply because, in circles which can command preferment, it is the refuge of the fool of the family; and that clergymen's sons are often conspicuous reactionists against the restraints imposed on them in childhood by their father's profession. These critics must know, too, from history if not from experience, that women as unscrupulous as Mrs Warren have distinguished themselves as administrators and rulers, both commercially and politically. But both observation and knowledge are left behind when journalists go to the theatre. Once in their stalls, they assume that it is "natural" for clergymen to be saintly, for soldiers to be heroic, for lawyers to be hard-hearted, for sailors to be simple and generous, for doctors to perform miracles with little bottles, and for Mrs Warren to be a beast and a demon. All this is not only not natural, but not dramatic. A man's profession only enters into the drama of his life when it comes into conflict with his nature. The result of this conflict is tragic in Mrs Warren's case, and comic in the clergymen's case (at least we are savage enough to laugh at it); but in both cases it is illogical, and in both cases natural. I repeat, the critics who accuse me of sacrificing nature to logic are so sophisticated by their profession that to them logic is nature, and nature absurdity.

Many friendly critics are too little skilled in social questions and moral discussions to be able to conceive that respectable gentlemen like themselves, who would instantly call the police to remove Mrs Warren if she ventured to canvass them personally, could possibly be in any way responsible for her proceedings. They remonstrate sincerely, asking me what good such painful exposures can possibly do. They might as well ask what good Lord Shaftesbury[1] did by devoting his life to the exposure of evils (by no means yet remedied) compared to which the worst things brought into view or even into surmise in this play are trifles. The good of mentioning them is that you make people so extremely uncomfortable about them that they finally stop blaming "human nature" for them, and begin to support measures for their reform. Can anything be more absurd than the copy of The Echo which contains a notice of the performance of my play? It is edited by a gentleman who, having devoted his life to work of the Shaftesbury type, exposes social evils and clamors for their reform in every column except one; and that one is occupied by the declaration of the paper's kindly theatre critic, that

---

1   Anthony Ashley Cooper, 7th Earl of Shaftesbury (1801-85), a Member of Parliament from 1826 to 1851, advocated reform in health, prison, education, housing, and employment.

the performance left him "wondering what useful purpose the play was intended to serve."...[1] [253-59]

... Many people have been puzzled by the fact that whilst stage entertainments which are frankly meant to act on the spectators as aphrodisiacs are everywhere tolerated,[2] plays which have an almost horrifying contrary effect are fiercely attacked by persons and papers notoriously indifferent to public morals on all other occasions. The explanation is very simple. The profits of Mrs Warren's profession are shared not only by Mrs Warren and Sir George Crofts, but by the landlords of their houses, the newspapers which advertise them, the restaurants which cater for them, and, in short, all the trades to which they are good customers, not to mention the public officials and representatives whom they silence by complicity, corruption, or blackmail. Add to these the employers who profit by cheap female labor, and the shareholders whose dividends depend on it (you find such people everywhere, even on the judicial bench and in the highest places in Church and State), and you get a large and powerful class with a strong pecuniary incentive to protect Mrs Warren's profession, and a correspondingly strong incentive to conceal, from their own consciences no less than from the world, the real sources of their gain. These are the people who declare that it is feminine vice and not poverty that drives women to the streets, as if vicious women with independent incomes ever went there. These are the people who, indulgent or indifferent to aphrodisiac plays, raise the moral hue and cry against performances of *Mrs Warren's Profession*, and drag actresses to the police court to be insulted, bullied, and threatened for fulfilling their engagements....

At all events, to prohibit the play is to protect the evil which the play exposes; and in view of that fact, I see no reason for assuming that the prohibitionists are disinterested moralists, and that the author, the managers, and the performers, who depend for their livelihood on their personal reputations and not on rents, advertisements, or dividends, are grossly inferior to them in moral sense and public responsibility.

It is true that in *Mrs Warren's Profession*, Society, and not any individual, is the villain of the piece; but it does not follow that the people who take offence at it are all champions of society. Their credentials cannot be too carefully examined. [262-64]

1　The editor of *The Echo* at this time was S.K. Ratcliffe. While the paper's theatre critic was condemning *Mrs Warren's Profession*, Ratcliffe was running a front-page campaign to raise funds for shoes and clothes for poor children.

2　Shaw has in mind, for example, popular music hall performances.

Appendix B: *The Expurgated Text of* Mrs Warren's Profession *(1898)*

[When, as anticipated by Shaw, the Lord Chamberlain refused to license *Mrs Warren's Profession* for public performance in England, Shaw submitted an expurgated text that transformed Mrs Warren from prostitute to pickpocket and eliminated all direct and indirect references and allusions to her sexual career and its consequences for her family and acquaintances. This "mutilated" (Shaw's word) version was licensed on 19 March 1898 and given a public reading (not full performance) on 30 March 1898 at the Victoria Hall, Bayswater, thus safeguarding Shaw's copyright on the play. The expurgated copy—a printed version of the full play, with Shaw's handwritten changes—is in the British Library, Add MS 53654. Shaw's changes are described here. (See also Introduction, above, pp. 54-55.)]

Act One

Approximately seventy lines are deleted, from Mrs Warren's exit into the cottage to join Vivie, to the entry of Frank (pages 98 to 99 of this edition)—the whole of the conversation between Crofts and Praed about the identity of Vivie's father. Shaw provides new stage directions to cover the deletion. After Mrs Warren's "Dont be cross, Praddy", the stage direction reads *She follows Vivie into the cottage*. In the expurgated version Shaw extends this to read *She follows Vivie into the cottage, Crofts accompanying her. Praed is following slowly when he is hailed by a young gentleman who has just appeared on the common & is making for the gate. He is pleasant, pretty*—and this links to the description of Frank (99)—*smartly dressed, cleverly good-for-nothing*, etc.

Act Two

The whole act is entirely cut—thus eliminating key incidents and discussions: Mrs Warren's kissing Frank; the revelation of the possibility that Frank and Vivie are half-siblings; Vivie's demands to know the identity of her father; Mrs Warren's account of her family background and upbringing; and Mrs Warren's decision to join her sister Liz in the business of "pleasing men".

Act Three

Act 3 becomes Act 2 in the expurgated version, the action moving straight from the end of Act 1 to the scene in the rectory garden at the beginning of Act 2 in the unexpurgated text. There are, however, major cuts in the new Act 2.

Much of the conversation between Frank and Vivie when they are alone near the beginning of the act is cut. In the licensed copy someone (presumably Shaw) has pasted blank paper over that section of the conversation beginning with Frank's "the two cases require different treatment" (133) up to and including the stage direction *babyishly, lulling her and making love to her with his voice* (134).

Several more pages are cut from the later conversation between Vivie and Crofts, in which Crofts (having had his marriage proposal rejected by Vivie) explains the nature of his investment in Mrs Warren's business, gives Vivie details about her mother's "private hotels" in Europe, and exposes the hypocrisy of an establishment—aristocracy, the church, politicians, the universities—that profits from Mrs Warren's business while expressing moral outrage.

The section that is cut (Shaw has simply glued the pages together!) runs from Crofts' *rising, after a final slash at a daisy, and coming nearer to her* (137) to the moment at the garden gate when Crofts *puts his hand heavily on the top bar to prevent its opening* (141).

And after Frank has entered with his rifle to send Crofts on his way, Crofts' dramatic exit lines are deleted: "Allow me, Mister Frank, to introduce you to your half-sister, the eldest daughter of the Reverend Samuel Gardner. Miss Vivie: your half-brother. Good morning."

Shaw replaces this with "This young lady's mother was convicted five times of shoplifting before she took to her present trade of training young girls to the profession of larceny."

Act Four
Act 4 becomes Act 3, still set in Honoria Fraser's chambers, but is significantly altered in many other ways.

That part of the early conversation between Vivie and Frank in which Frank professes feelings for Vivie that are "not the least in the world" fraternal is cut. Shaw has again glued the pages together and added a few words so that Frank's "Well, I want to know what youve done—what arrangements youve made" (144) becomes "Well I want to know what youve done—what our relations are to be in the future" and the dialogue then jumps immediately to Vivie's "I think brother and sister would be a very suitable relation for us" (146).

Shortly after Praed enters (147), another cut occurs, this time to remove the scene in which Vivie writes down the "two infamous words" that describe her mother. From Vivie's "You are very old fashioned in your delicacies, after all" (150) to Frank's "Dont stir, Viv, if you dont want to. Take it easy" (151) is again pasted over with blank paper, on which Shaw has written the following brief replacement dialogue:

VIVIE ... I know now that my mother is a convicted thief.
PRAED. But she has repented, and atoned for that one slip of her youth and poverty.
VIVIE. You are mistaken. She no longer steals; but she teaches others to steal.
PRAED. Great Heaven! And you have the courage to tell us this.

And Vivie then continues as in the original text with "Thank you. You can always depend on me for two things ...."

The removal of the "two infamous words" scene also eliminates the reference (151) to Crofts' £40,000 investment in Mrs Warren's business, so Praed's expression of disappointment in Crofts' behaviour (and values) also has to go, as does Frank's response. Praed still says (152) "What an amazing revelation" [about Mrs Warren's Faginesque career], but Shaw has drawn a line through his next words ("I'm extremely disappointed in Crofts: I am indeed") and through Frank's response ("I'm not in the least. I feel he is perfectly accounted for at last"). To keep things tidy, Shaw also changes the "But" of Frank's next sentence to "And".

A later reference to Crofts is also cut, this time in the conversation between Vivie and her mother. Another blank piece of paper is glued over Vivie's "Sir George Crofts has told me the whole business" to her "You did not tell me that it is still going on" (156).

And since Vivie's Aunt Lizzie has disappeared from the play with the deletion of Act 2, references to her in Act 4 also have to go. Three words ("and Lizzie's friends") are crossed out near the end of Mrs Warren's powerful speech (157) urging Vivie to continue to benefit from her mother's wealth, and a longer section of Vivie's response (158) is pasted over (from "I dont object to Crofts" to "without having a word said to me about it").

Shaw overlooked, however, Vivie's next reference to Liz ("Your sister, you told me, has left all that behind her") and Mrs Warren's "Oh, it's all very easy for Liz".

Appendix C: Contemporary Reviews

[This is a selection of reviews of performances of *Mrs Warren's Profession* from the first performance of the full, unexpurgated text in a private production by the Stage Society in London on 5 January 1902 to its first public performances in England (Birmingham and London) in 1925. Reviews of the notorious 1905 New York production are also included, as are reviews of the Canadian première in Winnipeg in 1907 and a brief review of a little-known Glasgow production in 1913.]

1. *St James's Gazette*, 7 January 1902

Yesterday afternoon the protracted efforts of the Committee of the Stage Society were at length crowned with success, and a performance was duly given of *Mrs Warren's Profession* ... at the theatre of the New Lyric Club. Everything that could possibly have happened to prevent the performance seems to have occurred. The Censor of Plays had long since refused to licence the play. Manager after manager had refused the Society the use of his theatre for its production. Notices of the date of the performance were sent out and cancelled in a lavish manner. There were difficulties about the cast. Even at the very last moment the time of the production had to be changed from the evening to the afternoon to the great inconvenience of the audience. And all for what? In order that a play might be performed which deals with an unmentionable subject in a manner that even the least squeamish might find revoltingly offensive. Mr Shaw, in one of his usual speeches after the fall of the curtain, congratulated the Society on having found a cast to interpret his play so admirably, and to overcome successfully the thousand and one obstacles which had arisen to its production. But this was doubtless Mr Shaw's humour. Had he been serious (and had he not been the author of the play) he might more fitly have condoled with the Society on having found a committee who recklessly sacrificed the convenience of members in order to carry through a performance which was very generally regretted and on having found a cast who were willing to expend really admirable acting on this dingy drama. The play is in its parts undeniably clever. But as Mr Shaw himself acknowledged in his speech, it is not the treatment but the subject which carries *Mrs Warren's Profession* successfully through the ordeal of even a private performance. For if you take a sufficiently disgusting theme it is comparatively easy to interest an audience so long as you select that audience carefully....

Some of Mr Shaw's audience yesterday probably went away under the impression that they had been interested by the play in spite of its subject. That is a delusion. The play interested because the subject is a tremendous one. Grossly unsuitable for stage treatment before a mixed audience, grossly unsuitable for tricking out in Mr Shaw's verbal humours with his pert youngsters and comic clergymen, it remains a theme of painful and absorbing interest, and, granted that you can find an audience willing to listen to it at all, their attention cannot help being riveted by it. That the tendency of the play is wholly evil we are convinced. The second act contains one of the boldest and most specious defences of an immoral life for poor women that has ever been written. But what a waste of a quite appreciable talent! What a theme for the stage! ... The excellent acting secured toleration for the performance, but it is to be hoped that the Stage Society, which has been responsible for several really interesting and valuable productions in the two years of its existence,[1] intends to eschew dramatic garbage in the future.

2. J.T. Grein, *The Sunday Special*, 12 January 1902

It was an exceedingly uncomfortable afternoon, for there was a majority of women to listen to that which could only be understood by a minority of men. Nor was the play fit for women's ears. By all means let us initiate our daughters before they cross the threshold of womanhood into those duties and functions of life which are vital in matrimony and maternity. But there is a boundary line, and its transgression means peril — the peril of destroying ideals. I go further. Even men need not know all the ugliness that vegetates below the surface of everyday life. To some male minds too much knowledge of the seamy side is poisonous, for it leads to pessimism, that pioneer of insanity and suicide. And, sure as I feel that most of the women and a good many of the men who were present at the production of *Mrs Warren's Profession* by the Stage Society did not at first know, and finally merely guessed, what was the woman's trade, I cannot withold the opinion that the representation was unnecessary and painful.

It is mainly for these reasons that, in spite of my great admiration for Bernard Shaw, the play was not brought out by the late Independent Theatre. As a "straight talk to men only" it is not sufficiently true to life and useful to be productive of an educational effect. As a drama it is

---

1 Among the early productions of the Stage Society were Shaw's *You Never Can Tell* (the Society's first production) and Maurice Maeterlinck's *Monna Vanna* (both in 1902). For more information on the Stage Society see Introduction, above, p. 57.

unsatisfactory because the characters have no inner life, but merely echo certain views of the author. As literature, however, the merits of *Mrs Warren's Profession* are considerable, and its true place is in the study....

The main point is whether the problem is worth discussing and whether it has been dealt with in an adequate, convincing manner. I say no on both counts. The problem is neither vital nor important.... The case of Mrs Warren has been invented with such ingenuity and surrounded by such impossibilities that it produces revolt instead of reasoning. For Mr Shaw has made the great mistake of tainting all the male characters with a streak of a demoralised tar brush; he has created a cold-blooded, almost sexless daughter as the sympathetic element; and he has built the unspeakable Mrs Warren of such motley material that in our own mind pity and disgust for the woman are constantly at loggerheads. If the theme was worth treating at all the human conflict was the tragedy of the daughter through the infamy of the mother. Instead of that we get long arguments—spiced with platform oratory and invective—between a mother really utterly degraded, but here and there whitewashed with sentimental effusions, and a daughter so un-English in her knowledge of the world, so cold of heart, and "beyond human power" in reasoning, that we end by hating both: the one who deserves it, as well as the other who is a victim of circumstances. Thus there are false notes all the time and apart from a passing interest in a few scenes, saved by the author's cleverness, the play causes only pain and wonderment, while it should have shaken our soul to its innermost chords....

If Mr. Shaw had fully known the nature of Mrs. Warren's profession he would have left the play unwritten or produced a tragedy of unsurpassable heartrending power. Now he has merely philandered around a dangerous subject; he has treated it half in earnest, half in that peculiar jesting manner which is all his own. He has given free reins to his brain and silenced his heart. He has therefore produced a play of a needlessly "unpleasant" understructure to no useful end. A play that interests in part, repels in others; a drama that plays fast and loose with our emotions, and will in some way awaken our curiosity which would have best been left in slumber....

3. *New York Times*, 31 October 1905

... *Mrs Warren's Profession*, as an acted play, bears about the same relation to the drama that the post-mortem bears to the science of which it is a part. Mr Shaw takes a subject, decayed and reeking, and analyzes it for the édification of those whose unhealthy tastes find satisfaction in morbific[1] suggestion.

As a play to be read by a limited number of persons capable of understanding its significance, of estimating Mr Shaw and his themes at their full value, and of discounting them through their personal knowledge of him and their general knowledge of the life he seeks to portray, it undoubtedly has a place. But as a play to be acted before a miscellaneous assemblage, it cannot be accepted.

If there had been any doubt upon that subject it was dispelled after seeing the performance last night. *Mrs Warren's Profession* is not only of vicious tendency in its exposition, but it is also depressingly stupid. And those who would be likely to condone the first fault will find it extremely difficult to forgive the latter. Lines that impressed themselves upon the mind as one read the play, and whole passages that impressed one in the reading as examples of Mr Shaw's brilliant capacity for argumentation, when delivered by the actors became simply long, dry, tedious shallows of nugatory[2] talk. The fact that the dialogue had been pruned to some extent was hardly apparent in the actual effect of the representation. The whole thesis involving Mr Shaw's value as a moralist, of *Mrs Warren's Profession* as a moral treatise, becomes ridiculous in the consideration of it as acted drama....

While we do not admit that Mr Shaw's works are as inscrutable or triple-plated with meanings as some of his critics would have us believe, and while there is every reason for attributing much credit to his magnificent powers of mentality, and while we feel that tragic seriousness, not willful flippancy, may be the motive for his work, we must exclude Mrs Warren from our theatre—reject her, as a moral derelict. She is of no use to us as a lesson or a study.

When she becomes a subject for laughter and amusement, as occurred last night, she is something more than useless—she is vicious. She may serve a purpose when we are free to ponder over her under our own vine and fig tree, without the uncomfortable conviction that others, not, perhaps, so earnest as we, are gaining a certain amount of unholy enjoyment from the utter profundity of the horror....

---

1   That which causes disease.
2   Worthless; futile.

4. *New York Herald*, 31 October 1905

"The lid" was lifted by Mr Arnold Daly[1] and "the limit" of stage indecency reached last night in the Garrick Theatre in the performance of one of Mr George Bernard Shaw's "unpleasant comedies" called *Mrs Warren's Profession*.

"The limit of indecency" may seem pretty strong words, but they are justified by the fact that the play is morally rotten. It makes no difference that some of the lines may have been omitted and others toned down; there was superabundance of foulness left. The whole story of the play, the atmosphere surrounding it, the incidents, the personalities of the characters are wholly immoral and degenerate. The only way successfully to expurgate *Mrs Warren's Profession* is to cut the whole play out. You cannot have a clean pig stye. The play is an insult to decency because—

It defends immorality.

It glorifies debauchery.

It besmirches the sacredness of a clergyman's calling.

It pictures children and parents living in calm observance of most unholy relations.

And, worst of all, it countenances the most revolting form of degeneracy, by flippantly discussing the marriage of brother and sister, father and daughter, and makes the one supposedly moral character of the play, a young girl, declare that choice of shame, instead of poverty is eminently right.

These things cannot be denied. They are the main factors of the story. Without them there would be no play. It is vileness and degeneracy brazenly considered. If New York's sense of shame is not aroused to hot indignation at this theatrical insult, it is indeed in a sad plight.

[There follows a summary of the plot of the play.]

Does not this literary muck leave a bad taste in the mouth? Does it not insult the moral intelligence of New York theatregoers and outrage the decency of the New York stage?

There was not one redeeming feature about it last night, not one ray of sunshine, of cleanliness, to lighten up the moral darkness of situation and dialogue; not the semblance of a moral lesson pointed. As

---

1   American actor-manager Arnold Daly (1875-1927) staged and acted in many of Shaw's early plays in the United States.

Letchmere says of his family in *Letty*, "We are rotten to the core,"[1] and the same might be said of the characters in *Mrs Warren's Profession*....

5. *Manitoba Free Press* (Winnipeg), 1 May 1907

No more unwholesome nor repulsive play has ever been seen in Winnipeg than George Bernard Shaw's *Mrs Warren's Profession*, produced at the Walker Theatre last night.[2] It has not one redeeming feature. True, there are one or two smart lines and a certain sort of brilliancy which one has learned to term Shawian [sic], but the bitter sewerlike flavor one carries away in the mouth is not compensated for by a false and meretricious glitter.

Mrs Warren's "profession" is the keeping of brothels in various capitals of Europe, where young girls are lured and ruined. The play is a beatification of evil living, a sermon on the advantages of vice, and the story of a woman whom to term a courtesan would be a compliment. The play is full of false sentiment and bathotic bosh, as, for interest, the scene in the last act, when the mother expatiates to the daughter on what an exemplary parent she has been and begs her to go on living on the money derived from her malodorous "profession."

... There are one or two strong scenes, especially between the mother and daughter in the second act, the father and son and the two young lovers in the third act, but they are all the same, like fly-blown meat, tainted....

6. *Glasgow News*, 11 April 1913

... *Mrs Warren's Profession* is a play that deserved the Censor's disapproval, and there is no need to labour the point. To those who saw it produced last night [at the Royalty Theatre, Glasgow] much of it appealed, it could scarcely fail to, for it is admirably well done in its way. But we do not like its way, and for the simple reason that while granting a full measure of sympathy to Mrs Warren, the prostitute, we decline to accept the defence of Mrs Warren, the procuress; it is a defence put up after the admission of guilt, the defence of a woman still engaged in a trade unspeakable, a defence absolutely nauseating. But we are not going to weave a network of argument. We know that Mr Shaw shows virtue triumphant, and that his

---

1 *Letty* is a play by Arthur Wing Pinero, first performed (in London) on 8 October 1903.

2 In a touring production by an American company, with Rose Coghlan (1850/3?–1932) as Mrs Warren.

sneers are not levelled against that. What we object to is that the procuress should be heard in public. Her case is one for closed doors....

7. *Birmingham Gazette*, 28 July 1925

Even the magic words: "Bernard Shaw's hitherto banned play" did not succeed in quite filling the Prince of Wales Theatre, Birmingham, last night for the first public performance in England of *Mrs Warren's Profession*. This was regrettable, for the Macdona Players[1] gave the best performance of their visit so far in one of the finest plays in the Shavian catalogue.

One is at a complete loss to understand why *Mrs Warren's Profession* was ever banned. It is, perhaps, the most truly moral play ever produced on the English stage, not excepting miracle plays, morality plays, or religious propaganda plays. A vicarage soirée, with an up-lift address from the rector, would be an orgy of licentiousness compared with this play. There is no suggestion that the profession of Mrs Warren is a desirable career, or that to live it whole one should necessarily be immoral. The play amounts to a scathing exposure of the society that tolerates Mrs Warren's profession and fattens on it....

8. *The Times*, 29 September 1925

Written more than thirty years ago ... Mr Bernard Shaw's *Mrs Warren's Profession* was given its first public performance in London last night, when the Macdona Players produced it at the Regent Theatre. When it was first seen, after what Mr Shaw himself described as a "delay of only eight years," the author took infinite pleasure in criticizing the criticisms of his work. According to him, many of those who saw the piece were very upset. Last night, however, the play was received with perfect equanimity. Mrs Warren's "profession" is still not a subject for drawing-room discussion, but many such subjects are discussed in plays in these days, and it is sufficient to say that Mr Shaw has taken a difficult theme and told as many truths about it as he felt inclined. There can be no question now of condemning it as an "immoral" play.

Whether it is a true work of art is a different matter, for the author has been so insistent on driving unpalatable truths and half truths over the footlights that his balances are sometimes upset. At any rate, *Mrs Warren's Profession* has not suffered the fate of many "up-to-date" plays;

---

1   A touring company founded by Charles Macdona (1860-1946) in 1921 to specialize in productions of Shaw's plays. Macdona toured extensively in the United Kingdom and internationally.

it has not "dated." Perhaps it was before its time when it was privately performed, for apart from certain superficialities, it might have been written quite recently. There is no question, moreover, of the stagecraft in it, for, even when the author is being most didactic, his sense of the stage carries him through again into clear dramatic waters.

It is the heroine herself who is the weakest part, and it is rather ironical that this "modern," strong-minded young woman should be the one dramatic fault of the play. She has not dated; that was impossible, for her unreality is not of one age, but of all time. She is merely a machine, perfect as only such a machine can be, but even such an artist as her creator cannot endow her with life. Miss Valerie Richards last night did her best with the part, but one simply could not believe in Vivie.

This inevitably turned a little too much sympathy in the direction of Mrs Warren, and Miss Florence Jackson's performance strengthened this tendency. After rather a false start, she acted well in her big scenes and so indeed did the other "villain of the piece," Sir George Crofts, played by Mr Charles Sewell, who, in the second act, gave an excellent study of cultured malice. Praed, Frank, and the Reverend Samuel Gardner are three more puppets, always expressing opinions which seldom seem their own, and all three actors who played them found them difficult to portray....[1]

---

[1] The cast for the London production was the same as for the Birmingham production: Florence Jackson (Mrs Warren), Valerie Richards (Vivie), Oliver Johnston (Praed), Charles Sewell (Crofts), George Bancroft (Frank), and Arthur Claremont (Reverend Samuel Gardner).

Appendix D: Prostitution in Victorian England

1. From *The Unknown Mayhew. Selections from the Morning Chronicle, 1849-50*. Edited by E.P. Thompson and Eileen Yeo. London: Merlin Press, 1971. "Prostitution Among Needlewomen."

[A prolific and successful playwright and novelist, and co-founder and co-editor of *Punch*, Henry Mayhew (1812-87) is now best remembered for his reports in the *Morning Chronicle* (supplemented with interviews) on the living and working conditions of London's poor in the late 1840s—about the time that Mrs Warren would have been growing up in London (she is, Shaw tells us, "between 40 and 50"). Mayhew collected his reports in *London Labour and the London Poor* (1851). For an explanation of British currency values and notations see A Note on British Currency, above, p. 79.]

"I make moleskin trowsers. I get 7d. and 8d. per pair. I can do two pairs in a day, and twelve when there is full employment, in a week. But some weeks I have no work at all. I work from six in the morning to ten at night; that is what I call my day's work. When I am fully employed I get from 7s. to 8s. a week. My expenses out of that for twist, thread, and candles are about 1s. 6d. a week, leaving me about 6s. per week clear. But there's coals to pay for out of this, and that's at the least 6d. more, so 5s. 6d. is the very outside of what I earn when I'm in full work. Lately I have been dreadfully slack; so we are every winter, all of us 'sloppers',[1] and that's the time when we wants the most money. The week before last I had but two pair to make all the week; so that I only earnt 1s. clear. For this last month I'm sure I haven't done any more than that each week. Taking one week with another, all the year round I don't make above 3s. clear money each week. I don't work at any other kind of slop work. The trowsers work is held to be the best paid of all. I give 1s. a week rent.

My father died when I was five years of age. My mother is a widow, upwards of 66 years of age, and seldom has a day's work. Generally once in the week she is employed pot-scouring—that is, cleaning publicans' pots. She is paid 4d. a dozen for that, and does about four dozen and a half, so that she gets about 1s. 6d. in the day by it. For the rest she is dependent upon me. I am 20 years of age the 25th of this month. We earn together, to keep the two of us, from 4s. 6d. to 5s. each week. Out

---

1 Workers in factories manufacturing cheap clothing ("slops").

of this we have to pay 1s. rent, and there remains 3s. 6d. to find us both in food and clothing. It is of course impossible for us to live upon it, and the consequence is I am obliged to go a bad way. I have been three years working at slop work.

I was virtuous when I first went to work, and I remained so till this last twelvemonth. I struggled very hard to keep myself chaste, but I found that I couldn't get food and clothing for myself and mother, so I took to live with a young man. He is turned 20. He is a tieman.[1] He did promise to marry me, but his sister made mischief between me and him, so that parted us. I have not seen him now for about six months, and I can't say whether he will keep his promise or not. I am now pregnant by him, and expect to be confined in two months' time. He knows of my situation, and so does my mother. My mother believed me to be married to him. She knows otherwise now. I was very fond of him, and had known him for two years before he seduced me. He could make 14s. a week. He told me if I came to live with him he'd take care I shouldn't want, and both mother and me had been very bad off before. He said, too, he'd make me his lawful wife, but I hardly cared so long as I could get food for myself and mother.

Many young girls at the shop advised me to go wrong. They told me how comfortable they was off; they said they could get plenty to eat and drink and good clothes. There isn't one young girl as can get her living by slop work. The masters all know this, but they wouldn't own to it, of course. It stands to reason that no one can live and pay rent, and find clothes, upon 3s. a week, which is the most they can make clear, even the best hands, at the moleskin and cord trowsers work. There's poor people moved out of our house that was making 3/4 d. shirts. I am satisfied there is not one young girl that works at slop work that is virtuous, and there are some thousands in the trade. They may do very well if they have got mothers and fathers to find them a home and food, and to let them have what they earn for clothes; then they may be virtuous, but not without. I've heard of numbers who have gone from slop work to the streets altogether for a living, and I shall be obliged to do the same thing myself unless something better turns up for me.

If I was never allowed to speak no more, it was the little money I got by my labour that led me to go wrong. Could I have honestly earnt enough to have subsisted upon, to find me in proper food and clothing, such as is necessary, I should not have gone astray; no, never—As it was I fought against it as long as I could—that I did—to the last. I hope to

---

1   A maker of beams or rods ("ties") used in construction of buildings.

be able to get a ticket for a midwife; a party has promised me as much, and, he says, if possible, he'll get me an order for a box of linen. My child will only increase my burdens, and if my young man won't support my child I must go on the streets altogether. I know how horrible all this is. It would have been much better for me to have subsisted upon a dry crust and water rather than be as I am now. But no one knows the temptations of us poor girls in want. Gentlefolks can never understand it. If I had been born a lady it wouldn't have been very hard to have acted like one. To be poor and honest, especially with young girls, is the hardest struggle of all. There isn't one in a thousand that can get the better of it. I am ready to say again, that it was want, and nothing more, that made me transgress. If I had been better paid I should have done better. Young as I am, my life is a curse to me. If the Almighty would please to take me before my child is born, I should die happy." [147-49]

2. From James Miller, *Prostitution Considered in Relation to its Cause and Cure*. Edinburgh: Sutherland and Knox, 1859.

[James Miller (1812-64) was Professor of Surgery at the University of Edinburgh.]

... In this country, the whole question of female labour and wages stands urgently in need of revision. It is a shame that, in these enlightened days, honest, industrious, able-bodied women, labouring with painful industry from morning to night, or oft-times far into night, cannot make a living; and may, from this cause alone, be driven into vice and self-debasement. Where the blame rests we are not prepared to say. At first sight, one is apt to think harshly of the man who employs these poor needlewomen to turn out his goods, and pays them the insufficient pittance of a few, very few, shillings a week. But further consideration lays the responsibility, at all events in some measure, on those public patrons on whom the trader depends, who run determinedly after "great bargains," buying only where cheapness is to be found, and consequently favouring or forcing the iniquitous system of insufficient wage. And this unwholesome state of things is not confined to our own country. Dr Sanger[1] tells us that on the other side of the Atlantic, the public sanction a system which enforces starvation or crime; and, for the sake of saving a few cents, add their influence to swell the ranks of prostitution, and condemn many a poor

---

1 Unidentified.

woman to eternal ruin. "Masters, give unto your servants that which is just and equal; knowing that ye also have a Master in heaven,"[1]—that is a solemn command of the Great Lawgiver, which may not be transgressed with impunity. "Behold, the hire of the labourers who have reaped down your fields, which is of you kept back by fraud, crieth; and the cries of them which have reaped are entered into the ears of the Lord of Sabaoth."[2] The cry of the starving, overwrought, sorely tempted needlewomen is great in the land: and one of the curses which their neglect and oppression bring, is the social evil of prostitution. We do not presume to dictate here the remedial means; but we earnestly call attention to the sorrowful facts, and entreat that steps in the right direction be taken actively and without delay. The buyer and the seller are both involved. Let both see to it. Follow a poor young widow from the workshop, where till late at night she has stitched and stitched—how wearily! In a comfortless home see her weeping over a wailing child, or paralytic mother, as in cold and hunger they share their wretched pittance of food. See her struggling day by day to remain virtuous and chaste, eking out their little all by harder and harder labour; but driven at length, in terrible desperation, to rush upon the streets, there to seek the hire which her lawful calling has cruelly denied, and which she can only purchase by the most loathsome of all vocations, and the sacrifice of all which she personally holds dear. Somebody must be to blame for this. Who is it? Let conscience answer the question and act out the remedy.... [15-16]

3. From *Parliamentary Papers, 1865, XX, Children's Employment Commission, 4th Report.*[3]

[It was normal practice for the several nineteenth-century Parliamentary investigations into employment conditions to hear directly from witnesses with first-hand experience. In this case the witness was a young woman named Agnes Hafferman, employed as a maker of artificial flowers. She gave her evidence to the commission in September 1864.]

I was employed eight months ago at an artificial flower maker's in Goswell Road.[4] I was there for one year. About 50 females worked there; 10 or 11 of them were under 13; none under 11; I was 19.

---

1   Colossians 4:1.

2   James 5:4.

3   Reprinted in Erna Olafson Hellerstein et al., eds., *Victorian Women* (Stanford: Stanford UP, 1981) 327-28.

4   Goswell Road was (and is) a busy thoroughfare in London's East End.

Our regular hours were from 9 to 9, but in the season they were always longer. I should say that for six months out of the year we worked from 7 a.m. to 10 p.m. every night but Saturday, and sometimes we began at 6, and even 5 a.m., and worked till 12 at night. I worked about two dozen times from 6 a.m. to 12 at night; the younger ones were not so long at work; they did not ever come before 7 a.m. nor stay after 11 p.m.; their usual time in the season was from 7 a.m. to 10 p.m. We left at 9 p.m. on Saturday, and sometimes earlier.

All but the learners were on piecework. I only did the best work, but I never earned more than 10s. a week even when I worked three nights a week from 6 a.m. till 12 at night. I worked all the night through once or twice. Once was a Friday night; I went on till 5 p.m. on the Saturday before I went home; another time was a Monday night, and I then worked on till 10 p.m. on the next day. We used to be very tired indeed with the work in the season; the constant sitting hurts the chest; but I don't find that I am any the worse for it now. Face-aches were very common among us; I still suffer from that, but I think not so much as I did....

It was not our own choice to work so; we were not allowed to leave till we had finished our work. Our being on piecework made us, perhaps, ready to stop, but we could not go whenever we wished.

The young ones breakfasted before they came: we, who began at 6 a.m., often had nothing to eat until 11 a.m.; but we did generally breakfast at about 8 a.m. Half an hour was allowed for that, and for tea at 4; an hour for dinner at 1 p.m.; and if we worked late we took some supper at 9 or 10 p.m. We often worked through the meal times, but the children did not. I think most of us ate our meals at the table where we worked.

The dust of the green, and the blue too, was bad; it used to fly about and get on our hands when we had to separate the 'pieces'; if we had a cut it made it sore; we used to tie a handkerchief over our mouths and noses, so that nothing got down our throats. We had nothing to do with preparing or putting on the colours; men did that. We used to draw the poison out of our hands with soap and sugar.

Our fingers often got cut by the silk and wire; I have known a girl ill for a fortnight through sores made by winding the stalks.

I have been at other flower makers; at one where I was for six months, three years ago, there were 40 at work; I was the youngest, and was 17 then. We never worked longer than from 8 to 8; but I was not there in their busiest time.

4. From William Acton, *Prostitution Considered in its Moral, Social, and Sanitary Aspects in London and other Large Cities and Garrison Towns with Proposals for the Control and Prevention of its Attendant Evils*. 2nd ed. London: John Churchill and Sons, 1870.

[William Acton (1814-75) was a surgeon, medical author, and social reformer. His account of life in a Paris bordello is particularly relevant to Mrs Warren's chain of European brothels. See also Appendix D5.]

(a) Prostitution Abroad [France]

... The life of these women must be monotonous enough. They rise about ten, breakfast at eleven (*à la fourchette*),[1] dine at half-past five, and sup at about two; they seldom go out walking, and when they do 'it is in the company of the mistress or sub-mistress. They pay great and minute attention to their persons, taking baths very frequently, and spending the greater part of the day between breakfast and dinner in preparing their toilette, gossiping together, and smoking cigarettes; some few can play the piano (an instrument usually to be found in these houses), but, as a rule, they are, as might be expected, totally devoid of accomplishments. They have no rooms to themselves, but live *en pension*, taking their meals together; the mistress of the house, or her husband, or lover, as the case may be, presides, and the women take precedence at a table among themselves, according to the time that they have been in the establishment. After dinner, commences the operation of dressing, and otherwise preparing themselves for the public, who chiefly frequent these houses in the evening, and after midnight. By half-past seven or eight o'clock they are ready to make their appearance immediately on the bell being rung.

They are generally dressed in accordance with the latest fashion in vogue at balls and *soirées*, and leave untried no device of art for improving or supplementing nature, spending large sums of money on cosmetics and perfumery, often dyeing their hair and darkening their eyebrows and lashes, and in some cases having sores painted over to conceal them from their medical attendant.

These women are undoubtedly, as a rule, well-fed and well-dressed. There is usually a debtor and creditor account between them and the mistress of the house, with whom it is always an object to keep her lodgers in her debt, this being the only hold she can have upon them. They are supposed, by a pleasing fiction, to pay nothing for their lodging,

---

1   A knife-and-fork meal.

firing, and light, and there is certainly no actual charge made on this account; but, as a makeweight, one-half of what they earn is considered to be the mistress's portion, while the other half is paid over to these avaricious duennas, and goes towards defraying the boarding and other expenses. Such a bargain can only be struck by utterly improvident and reckless persons, and goes far towards proving them incapable of regulating their expenses for themselves; it is believed in France that, if they were not cared for by their mistresses, they would sink at once into the extreme of poverty, and this affords, to my mind, one of the few excuses that can be made for the toleration of such houses. I have read in a French work upon prostitution some horrid paragraphs that I do not care to extract, showing the fearful depth of infamy into which these miserable women are sunk, it being even hinted that their mistresses compel them to practise unnatural crimes by threats of expulsion, to which also they are encouraged by extra *douceurs*[1] from the debauched *habitués*. So long as a woman is much sought after, the mistress proves obsequious and kind, taking her occasionally to the theatre, and permitting her other indulgences; but so soon as the public desert the waning prostitute, a cause of quarrel is found, and she is brutally turned out of doors, often with no better covering than an old petticoat or worn-out dress. Thus it is that the public prostitutes step at once from luxurious *salons* to dirty hovels.... [109-10]

(b) Causes of Prostitution

... What is a prostitute? She is a woman who gives for money that which she ought to give only for love; who ministers to passion and lust alone, to the exclusion and extinction of all the higher qualities and nobler sources of enjoyment which combine with desire, to produce the happiness derived from the intercourse of the sexes. She is a woman with half the woman gone, and that half containing all that elevates her nature, leaving her a mere instrument of impurity; degraded and fallen she extracts from the sin of others the means of living, corrupt and dependent on corruption, and therefore interested directly in the increase of immorality—a social pest, carrying contamination and foulness to every quarter to which she has access, who—

> like a disease,
> Creeps, no precaution used, among the crowd,

---

1 Gifts.

Makes wicked lightnings of her eyes,
... and stirs the pulse,
With devil's leaps, and poisons half the young.[1]

Such women, ministers of evil passions, not only gratify desire, but also arouse it. Compelled by necessity to seek for customers, they throng our streets and public places, and suggest evil thoughts and desires which might otherwise remain undeveloped. Confirmed profligates will seek out the means of gratifying their desires; the young from a craving to discover unknown mysteries may approach the haunts of sin, but thousands would remain uncontaminated if temptation did not seek them out. Prostitutes have the power of soliciting and tempting. Gunpowder remains harmless until the spark falls upon it; the match, until struck, retains the hidden fire, so lust remains dormant till called into being by an exciting cause....
[166]

We have seen that many women stray from the paths of virtue, and ultimately swell the ranks of prostitution through being by their position peculiarly exposed to temptation. The women to whom this remark applies are chiefly actresses, milliners, shop girls, domestic servants, and women employed in factories or working in agricultural gangs. Of these, many, no doubt, fall through vanity and idleness, love of dress, love of excitement, love of drink, but by far the larger proportion are driven to evil courses by cruel biting poverty. It is a shameful fact, but no less true, that the lowness of wages paid to workwomen in various trades is a fruitful source of prostitution; unable to obtain by their labour the means of procuring the bare necessaries of life, they gain, by surrendering their bodies to evil uses, food to sustain and clothes to cover them. Many thousand young women in the metropolis are unable by drudgery that lasts from early morning till late into the night to earn more than from 3s. to 5s. weekly. Many have to eke out their living as best they may on a miserable pittance for less than the least of the sums above-mentioned. What wonder if, urged on by want and toil, encouraged by evil advisers, and exposed to selfish tempters, a large proportion of these poor girls fall from the path of virtue? Is it not a greater wonder that any of them are found abiding in it? .... [180-81]

---

1   Tennyson, *Idylls of the King*, Book 10, *Guinevere*, lines 515-19.

5. From Alfred S. Dyer, *The European Slave Trade in English Girls. A Narrative of Facts*. 6th edition. London: Dyer Brothers, 1882.

[Dyer's pamphlet was first published in 1880, and quickly went through several editions. Dyer's investigations supported the work of the London Committee for the Suppression of the Foreign Traffic in British Girls, a group dedicated to halting "the systematic abduction and enslavement of our countrywomen" (2). One of Mrs Warren's brothels is in Brussels.]

... In Continental countries ... houses devoted to prostitution are licensed, and publicly and conspicuously distinguished; and their inmates are forbidden to appear alone in the streets. Other fallen women are licensed to live in private apartments. It is not surprising that such an unblushing recognition by the authorities of the necessity of prostitution demoralises the population. In Brussels, where the system is said to have reached its highest degree of perfection, the Chief of Police advises that licensed houses be situated at convenient places, because "men, for whom houses of debauchery are a necessity, seldom care to take long journeys to find them," and failing to find licensed houses would resort to unregulated prostitution. Immorality, indeed, becomes so general under this system that it loses its shames. A cynicism is induced which refuses to believe in the possibility of virtue. The women in families reputed respectable become familiar with the immoral practices of their male relatives, which practices they are led to regard as universal amongst men. Instead of chastity being inculcated, boys are early introduced to dens of sin, with the knowledge and consent of their parents, and grow up under the unrestrained influence of their passions. Thus society is corrupted, and the patrons of houses of debauchery are to be found everywhere, in high official as well as non-official circles.

The female inmates of houses of prostitution are in a state of veritable slavery. Whatever may be the varying official ordinances in regard to the regulation of debauchery, the women and children who are its victims are practically without rights and protection, either of person or property. From the day they enter these houses they are not allowed to wear their own clothing, but are forced to accept garments of a disgusting nature, for the hire of which, and also for everything they require, they are charged exorbitant prices. They are thus kept deeply in debt and terrified with the threat of imprisonment if they dare attempt to leave without paying. They are frequently brutally treated and beaten if they show any signs of insubordination, or resist the wishes of the profligates who frequent the houses. Moreover, as the letter of the law forbids the reception of girls who are minors, such girls are registered by their buyers or betrayers under false names, with false certificates of birth, with or without the connivance of the officials, for which registration the girls are liable to imprisonment for forgery—a penalty which the keepers of the houses hold over them as a means of maintaining them in subjection.

If suspected of an intention to escape, they are re-sold to keepers of similar houses in other towns, sometimes hundreds of miles distant. Hired bullies, frequently ex-convicts, are at hand to frustrate any attempt at their rescue. In order to make escape or rescue more difficult, the street doors are so constructed that while entrance is easy, exit is impossible without the door being unlocked by the person in charge within. The windows of the houses in most cities are fitted with venetian blinds on the outside, which are kept always closed, so that the inmates are unable to see into the street, and, in many cases, daylight is never visible from one month's end to another. In some houses, where the inmates are treated with exceptional violence and brutality, the walls of the rooms and the outer doors are padded, to prevent the cries of the victims and the sounds of drunken orgies reaching the street.

It is well known on the Continent that the patrons of these places soon become satiated with the ordinary forms of immorality, and, in the craving of their lust for novelty, the poor inmates are made the subjects of the most inhuman, unnatural, and diabolical outrages, the nature of which it is impossible to mention in print, and difficult to allude to even in private conversation. To pander to this craving for novelty, the keepers of the houses provide a constant succession of fresh victims, including sometimes a negress, and in a recent case in Brussels, a Zulu girl. The more childish and innocent the victims, the more profitable they are. The wealthy Continental debauchee, reared under the influence of the moral blight of licensed debauchery, whose respect for womanhood has dwindled to an outward politeness of behaviour, but whose unrestrained and now uncontrollable passions have sunk him to a position in which, notwithstanding his outward politeness, he is morally half brute and half devil, will pay an amount equal to a poor man's annual income for the opportunity of violating a betrayed, terrified and helpless virgin. Hence, as the head of the police of Brussels acknowledges, the keepers of licensed houses of prostitution enter into costly researches for new, and, if possible, perfectly innocent victims; and hence also, English-speaking girls, who are perhaps the most valuable because the most in request by Continental debauchees, are systematically sought after, entrapped, and sold into a condition of slavery infinitely more cruel and revolting than negro servitude, because it is slavery not for labour but for lust; and more cowardly than negro slavery because it falls on the young and helpless of one sex only. The public have been known to have been informed of the arrival of an English girl by an advertisement in a newspaper; and the keepers of licensed dens of infamy have their cards like ordinary tradesmen, which are widely circulated, some of them being handsomely printed, and in the preparation of which, Art is prostituted to produce figures designed to excite the passions.... [3-6]

6. From *An Act to Make Further Provision for the Protection of Women and Girls, the Suppression of Brothels, and Other Purposes* **[***The Criminal Law Amendment Act***], 1885. (***The Statutes.*** 3rd Revised Edition. XI, 1884-1890. London: His Majesty's Stationery Office, 1950, pp. 129-35.)**

...

2. Any person who —

(1) Procures or attempts to procure any girl or woman under twenty-one years of age, not being a common prostitute, or of known immoral character, to have unlawful carnal connexion, either within or without the Queen's dominions, with any other person or persons; or

(2) Procures or attempts to procure any woman or girl to become, either within or without the Queen's dominions, a common prostitute; or

(3) Procures or attempts to procure any woman or girl to leave the United Kingdom, with intent that she may become an inmate of a brothel elsewhere; or

(4) Procures or attempts to procure any woman or girl to leave her usual place of abode in the United Kingdom (such place not being a brothel), with intent that she may, for the purposes of prostitution, become an inmate of a brothel within or without the Queen's dominions,

shall be guilty of a misdemeanor, and being convicted thereof shall be liable at the discretion of the court to be imprisoned for any term not exceeding two years, with or without hard labour....

6. Any person who, being the owner or occupier of any premises, or having, or acting or assisting in, the management or control thereof—

induces or knowingly suffers any girl of such age as is in this section mentioned to resort to or be in or upon such premises for the purpose of being unlawfully and carnally known by any man, whether such carnal knowledge is intended to be with any particular man or generally,

(1) shall, if such girl is under the age of thirteen years, be guilty of felony, and being convicted thereof shall be liable to be kept in penal servitude for life, or for any term not less than five years, or to be imprisoned for any term not exceeding two years, with or without hard labour; and

(2) if such girl is of or above the age of thirteen and under the age of sixteen years, shall be guilty of a misdemeanor, and being convicted thereof shall be liable at the discretion of the court to be imprisoned for any term not exceeding two years, with or without hard labour....

13. Any person who —

(1) keeps or manages or acts or assists in the management of a brothel, or

(2) being the tenant, lessee, or occupier of any premises, knowingly permits such premises or any part thereof to be used as a brothel or for the purposes of habitual prostitution, or

(3) being the lessor or landlord of any premises, or the agent of such lessor or landlord, lets the same or any part thereof with the knowledge that such premises or some part thereof are or is to be used as a brothel, or is wilfully a party to the continued use of such premises or any part thereof as a brothel,

shall on summary conviction ... be liable —

(1) to a penalty not exceeding twenty pounds, or, in the discretion of the court, to imprisonment for any term not exceeding three months, with or without hard labour, and

(2) on a second or subsequent conviction to a penalty not exceeding forty pounds, or, in the discretion of the court, to imprisonment for any term not exceeding four months, with or without hard labour....

7. From General [William] Booth. *In Darkest England and the Way Out.* **London: The Salvation Army, 1890.**

[William Booth (1829-1912) was founder of the Salvation Army. The Salvation Army's "Rescue Homes" provided support for destitute prostitutes, for whom Booth—for good reason—felt particular compassion.]

...There are many vices and seven deadly sins.[1] But of late years many of the seven have contrived to pass themselves off as virtues.... There are still two vices [however] which are fortunate, or unfortunate, enough to remain undisguised, not even concealing from themselves the fact that they are vices and not virtues. One is drunkenness; the other fornication. The viciousness of these vices is so little disguised, even from those who habitually practise them, that there will be a protest against merely describing one of them by the right Biblical name. Why not say prostitution? For this reason: prostitution is a word applied to only one half of the vice, and that the most pitiable. Fornication hits both sinners alike. Prostitution applies only to the woman.

When, however, we cease to regard this vice from the point of view of morality and religion, and look at it solely as a factor in the social problem, the word prostitution is less objectionable. For the social burden of this vice is borne almost entirely by women. The male sinner does not, by the mere fact of his sin, find himself in a worse position in obtaining employment, in finding a home, or even in securing a wife. His wrong-doing only hits him in the purse, or, perhaps, in his health. His incontinence, excepting in so far as it relates to the woman whose degradation it necessitates, does not add to the number of those for whom society has to provide. It is an immense addition to the infamy of this vice in man that its consequences have to be borne almost exclusively by woman.

The difficulty of dealing with drunkards and harlots is almost insurmountable....

... The problem of what to do with our half of a million drunkards remains to be solved, and few more difficult questions confront the social reformer.

The question of the harlots is, however, quite as insoluble by the ordinary methods. For these unfortunates no one who looks below the surface can fail to have the deepest sympathy. Some there are, no doubt,

---

1 In Christian belief the seven deadly sins are pride, covetousness, lust, envy, gluttony, anger, and sloth.

perhaps many, who—whether from inherited passion or from evil education—have deliberately embarked upon a life of vice, but with the majority it is not so. Even those who deliberately and of free choice adopt the profession of a prostitute, do so under the stress of temptations which few moralists seem to realise. Terrible as the fact is, there is no doubt it is a fact that there is no industrial career in which for a short time a beautiful girl can make as much money with as little trouble as the profession of a courtesan. The case recently tried at the Lewes assizes,[1] in which the wife of an officer in the army admitted that while living as a kept mistress she had received as much as £4,000 a year,[2] was no doubt very exceptional. Even the most successful adventuresses seldom make the income of a Cabinet Minister. But take women in professions and in businesses all round, and the number of young women who have received £500 in one year for the sale of their person is larger than the number of women of all ages who make a similar sum by honest industry. It is only the very few who draw these gilded prizes, and they only do it for a very short time. But it is the few prizes in every profession which allure the multitude, who think little of the many blanks. And speaking broadly, vice offers to every good-looking girl during the first bloom of her youth and beauty more money than she can earn by labour in any field of industry open to her sex. The penalty exacted afterwards is disease, degradation and death, but these things at first are hidden from her sight....

There is no need for me to go into the details of the way in which men and women, whose whole livelihood depends upon their success in disarming the suspicions of their victims and luring them to their doom, contrive to overcome the reluctance of the young girl without parents, friends, or helpers to enter their toils. What fraud fails to accomplish, a little force succeeds in effecting; and a girl who has been guilty of nothing but imprudence finds herself an outcast for life.

The very innocence of a girl tells against her. A woman of the world, once entrapped, would have all her wits about her to extricate herself from the position in which she found herself. A perfectly virtuous girl is so often overcome with shame and horror that there seems nothing in life worth struggling for. She accepts her doom without further struggle, and treads the long and torturing path-way of "the streets" to the grave.

---

1   Not traced.
2   This is a massive sum. See p. 90, note 3 for an account of what Vivie Warren's £50 could buy at about the same date.

"Judge not, that ye be not judged"[1] is a saying that applies most appropriately of all to these unfortunates. Many of them would have escaped their evil fate had they been less innocent. They are where they are because they loved too utterly to calculate consequences, and trusted too absolutely to dare to suspect evil. And others are there because of the false education which confounds ignorance with virtue, and throws our young people into the midst of a great city, with all its excitements and all its temptations, without more preparation or warning than if they were going to live in the Garden of Eden.

Whatever sin they have committed, a terrible penalty is exacted. While the man who caused their ruin passes as a respectable member of society, to whom virtuous matrons gladly marry—if he is rich—their maiden daughters, they are crushed beneath the millstone of social excommunication.

Here let me quote from a report made to me by the head of our Rescue Homes as to the actual life of the unfortunates.

> ... The girls suffer so much that the shortness of their miserable life is the only redeeming feature. Whether we look at the wretchedness of the life itself; their perpetual intoxication; the cruel treatment to which they are subjected by their task-masters and mistresses or bullies; the hopelessness, suffering and despair induced by their circumstances and surroundings; the depths of misery, degradation and poverty to which they eventually descend; or their treatment in sickness, their friendlessness and loneliness in death, it must be admitted that a more dismal lot seldom falls to the fate of a human being....
>
> This life induces insanity, rheumatism, consumption, and all forms of syphilis. Rheumatism and gout are the commonest of these evils. Some were quite crippled by both—young though they were. Consumption sows its seeds broadest. The life is a hot-bed for the development of any constitutional and hereditary germs of the disease. We have found girls in Piccadilly at midnight who are continually prostrated by haemorrhage, yet who have no other way of life open, so struggle on in this awful manner between whiles.
>
> [Drink] is an inevitable part of the business. All confess that they could never lead their miserable lives if it were not for its influence.

---

1 Matthew 7:1.

A girl, who was educated at college, and who had a home in which was every comfort, but who, when ruined, had fallen even to the depth of Woolwich "Dusthole",[1] exclaimed to us indignantly—"Do you think I could ever, ever do this if it weren't for the drink? I always have to be in drink if I want to sin." . . .

The devotion of these women to their bullies is as remarkable as the brutality of their bullies is abominable. Probably the primary cause of the fall of numberless girls of the lower class is their great aspiration to the dignity of wifehood;—they are never "somebody" until they are married, and will link themselves to any creature, no matter how debased, in the hope of being ultimately married to him. This consideration, in addition to their helpless condition once character has gone, makes them suffer cruelties which they would never otherwise endure from the men with whom large numbers of them live....

The state of hopelessness and despair in which these girls live continuously makes them reckless of consequences, and large numbers commit suicide who are never heard of. A West End policeman assured us that the number of prostitute-suicides was terribly in advance of anything guessed by the public....

In hospitals it is a known fact that these girls are not treated at all like other cases; they inspire disgust, and are most frequently discharged before being really cured.

Scorned by their relations, and ashamed to make their case known even to those who would help them, unable longer to struggle out on the streets to earn the bread of shame, there are girls lying in many a dark hole in this big city positively rotting away, and maintained by their old companions on the streets.

Many are totally friendless, utterly cast out and left to perish by relatives and friends. One of this class came to us, sickened and died, and we buried her, being her only followers to the grave.

It is a sad story, but one that must not be forgotten, for these women constitute a large standing army whose numbers no one can calculate. All estimates that I have seem purely imaginary. The ordinary figure given for London is from 60,000 to 80,000. This may be true if it is meant to include all habitually unchaste women. It is a monstrous exaggeration if it is meant to apply to those who make their living solely and habitu-

---

1   Woolwich was a flourishing district of southeast London until its dockyards closed in
    1869, creating widespread unemployment and poverty. Woolwich was also a centre
    for arms manufacturing, and the site of an army barracks.

ally by prostitution. These figures, however, only confuse. We shall have to deal with hundreds every month, whatever estimate we take. How utterly unprepared society is for any such systematic reformation may be seen from the fact that even now at our Homes we are unable to take in all the girls who apply. They cannot escape, even if they would, for want of funds whereby to provide them a way of release. [46–56]

8. From Clementina Black, *Married Women's Work*. London: Bell, 1915.

[Clementina Black (1855?–1923) was a prominent social reformer, feminist, and Fabian colleague of Shaw. A trade union advocate, she worked in the East End of London to improve working conditions for women. Two of her most influential books were *Sweated Industry and the Minimum Wage* (1907) and *Married Women's Work*, which gives detailed information on the cost of living for low-income families. The data, gathered in 1909–10, provide useful comparisons with the wage figures given by Mrs Warren in Act 2 of *Mrs Warren's Profession*. For an explanation of British currency values and notations see A Note on British Currency, above, p. 79.]

MISCELLANEOUS WORKER No. 5

This is a young married woman of 24, whose husband has gone to America in hopes of "making a fortune for her," but she has had no money from him for four months. She earns 11/- as a paper sorter, and employers occasionally give her some food. She has 2 children.

Expenditures in a week: 3 to keep.

	s. d.	s. d.	Percentages
Rent		3 6	35.3
Child-minding		3 0	30.3
Coal		0 6	5.0
Flour and Yeast	1 3		
Potatoes	0 2		
¼ lb. Tea	0 5		
¼ lb. Dripping	0 2		
Jam	0 1		
Milk	0 10	2 11	29.4
		9 11	100.0

Remarks.—Here the income exceeds expenditure by 1/-,[1] and has to account for wood, light, soap, and clothing. The food expenditure appears very inadequate for a young working woman and 2 children, but it is supplemented by the employer.

MISCELLANEOUS WORKER NO. 7

This is a young woman aged 25, [who] works in a packing warehouse, but has not yet resumed work since her baby's birth, 5 weeks previously. Her husband earns only 18/- a week; he is good to her, and gives her 17/- for the house. Both parents need better food, and the baby is not thriving.

Expenditures in a week: 3 to keep.

	s. d.	s. d.	Percentages
Rent		4 9	29.4
Furniture Instalment		2 6	15.5
Insurance		0 8	4.1
Coal		1 1	6.7
Flour and Yeast	2 1		
Tea	0 5½		
1 lb. Butter	1 2		
2 lbs. Sugar	0 4		
Condensed Milk	0 2½		
Potatoes	0 4		
Stew Meat	9		
Meat for Husband	1 10	7 2	44.3
		16 2	100.0

Remarks. — 9½d.[2] is left over for light, wood, soap, and clothing. Note the inadequacy of the amount spent on fatty foods for a young nursing mother, and the absence of cheese, fruit, or vegetables other than potatoes. [268-69]

---

1 Actually 1s. 1d.
2 Actually 10d.

Appendix E: Incest

[Public hostility towards *Mrs Warren's Profession* and the official sanctions against the play arose in part from brief references in the dialogue to the potentially incestuous relationship between Vivie and Frank, who may be half-siblings, and to the possibility that Crofts may be Vivie's father as well as her suitor (see Introduction 55-57). When Shaw completed the play in 1894 incest was not a crime in England, though it was in Scotland (and had been in England during the Puritan interregnum in the mid-seventeenth-century). Based on Biblical decree, incest—including between half-siblings—was forbidden under church law, and momentum grew in the early years of the twentieth century to bring incest into the sphere of criminal law. Parliamentary debates exposed serious differences of opinion on the advisability of using criminal law to deal with matters of morality, but legislation (*An Act to Provide for the Punishment of Incest*) was finally effected on 21 December 1908. If Vivie and Frank were indeed half-siblings, they could never have married. They would not, however, have faced criminal prosecution at the time Shaw wrote the play had they engaged in a sexual relationship. But after 1908 both Vivie and Frank would have faced up to seven years in prison.]

1. From the Old Testament: Leviticus 18. 6-18

6. None of you shall approach to any that is near of kin to him, to uncover their nakedness: I am the LORD.

7. The nakedness of thy father, or the nakedness of thy mother, shalt thou not uncover: she is thy mother; thou shalt not uncover her nakedness.

8. The nakedness of thy father's wife shalt thou not uncover: it is thy father's nakedness.

9. The nakedness of thy sister, the daughter of thy father, or daughter of thy mother, whether she be born at home, or born abroad, even their nakedness thou shalt not uncover.

10. The nakedness of thy son's daughter, or of thy daughter's daughter, even their nakedness thou shalt not uncover: for theirs is thine own nakedness.

11. The nakedness of thy father's wife's daughter, begotten of thy father, she is thy sister, thou shalt not uncover her nakedness.

12. Thou shalt not uncover the nakedness of thy father's sister: she is thy father's near kinswoman.

13. Thou shalt not uncover the nakedness of thy mother's sister: for she is thy mother's near kinswoman.

14. Thou shalt not uncover the nakedness of thy father's brother, thou shalt not approach to his wife: she is thine aunt.

15. Thou shalt not uncover the nakedness of thy daughter in law: she is thy son's wife; thou shalt not uncover her nakedness.

16. Thou shalt not uncover the nakedness of thy brother's wife: it is thy brother's nakedness.

17. Thou shalt not uncover the nakedness of a woman and her daughter, neither shalt thou take her son's daughter, or her daughter's daughter, to uncover her nakedness; they are her near kinswomen: it is wickedness.

18. Neither shalt thou take a wife to her sister, to vex her, to uncover her nakedness, beside the other in her life time.

2. From the House of Lords Debate on the Incest Bill, 16 July 1903 (*The Parliamentary Debates*, 4th Series, vol. 125, 1903, pp. 819–26)

THE EARL OF DONOUGHMORE.... The object is to punish as a misdemeanour what is one of the most horrible and unnatural crimes conceivable, but which at present is no crime at all according to English law.

Since the Restoration[1] the punishment of this crime has been left to what has been described as the "feeble coercion of the ecclesiastical Courts." Incest is, at present, only a crime by ecclesiastical law; it is not a crime under the criminal law. I am sure I am not saying too much when I assert that their most strenuous advocates will not claim that the ecclesiastical Courts are a proper tribunal to deal with such cases. It is an undoubted fact that this offence is committed. I have made careful enquiries in many directions and have ascertained from many people who have had experience both in large towns and rural districts that cases do very often occur. I was talking only this afternoon to a minister of the Roman Catholic Church who has had very great experience on the other side of the river, in Southwark. He tells me that cases are frequently coming to his notice. I have also had a conversation with a

---

1   The historical reference is to the restoration of the monarchy (Charles II) in 1660. Between 1649 and 1660 England was governed as a Commonwealth and (from 1653) as a Protectorate, led by Oliver Cromwell (1599–1658), whose strict Puritanical views were reflected in English law.

magistrate in the County of Essex, and he says he has known of three undoubted cases of incest. There are many others which must occur, and yet there is absolutely no power of dealing with them criminally. In Scotland, ever since 1857, a punishment has been provided for this offence, and, indeed, until 1887 the punishment by law was death. I believe that in practice the punishment was generally penal servitude, and I have ascertained, in the course of the few researches I have made, that last century there was one case of penal servitude for life. I might mention, further, that many States in the United States of America also recognise incest as a criminal offence, but it is to the Scottish example that I appeal chiefly. If it is a crime in Scotland it should be so in England. We do already indirectly recognise it as a crime in this country, for incest is one of the aggravations which enable a wife to divorce her husband. This Bill is only really a logical and practical extension of this partial recognition, and I trust that it will commend itself on its merits to your Lordships. The passing of this measure would act as a most salutary preventive....

3. From the House of Commons Debate on the Incest Bill, 26 June 1908 (*The Parliamentary Debates*, 4th Series, vol. 191, 1908, pp. 278–90)

... The first consideration he [J.F.P. Rawlinson, Member of Parliament for the University of Cambridge] would put before the House was that up to the present time these offences against morality had never been made a crime. The House, therefore, should hesitate before making a sweeping addition to the criminal law of England.... If the criminal law was brought in to deal with offences against morals they would be met at every turn with the difficulty that it was adults who committed these immoral offences. The words brother and sister in this Bill included half brother and sisters. Let them take the case of a brother and half-sister. Was it right to make such an offence a crime; was it desirable?... Here was a brother and half-sister living in one house and any person for reasons of enmity or blackmail could give any information against them. It was a grossly immoral offence, and though he felt it was unpopular to oppose a Bill of this kind in the House, he ventured to submit that before this offence was made a crime the House should see to it that they did not take any step that might do more harm than good.... What case was there? There was no suggestion that this offence was on the increase; indeed, it was far less known now than it was twenty or thirty years ago in parts of England, and only now or then was there a case in the criminal Courts. Was there the slightest reason to doubt that the spread of education and of civilising influences was doing away with this evil, and that there was, therefore, less need to deal with the matter so drastically as was proposed by this Bill?....

[D. MacLean, M.P. for Bath] thought the whole sense of the community was in favour of making this grave moral offence a crime. Out of every 1,000 people, 999 were under the impression that it was a crime, and most people would be astonished to hear that it was not. His professional experience had led him to know a good deal about this offence. No less than thirty-five cases, really of a most gross character, had come under his personal notice within the last twelve months, and he had known instances producing no less than three or four children of weak intellect, idiots and imbeciles. The cases were of the most grave kind.... In regard to the objection that they were creating a new crime by this Bill, he would point out that at one time this offence was a crime under the law of England. When the Puritans had sway over things in this country they made a long list of capital offences, which included adultery and incest. At the Restoration they swept away these penal offences, including that with which they were now dealing. It was a pure oversight, owing to what happened at the Restoration, that it was not a crime in England today.

[Herbert Samuel, M.P. for Yorkshire, Cleveland, and Under-Secretary of State for the Home Department] said he desired on the part of the Home Office to say a few words in support of the principle of the Bill. The Home Office had been long aware, from the reports they had received from the police and other sources, that it was exceedingly necessary to add to the law provisions of the character proposed by this Bill. The hon. and learned Member for Cambridge University said the offence was probably less rife than it was in the past. He doubted whether anyone could say with any degree of certainty either that it was increasing or that it was decreasing, but it was quite certain that the offence was by no means rare, and it was essential that some steps should be taken by the Legislature to put a stop to it. It was not merely the case of a moral offence affecting grown-up people, but it might entail consequences of a disastrous kind on the offspring which sometimes followed from such intercourse, and from that point of view society had a special interest that should lead to steps being taken to put a stop to it....

[A. Lupton, M.P. for Lincolnshire, Sleaford] said he was surprised that they were asked to pass a Bill of this sort. Poor people were forced to live together, men and women often in the same room, and it was easy enough for anybody to make accusations which could not be disproved against parties who were totally innocent. They would make family life impossible if they passed such legislation. They would make it impossible for members of a family to live at home without running the risk of terrible accusations being brought against them.... [H]e asked the House to pause before they tried to make the world good by legislation passed in a headlong rush. They might thrash and imprison people, but they would not make them good. There were appointed ways of dealing with immorality, and that was to try and lead people kindly by preaching religion and morality to them. When they left that path, which on the whole had answered so well, and had made us a great, a glorious, and a good nation, when they turned aside from the assistance of the clergy, the schoolmaster, and all the ladies and gentlemen who went about doing good, and simply relied upon the policeman, then they took the wrong course, and would make the world not better, but he was afraid very much worse.

4. From *An Act to Provide for the Punishment of Incest*, 1908 (*The Statutes. 3rd ed. Vol. 14, 1906-11*. London: His Majesty's Stationery Office, 1950, pp. 444-46)

1. (1) Any male person who has carnal knowledge of a female person, who is to his knowledge his grand-daughter, daughter, sister, or mother, shall be guilty of a misdemeanour, and upon conviction thereof shall be liable, at the discretion of the court, to be kept in penal servitude for any term not less than three years, and not exceeding seven years, or to be imprisoned for any time not exceeding two years with or without hard labour: Provided that if, on indictment for any such offence, it is alleged in the indictment and proved that the female person is under the age of thirteen years, the same punishment may be imposed as may be imposed under section four of the Criminal Law Amendment Act, 1885 (which deals with the defilement of girls under thirteen years of age).[1]

(2) It is immaterial that the carnal knowledge was had with the consent of the female person.

(3) If any male person attempts to commit any such offence as aforesaid, he shall be guilty of a misdemeanour, and upon conviction thereof shall be liable at the discretion of the court to be imprisoned for any time not exceeding two years with or without hard labour.

(4) On the conviction before any court of any male person of an offence under this section, or of an attempt to commit the same, against any female under twenty-one years of age, it shall be in the power of

---

1   See Appendix D6.

the court to divest the offender of all authority over such female, and, if the offender is the guardian of such female, to remove the offender from such guardianship, and in any such case to appoint any person or persons to be the guardian or guardians of such female during her minority or any less period....

2. Any female person of or above the age of sixteen years who with consent permits her grandfather, father, brother, or son to have carnal knowledge of her (knowing him to be her grandfather, father, brother, or son, as the case may be) shall be guilty of a misdemeanour, and upon conviction thereof shall be liable, at the discretion of the court, to be kept in penal servitude for any term not less than three years, and not exceeding seven years, or to be imprisoned with or without hard labour for any term not exceeding two years.

3. In this Act the expressions "brother" and "sister," respectively, include half-brother and half-sister, and the provisions of this Act shall apply whether the relationship between the person charged with an offence under this Act and the person with whom the offence is alleged to have been committed, is or is not traced through lawful wedlock....

Appendix F: Censorship of the Stage

[Formal government censorship of drama in England was initiated by the Stage Licensing Act of 1737. The legislation in force when the manager of the Victoria Hall, Bayswater, was denied a licence in 1898 to produce *Mrs Warren's Profession* was the Theatres Act (*An Act for Regulating Theatres*) of 1843. The relevant sections of the Act are given here, as is a description of the responsibilities of the Examiner of Plays, the official in the Lord Chamberlain's Office — the Lord Chamberlain was (and is) the appointed head of the royal household — who read all new plays (and alterations to previously performed plays) and determined whether or not they were suitable for public performance. When a joint committee of the House of Lords and the House of Commons reviewed the stage censorship system in 1909, Shaw, a lifelong and eloquent opponent of the system, was a major witness. His eloquence (and good sense) were, however, to no avail. Although the committee recommended several changes, they were largely ignored by the government, and the system remained in force until repealed in 1968. See Introduction, above, 67-69.]

1. From *An Act for Regulating Theatres*, 1843. (*The Statutes*. 3rd Revised Edition. IV, 1836-1844. London: His Majesty's Stationery Office, 1950, pp. 638-40)

12. One copy of every new stage play, and of every new act, scene, or other part added to any old stage play, and of every new prologue or epilogue, and of every new part added to an old prologue or epilogue, intended to be produced and acted for hire at any theatre in Great Britain, shall be sent to the lord chamberlain of her Majesty's household for the time being, seven days at least before the first acting or presenting thereof, with an account of the theatre where and the time when the same is intended to be first acted or presented, signed by the master or manager, or one of the masters or managers, of such theatre; and during the said seven days no person shall for hire act or present the same, or cause the same to be acted or presented; and in case the lord chamberlain, either before or after the expiration of the said period of seven days, shall disallow any play, or any act, scene, or part thereof, or any prologue or epilogue, or any part thereof, it shall not be lawful for any person to act or present the same, or cause the same to be acted or presented, contrary to such disallowance.

13. It shall be lawful for the lord chamberlain to charge such fees for the examination of the plays, prologues, and epilogues, or parts thereof, which shall be sent to him for examination as to him from time to time shall seem fit, according to a scale which shall be fixed by him, such fee not being in any case more than two guineas, and such fees shall be paid at the time when such plays, prologues, and epilogues, or parts thereof, shall be sent to the lord chamberlain; and the said period of seven days shall not begin to run in any case until the said fee shall have been paid to the lord chamberlain, or to some officer deputed by him to receive the same.

14. It shall be lawful for the lord chamberlain for the time being, whenever he shall be of opinion that it is fitting for the preservation of good manners, decorum, or of the public peace to do so, to forbid the acting or presenting any stage play, or any act, scene, or part thereof, or any prologue or epilogue, or any part thereof, anywhere in Great Britain, or in such theatres as he shall specify, and either absolutely or for such time as he shall think fit.

15. Every Person who for hire shall act or present, or cause to be acted or presented, any new stage play, or any act, scene, or part thereof, or any new prologue or epilogue, or any part thereof, until the same shall have been allowed by the lord chamberlain, or which shall have been disallowed by him, and also every person who for hire shall act or present, or cause to be acted or presented, any stage play, or any act, scene, or part thereof, or any prologue or epilogue, or any part thereof, contrary to such prohibition as aforesaid, shall for every such offence forfeit such sum as shall be awarded by the court in which or the justices by whom he shall be convicted, not exceeding the sum of fifty pounds; and every licence (in case there be any such) by or under which the theatre was opened, in which such offence shall have been committed, shall become absolutely void.

2. A Memorandum from the Lord Chamberlain to the Examiner of Plays, G.A. Redford, 13 March 1895[1]

[G.A. Redford was the newly appointed Examiner of Plays. It was Redford, formerly a bank manager, who rejected the licence application for *Mrs Warren's Profession* in 1898.]

---

1   From John Johnston, *The Lord Chamberlain's Blue Pencil* (London: Hodder & Stoughton, 1990) 266.

The Examiner of Plays is an Officer appointed to examine all Theatrical Entertainments on the part of the Lord Chamberlain who is responsible to Parliament, and generally to advise with him, and the Officers of his Department, upon all matters relating to the Stage.

With regard to the reading of Plays, the Examiner is solely responsible to the Lord Chamberlain for the pieces which he recommends for Licence.

The Manuscripts pass through the Examiner's hands alone, excepting in cases of doubt, when he is bound to consult the Lord Chamberlain, who in all other cases has been in the habit of accepting without question the recommendations of the Examiner.

As a matter of convenience the Licences for Pieces pass through the Office to be registered, and the manuscripts and correspondence are retained for reference with other records of the Department.

The Examiner is further expected to visit the Theatres constantly to see that the rules of the Lord Chamberlain are carried out with regard to the Pieces licensed by him.

In all other Theatrical matters the Examiner is an Officer of the Department, and as such is expected to attend at the Office and to co-operate with his colleagues there. It is his duty to keep himself informed, and to report to the Lord Chamberlain anything that may come to his knowledge through the Press or any other channel with regard to the conduct of Theatres generally, and be present at the annual inspection, and to assist the officers of the Lord Chamberlain in all matters relating to Theatres, whether in licensing or any other question which may arise.

He is expected to appear at subpoenas in Law Cases, more especially those having reference to the Licensing of Plays, and it is his duty also to examine the Play Bills with reference to the performance of unlicensed Pieces at the Theatres, and to see that they are sent regularly to the Lord Chamberlain's Office for this purpose.

3. "The Censorship of Plays," *The Times*, 29 October 1907

Sir,

The Prime Minister has consented to receive during the next month a deputation from the following dramatic authors on the subject of the censorship of plays.[1] In the meantime may these authors, through your

---

1   The deputation was in fact received not by the Prime Minister (Henry Campbell-Bannerman), but the Home Secretary (Herbert Gladstone).

columns, enter a formal protest against this office, which was instituted for political, and not for the so-called moral ends to which it is perverted—an office autocratic in procedure, opposed to the spirit of the Constitution, contrary to common justice and to common sense?

They protest against the power lodged in the hands of a single official—who judges without a public hearing, and against whose dictum there is no appeal—to cast a slur on the good name and destroy the means of livelihood of any member of an honourable calling.

They assert that the censorship has not been exercised in the interests of morality, but has tended to lower the dramatic tone by appearing to relieve the public of the duty of moral judgment.

They ask to be freed from the menace hanging over every dramatist of having his work and the proceeds of his work destroyed at a pen's stroke by the arbitrary action of a single official neither responsible to Parliament nor amenable to law.

They ask that their art be placed on the same footing as every other art.

They ask that they themselves be placed in the position enjoyed under the law by every other citizen.

To these ends they claim that the licensing of plays shall be abolished. The public is already sufficiently assured against managerial misconduct by the present yearly licensing of theatres, which remains untouched by the measure of justice here demanded.

[Signed by 71 authors, including Shaw, Harley Granville Barker, Joseph Conrad, John Galsworthy, W.S. Gilbert, Thomas Hardy, Henry James, W.S. Maugham, Arthur Wing Pinero, J.M. Synge, H.G. Wells, and W.B. Yeats.]

4. From the *Report from the Joint Select Committee of the House of Lords and the House of Commons on Stage Plays (Censorship); Together with the Proceedings of the Committee, Minutes of Evidence, and Appendices.* London: His Majesty's Stationery Office, 1909.

[Shaw appeared as a witness before the Joint Select Committee on 30 July 1909. The Chairman was Herbert Samuel, M.P., Postmaster-General.]

CHAIRMAN. Both as a result of your own experience and on broad considerations of general policy, do you think that the censorship ought to be abolished?

SHAW. I think that the censorship ought to be abolished. I would not say so much on broad questions of general policy in the ordinary sense;

but owing, if I may put it so, to my abhorrence of anarchism, I want the drama to be brought under the law and the author to be brought under the law. That is really my meaning. I only mention it because the words "general policy" do not quite convey my feeling about it.

CHAIRMAN. I notice in the statement of your evidence[1] that you have been good enough to submit to the Committee the following passage: "Accordingly there has arisen among wise and far-sighted men a perception of the need for setting certain departments of human activity entirely free from legal interference"?

SHAW. Yes.

CHAIRMAN. That is in reference especially to the drama and dramatists?

SHAW. To liberty of the Press, liberty of speech, and liberty of conscience.

CHAIRMAN. Is not that in some degree inconsistent with the doctrine that you desire to bring them under further control?

SHAW. No, because I conceive law to be the guarantee of liberty. I have no objection whatever if you will make a law that I shall not mention a certain subject, or that I shall not deal with a certain subject. If you pass that law, I am prepared to obey it, or, at any rate, I am only prepared to defy it under conditions under which a man is a martyr, but I object to there being no law. That is the point, and there is no law. There is not even any usage.

CHAIRMAN. You do not object to a regulated control of the theatre, but you object to an unregulated control of the theatre?

SHAW. I object to any control of the theatre that is not the ordinary control which is applied to all citizens. I object to a control of the theatre which excludes rights which are accorded to all other citizens in the conduct of their business and the pursuit of their livelihood.

CHAIRMAN. You consider that there should be some form of control in the social interest?

SHAW. Yes, the law of the land.

....

CHAIRMAN. To come back to the first point, whether it is advisable to have any form of social control whatever over the drama and the production of performances—you would admit that some control is necessary?

---

1 Shaw submitted a long (11,000 words) statement to the committee, but it was not accepted as formal evidence. Shaw published it as part of the preface to *The Shewing-up of Blanco Posnet* (1911). In the statement Shaw elaborates and expands on the key points he made orally to the committee.

SHAW. Yes, there should be social control over every possible sphere of human activity, but I contend that the control should be the control of law.

CHAIRMAN. Then the question arises, What should that law be? Should you consider that things which all mankind would condemn as grossly indecent should be prohibited from performance, or stopped from performance?

SHAW. Well, you know that there is not anything at all which all mankind would consider grossly indecent. But I think you must accept as a necessary thing that there are certain things which the community at large will not tolerate. Even with the strongest conviction that you must allow liberty of speech and liberty of conscience, there are certain things which would create an irresistible demand to have them prosecuted under the ordinary law dealing with obscenity or blasphemy. But I contend that the ordinary laws, so far from not being stringent enough, are, on the contrary, far too stringent, especially the blasphemy laws, which would put us all in prison if carried out.

CHAIRMAN. You admit that in all ages and all countries there have been representations on the stage deliberately intended to incite to sexual immorality?

SHAW. Almost all performances—that is too strong—but I should say a very large percentage of the performances which take place at present on the English stage under the censorship licence have for their object the stimulation of sexual desire.

CHAIRMAN. Should you say that any of these dramas ought to be prohibited from performance, or stopped when they have been performed?

SHAW. That is altogether a question to be decided by legal prosecution.

CHAIRMAN. But you can conceive cases in which it would be right in the public interest to suppress certain plays?

SHAW. Certainly, if their production is found to be a legal offence. I do not claim exemption for the drama from the law in any sense. For instance, I myself am not only a playwright, but a journalist. I am an author, and I am a public speaker. In all these capacities I may offend against the law, and I am responsible for what I do; but I am responsible to the law and not to Mr Redford or the Lord Chamberlain.

. . . .

CHAIRMAN. Could you conceive cases in which a play, having been produced, ought properly to be suppressed on the ground that it was deeply offensive to the dearest religious feelings of a large proportion of the community?

SHAW. No, certainly not.

CHAIRMAN. You think that any outrage on religion, or ridicule of sacred personages, should be allowed on the stage?

SHAW. I think it should. I think that the public would look after that. I think that the danger of crippling thought, the danger of obstructing the formation of the public mind by specially suppressing such representations is far greater than any real danger that there is from such representations. The real difficulty, of course, is not to suppress such representations, but, on the contrary, to bring them about. It is an extremely difficult thing to put on the stage anything which runs contrary to the opinions of a large body of people. The danger is that way, not the other way.

CHAIRMAN. Should you say that the danger of causing riot and tumult was a proper reason for preventing the performance of drama?

SHAW. No, I put it on exactly the same footing as political meetings, which, in my experience, very often have ended in riot.

CHAIRMAN. But is not a stage performance to some extent different from propaganda by the printed word in that no disorder and tumult can arise through the mere purchase of a book. It may ultimately and indirectly arise, but not directly, while in the case of the stage in time past serious riots and disturbances have taken place owing to the character of certain plays that have been performed.

SHAW. Yes, but riots and disturbances have occurred owing to political speeches, and I say that there is no difference. They are not special to the theatre. The same rights and liberties apply to both.

CHAIRMAN. What you have said with regard to religious plays would, I presume, apply also to political plays?

SHAW. Certainly.

CHAIRMAN. Would you apply that equally to plays that touch upon foreign relations? For example, supposing that one of the characters in a play was made up to represent the Sovereign of a foreign country and was placed in an ignominious and ridiculous situation, could the State properly interfere there, do you think, or not?

SHAW. The State might interfere by prosecution possibly. I should object to a censor interfering.

. . . .

CHAIRMAN. I gather that while you think that the theatre should be uncontrolled in relation to religious representations and political representations, there should be power of prosecution if incitements to sexual vice take place on the stage, or if grossly offensive allusions are made to foreign Sovereigns, or indeed to other persons?

SHAW. No, I could not admit that, because if you prosecute for incentives to sexual vice you immediately make it possible to prosecute a manager because the principal actress has put on a pretty hat or is a pretty woman. I strongly protest against anything that is not quite definite. You may make any law you like defining what is an incentive to sexual vice, but to lay down a general law of that kind with regard to unspecified incentives to sexual vice is going too far, when the mere fact of a woman washing her face and putting on decent clothes, or anything of the kind, may possibly cause somebody in the street who passes to admire her and to say, "I have been incited to sexual vice." These definitions are too dangerous. I do not think that any lawyer should tolerate them.

CHAIRMAN. Assuming with regard to that the very narrowest definition phrased with the utmost care by a most enlightened man, you can assume cases that ought properly to be penalised?

SHAW. Cases that ought properly to be penalised, but not specially in the theatre more than elsewhere. That is the point.

CHAIRMAN. You say in your printed statement: "The abolition of the censorship does not involve the abolition of the magistrate and of the whole civil and criminal code. On the contrary, it would make the theatre more effectually subject to them than it is at present." The theatre would be subject to the magistrate and the civil and the criminal code in relation to these things?

SHAW. Yes, but at present you see their amenability to the civil and criminal code is cut off by the fact that they practically get a certificate from the Lord Chamberlain.

CHAIRMAN. I want to get your alternative to censorship and see how far you would go with regard to public control supposing that censorship were abolished.

SHAW. I do not propose any substitute: I propose the bringing of the theatre under the ordinary law of the land.

CHAIRMAN. You say that "The abolition of the censorship does not involve the abolition of the magistrate and of the whole civil and criminal code." That means that the magistrate and the civil and criminal code will be left standing?

SHAW. Yes.

CHAIRMAN. And indeed more conspicuous and more active through the elimination of the censorship?

SHAW. Yes.

CHAIRMAN. Prosecutions might take place on the ground of gross indecency or on the ground of offences to foreign Sovereigns after the censorship had been abolished, and might indeed take place more frequently than they do now?

SHAW. Yes, possibly.

CHAIRMAN. Therefore you are merely shifting one part, at all events, of the control from the Censor to the magistrate?

SHAW. Yes, I am doing that, but I am substituting the magistrate for the Censor. I attach enormous importance to the distinction. The Censor is a species of anarch[ist], if I may say so. He is not a person administering the law in any sense. When you go to the magistrate you have not only shifted the control, but, for the first time, you have created what is real legal control. You have created law where there was nothing before but the chaos of the Censor's mind.... [46-50]

Appendix G: Vivie Warren's Cambridge

[Women contemporaries of Vivie Warren at Cambridge were allowed to attend lectures and to write examinations. Their examination results were published alongside those of their male counterparts, but regardless of academic success achieved by women they were not granted a degree by the University. Vivie has excelled in her final examinations, but she does not leave Cambridge with a degree. In 1896 a concerted effort was made by those women and men at Cambridge and elsewhere who believed that such discrimination against women should cease. The turbulence caused by this issue in the male-dominated University is reflected in the petitions, resolutions, and debates of 1896–97, and in the ensuing riots by Cambridge male undergraduates in celebration of the defeat of the resolution to grant degrees to women. Women were not granted degrees at Cambridge until 1921 (when there were further riots), and they were not granted full membership of the University (i.e. the right to participate in the academic administration of the University and vote on policy issues) until 1948. Other forms of discrimination against Vivie Warren and her female contemporaries at Cambridge are reflected in the extracts (G4, below) from the recollections of a Newnham student.]

1. Petitions and Resolutions on Degrees for Women, 1896–97

(a) TO THE VICE-CHANCELLOR AND THE COUNCIL OF THE SENATE OF THE UNIVERSITY OF CAMBRIDGE

We the undersigned students of Girton and Newnham Colleges,[1] knowing that a Memorial from Members of the Senate has been presented to you, praying for the admission of women to Degrees, beg respectfully to lay before you the following considerations in support of that petition. While appreciating to the full the privileges accorded by the Graces of the Senate, February 24, 1881,[2] we feel that women are without the encouragement and support which status in the University confers. Since

---

1   Girton and Newnham were founded as women's colleges at Cambridge in 1869 and 1871 respectively. All other Cambridge colleges admitted men only.

2   The Grace (i.e. Senate resolution) that gave women the formal right to take examinations.

at the present time the official relation of the University to the education of women is that of an examining body only, they owe the privileges of an academic education to the courtesy of the teachers of the University. We are conscious that women do not share fully in the great benefits which the University has the power to bestow upon education, learning, and research. While women who study at Cambridge are without the usual academic recognition which the students of other Universities receive,[1] we believe that they suffer a disability which not only places many of them at a disadvantage in their professional work, but also affects injuriously the widest interests of education. We therefore pray that such steps as may be deemed necessary be taken to provide for the admission of duly qualified women to the Degrees of the University of Cambridge.

[Signed by 1,172 students of Girton and Newnham Colleges. *Cambridge University Reporter*, 18 February 1896.]

(b) TO THE VICE-CHANCELLOR

We, the undersigned members of the Senate of the University of Cambridge, earnestly deprecate the admission of women to membership of the University or to any of the Degrees which are conferred on members of the University.

[Signed by 1,992 members of Senate. *Cambridge University Reporter*, 20 October 1896.]

(c) TO THE VICE-CHANCELLOR

We, the undersigned members of the Senate of the University of Cambridge, are prepared to support a proposal for conferring some title which does not imply membership of the University on women who, having satisfied the requirements of the University, have already passed or shall hereafter pass a Tripos Examination.[2]

[Signed by 1,369 members of Senate. *Cambridge University Reporter*, 20 October 1896.]

---

1 With the sole exception of Oxford, all other British universities at this time admitted women to degrees. See p. 222, note 1.
2 i.e. (in the Cambridge system) the final degree examination. See p. 91, note 2.

(d) TO THE VICE-CHANCELLOR

We, the undersigned members of the University "in statu pupillari,"[1] respectfully beg leave to approach through you the Members of the Senate in view of the proposed legislation with regard to Women Students. We desire to express our conviction that the giving of Titles of Degrees to Women would prove injurious to the position and efficiency of this University as a University for Men.

Signed by 2,137 students. (*Cambridge University Reporter*, 11 May 1897.)

(e) TO THE VICE-CHANCELLOR

We, the undersigned members of the University "in statu pupillari," respectfully beg leave to approach through you the Members of the Senate in view of the proposed legislation with regard to Women Students. We desire to express our conviction that the giving of Titles of Degrees to Women would not prove injurious to the position and efficiency of this University as a University of Men.

[Signed by 298 students. *Cambridge University Reporter*, 11 May 1897.]

(f) RESOLUTION TO THE SENATE

That it is desirable that the title of the Degree of Bachelor of Arts be conferred by diploma upon women who, in accordance with the now existing Ordinances, shall hereafter satisfy the Examiners in a Final Tripos Examination and shall have kept by residence nine terms at least.

[Proposed by a specially constituted Syndicate (i.e. committee) of the Senate. (*Cambridge University Reporter*, 1 March 1897.) The resolution was subsequently amended to add the phrase "provided that the title so conferred shall not involve membership of the University," in which form it was voted upon on 21 May 1897: 661 for, 1,707 against.]

---

1   "In the status of a pupil" (Latin); i.e. an undergraduate member of the University.

2. From the Senate Debate on Degrees for Women, March 1897[1]

DR FORSYTH.... It seems to be more or less admitted that there is something of a grievance. [No! No!] A great many people admit that there is something of a grievance. Dr Mayo and Mr Wyse do not admit it; and I dare say there may be others who do not admit it, but there are many people who do admit that there may be something of a grievance.... But for myself it does seem to me a very distinct claim of justice, when women have shown that they have the same intellectual power as men, and when they have gone through a training every bit as good as the men, that we should not refuse to allow them compendiously to express that fact, just as we allow men to do.... On the other hand we do not propose to give to women incorporation into the University. Incorporation into the University is what would make a real difference to our body, to our constitution, which might seriously affect us. Obviously that is the point on which the most anxious deliberation and the most careful consideration are most required; and personally I am not prepared to say that I think the time has come for any decision upon it. I can conceive that some day it may be the right way, but I do think it will be a very grave mistake to prejudge that matter now. I can quite conceive that the development of women's education might take more than one line different from that. It may grow to a women's University; or again it is conceivable that the Colleges in and near Cambridge might be formed into a separate corporation, which might stand in various kinds of relation, such as could be determined by experience, with the corporation of the University; in part perhaps united to it, and in part distinct. All these things are possible, and all these things we completely reserve and put on one side. Here is a real vital distinction, and we ought to trust our own successors sufficiently to be able to see a vital distinction of that kind....

MR ROBERTS.... Now every woman that leaves Cambridge under the present conditions, having passed the Tripos Examinations, carries with her down to the country what we may call a personal grievance. She finds she is handicapped in earning her daily bread because she is not able to use the symbol.

MEMBERS OF THE SENATE. No, No.

MR ROBERTS. I say she is handicapped in her efforts to obtain her daily

---

1 Participants in the debate (speakers shown here and others referred to) were all senior academic members of the University. Women were not allowed to participate in the debate or vote.

bread by the fact that she is not able to use the symbol which is intelligible to the average man, to the public generally, as setting out what course of training she has passed through. Now if you grant this title you will have removed that grievance.

A MEMBER OF THE SENATE. There is no grievance.

MR ROBERTS. You will have removed it in so far as it is felt by the women themselves, and you will remove it in so far as the public recognise it. The average man cannot understand our position because he does not realise that associated with these higher degrees is this large power of legislation, which is in a sense accidental, that is to say it is peculiar to Oxford and Cambridge. But it is not so in the case of other Universities. If you were to say to him: "Now these women have passed the examination and have resided three years but they cannot use the symbol," he would say "That is an injustice;" but if we say "We give them the symbol; they have all that is educationally needed to enable them to use their training, to their advantage, but they want a share in the management of the University," he would say "Unless you choose to give a share in the management of the University, why should they have it?" and I think he would be perfectly right. I say therefore there is a sharp line between the symbol which sets out what work they have done, and what standard they have attained, and the powers of legislation which are associated with the higher degree by this accident of our constitution. Even of the men who take their degree, a very small number practically use their privilege as Masters of Arts;[1] they do not care for it, and they do not use it. If the women were admitted to the degrees of this University tomorrow, I do not believe that a large proportion of them would care to use their privileges, and take part in the management of the University, and therefore the average woman who goes down from here with her title will have no sense of grievance. I will not say that every one of them won't, but the majority of them won't. There will be nothing practically pressing upon her day by day showing that she is under a disadvantage which might easily be removed, as is the case now, where she is not able to use a title.

Then finally I will say one thing more: you ask me whether this is final or not; I say it is final, because the question whether it be final or not rests with you, and you are persuaded it must be final; and therefore it must be final. Do you think that anybody could coerce

---

1 The M.A. degree at Cambridge is normally awarded (for a fee, not by examination) six years after matriculation. It entitles the holder to participate (and vote) in Senate debates.

this University into giving what it does not want to give? You will only grant this title if you are persuaded that it is a right and just thing; anybody persuaded that it is wrong will not vote for it; and anyone who is persuaded that women ought not to have a share in the management of this University would not vote for that however often it might be proposed. Therefore as I see no prospect that the University is likely to change its mind on the question of full membership, this will I believe be a final solution....

PROFESSOR RIDGEWAY..... Dr Sidgwick tried to persuade us on Saturday, if I rightly understood him, that the proposals of the Syndicate will be accepted by the women students and their supporters, or at least by the majority of them, in satisfaction of their claims. I must say that this is hard to believe when one remembers what took place last year. Look at the letters written so late as last November by representatives of Newnham and Girton Colleges, in which nothing was withdrawn of the demands made at the beginning of the year, and then look at what the Syndicate actually proposes to give, "the little modicum" as Dr Stanton called it. Is it possible that the little modicum can satisfy them? If so, what was the meaning of the sweeping demands which were made? After asking for "full recognition"[1] can they rest satisfied with exclusion and a bare title? They will accept what is offered, I dare say, but as what? As a full discharge? I fear not, but only as an instalment, and when they have succeeded, if they do unfortunately succeed, in getting a footing in the Statutes of the University, they will press on towards the goal which, as we are told on the best authority, they have in view.

I think therefore that in pronouncing an opinion upon the proposals of the Syndicate we cannot shut out of view the probability that they will, if approved, act as an encouragement to renewed efforts on the part of those who wish to bring about the admission of women to membership of the University.

It is too difficult and delicate an undertaking to discuss the question of the effect which the admission of female students into the University on equal terms with men would have. It must be left for each one to imagine and judge for himself. But I do not think the experience we have already had of the attendance of women at University lectures affords any adequate criterion of the results which might be expected to follow from their admission to membership,

---

1   i.e. equal rights with men (including full participation in the administration of the University).

for it must be remembered that they have hitherto been in the position of honoured guests and are always so treated. They have never been on the footing of fellow-students with our undergraduates. It must be borne in mind too that the experience we have already had of mixed classes has been by no means wholly favourable. I think no one can read the answers of lecturers printed in the Appendices to this Report without being convinced that serious inconveniences have been felt and the effectiveness of the teaching to some extent impaired.[1]

The admission of women to membership would also destroy the homogeneousness of our student body, and this is a serious matter. You will find that some of the lecturers complain of difficulties caused by the heterogeneousness of classes to which female students are admitted. This heterogeneousness would be greatly increased, and would extend to all parts of University life.

It is urged, I know, that even if women be admitted to membership of the University it is not at all likely that there will be many women students.... But this is surely the weakest possible plea. Indeed, it amounts to a confession that there might be just ground for objection if larger numbers were to come in response to the increased privileges. Surely if the admission of women is really desirable then it must be wished that it will be successful, and it would be the height of folly to admit women at all if we thought that the admission of a large number of women would be injurious to the University.

I submit that no sufficient reason has been shown for the disturbance of the constitution of the University which is proposed, and that the true method of providing for the academical requirements of women is the establishment of a women's University. I would earnestly implore those who have influence in women's colleges not to encourage the students in the miserable desire of doing exactly what the men do, but to seek to provide them with an academical organization which may inspire them with nobler ideas of their own.

I appeal to members of the Senate to reject the proposals of the Syndicate. Let us not be led away by attempts to minimise the importance of the concession we are asked to make in order to silence the cry that has been raised. It may seem to some to be a "little

---

1   A survey among lecturers revealed that some lecturers (and students) felt that the teaching and learning experience was compromised by the presence of women (e.g. in biology classes). Many lecturers, however, either welcomed the presence of women or detected no impact one way or the other from their attendance.

modicum," but the fact that it involves a change in the Statutes proves that it is more serious than at first sight, perhaps, it appears. A great responsibility lies upon us. We have to "keep our noble Cambridge whole." Do not let us make what is at best a very doubtful and risky experiment on the body of our beloved and time-honoured University....

PROFESSOR MARSHALL.... Some years ago there was no education of University rank open to women in England; it was right therefore that education should be offered here, as freely as might be, to all those who wanted it, and who could manage to come here.... The number of students at first was small; they were enthusiasts for learning for its own sake. They were pioneers to help other women to understand what thorough work means. By teaching them, Cambridge rendered a very great service to the country and did itself no harm. Since then great changes have taken place. There are now, I think, seven teaching Universities which have opened their doors to women.[1] Those Universities differ from Oxford and Cambridge very much as a church differs from a monastery. In connection with those Universities we have women living studious and intellectual lives, but their social life is entirely outside the University. On the other hand, the essence of these monasteries from which Oxford and Cambridge have inherited their unique structure lies in their social life. The essence of our system lies in the fact that our social life is carried on in our lecture rooms as well as outside it. The lecturer is not a mere preacher to a congregation; he is a senior student working with and helping junior students. For these and for other reasons the presence of a large number of women is a greater disturbance to our system than to that of the seven other teaching universities.

The question of the admission of women has therefore changed its form. Now we have to balance the gain to them of an increase in their numbers here against the loss to us. The gain to them steadily diminishes because of the excellent opportunities opened out for them elsewhere. And the loss to us increases; for their number has now become so great as frequently to divert the attention of our

---

1 A survey conducted on behalf of the Cambridge Senate lists eight English universities that admitted women to degrees (Durham, London, Manchester, Birmingham, Bristol, Nottingham, Exeter, Sheffield). The University of Wales admitted women to degrees, as did the Scottish universities. Trinity College, Dublin, reported that "women are not admitted as students, nor to degrees." (*Cambridge University Reporter,* 1 March 1897.)

undergraduates in class from the special purposes for which they are here. It causes undergraduates some little inconvenience in the matter of places in the lecture room; and it almost puts a stop in some cases to the best instruction, that is conversational instruction. In many cases, it diminishes the thoroughness and extent of teaching by paper work; and lastly it tends to make the teacher adapt his teaching to minds which, though splendid for examination purposes, in some respects better than most men's, are receptive rather than constructive. These evils are real and are not sentimental; others loom in the future, but one cannot speak of them without prophesying, and one may leave them. Those evils which already exist are sufficient to make us pause to inquire whether the limit has not been reached at which any further increase in the number of women students will do more harm to men than good to women....

[*Cambridge University Reporter*, 26 March 1897]

3. The May 1897 Riots

[The vote on the Senate resolution to admit women to degrees was held on 20 May 1897. The occasion and its aftermath were reported in the local press.]

At noon the roadway in front of the Senate House began to be occupied with a mixed crowd of people, undergraduates largely predominating, with a fair number of non-resident M.A.s, evidently enjoying the renewal of their acquaintance with Cambridge and their minds carried back to pre-graduate days. A vigorous cock crowing from the roof of Caius College,[1] emanating from an enterprising undergrad, and done with marvellous fidelity, was the signal for the commencement of operations. Forthwith the occupants of the front rooms in Caius began to hang out their banners on the outer walls, and a roar of laughter went up as there slowly descended from an upper window the lay figure of a woman with aggressively red hair, dressed in cap and gown. As the figure swung to and fro in the breeze, limp and lank, the remarks made were the reverse of complimentary to the sex. Meanwhile from the same window a string of gaudily got-up hats, brilliant enough to turn a coster girl[2] green with envy, were lowered, with

---

1   Gonville and Caius College (founded in 1348) is located adjacent to Senate House, in the centre of Cambridge.
2   A woman who sells fruit and vegetables from a street barrow.

the inscription, "Lecture Hats — Latest Designs." From another window at the corner of Trinity-street, and stretching across to Messrs Macmillan and Bowes' premises,[1] was a broad band of canvas, bearing the words,

GET YOU TO GIRTON, BEATRICE;[2] GET YOU TO NEWNHAM! HERE'S NO PLACE FOR YOU MAIDS.

Another enterprising group lowered a board, on which was printed in red and black letters:—

WHAT SHAKESPEARE SAYS
"I SEE SHE'S LIKE TO HAVE NEITHER CAP NOR GOWN." — *Taming of the Shrew*.[3]

"NO WOMAN SHALL COME WITHIN A MILE OF MY COURT." — *Love's Labour's Lost*.[4]

At the end of Caius College, in Trinity-street, stretching right across to the house opposite, was the legend: —

"ENGLAND EXPECTS EVERY **MAN** TO DO HIS DUTY."[5]

At the corner of Market-place the effigy of a woman arrayed in blue bloomers and pink bodice, sitting astride a bicycle, was run out from an upper window and received with cheers and groans. Other placards were, "The 'Varsity for Men and Men for the 'Varsity," "No Gowns for the Girtonites! Non-plus the Newnhamites! Frustrate the Feminine Fanatics! Prudent Proctors[6] prance on physical impossibilities! Satisfied Angels want to supersede beaten Apollos!" Yet another proclaimed "Firm and irrevocable is my doom which I have passed upon her. She is banished!"[7] A large dog strutted about, with tail proudly erect, from which drooped a Union Jack. Clouds of confetti, mixed with flour, showered upon the crowd, to the accompaniment of horn blowing, rattle springing, and other discordant noises.

---

1   Publishers and booksellers.
2   Presumably a reference to Shakespeare's Beatrice in *Much Ado About Nothing*.
3   *Taming of the Shrew*, 4.3.93.
4   *Love's Labour's Lost*, 1.1.119.
5   Nelson's command to his navy at the Battle of Trafalgar (1805).
6   University officers responsible for student discipline.
7   *As You Like It*, 1.3.77-78.

Up till about two o'clock nothing worse than confetti and flour had been thrown. The dons, after voting, stood in solemn and serried array within the Senate House yard, waiting for the verdict. Someone threw a cracker over the palings, and this was the signal for the commencement of a general bombardment. Cooped up like sheep in a pen, the devoted dons, some thousands in number, were pelted with fireworks of every description, while the smoke rose in clouds above their heads. The noise of the explosions and the cheers and counter-cheers were deafening. There was no help for it. The M.A.s were in for a lively time, and they got it. Some of them picked up the empty cases and threw them at their tormenters, but the majority had to stand a terrible fire, and look as dignified as they could.

As the hour approached three o'clock, matters became much more lively. The dons and voters on the Senate House Green were subjected to a continual fire of crackers, bombs, and rockets, the latter being with some ingenuity fired from bottles. The figure of Dr Caius in front of the college above the gate was decorated with a lady's gown of light terra cotta, and a flaxen wig and other female head gear almost hid the face of the statue. Squibs and bombs were thrown into the windows of the Senate House, of Caius College, and those tenanted by undergraduates at No. 6, Trinity-street. At the corner of Trinity-street, water from a garden hose was threatened, and liquid from a syphon flowed from one of the Caius windows upon the crowd below. The water was turned on at the corner house and the men below retaliated with decayed oranges and rotten eggs, and smashed most of the glass in the windows. While this was going on the result of the polling was announced at the entrance to the Senate House, which faces the green. The figures were received with loud cheering, but it was impossible for those in the street to hear them. They were hoisted at the front of the building, however, the result being—

NON-PLACETS [against] 1,713
PLACETS [for] 662

It will thus be seen that the cause of the women has been lost by nearly three to one.

The cheering continued for a considerable time, and while one section of the undergrads near Caius College were pelting the windows with fireworks, eggs, and oranges, another was cheering the M.A.s, who were trooping across from the gate to the University buildings to St Mary's-passage. When as many as seemed inclined had left, a body of undergrads suddenly rushed into the Senate House Green. The police were taken by surprise, and a good number got through before sufficient officers were on the spot to stop them. The police, however, got the gates closed, but they were subsequently opened, and the crowd allowed to pass through. A group cheering and yelling gathered round a few dons and a University constable or two who were on the steps of Senate House. The dons disappeared on one side, and the undergraduates rushed behind the Senate House into Senate House-passage and back on to Senate House-hill. A moment or two later the Lady Cyclist came down from the corner of Trinity-street, a piece of the balcony being carried away with it. The figure lost his [sic] head and hands and showed what it was made of. It was rushed away and on the Market-hill appeared on the top of a cab, an excited mob of undergraduates surging below. The cabby struggled frantically, for about a dozen men were soon in the cab, on the top, and on the horse. After some persuasion, the horse was taken out, the undergrads descended, and leaving the cabby in possession, with about a score of men tugging at the shafts, the cab with the remains of the figure, the bicycle, and the cabby on the top proceeded on a journey round the town, accompanied by horn blowing, wooden rattles, and discordant noises from human throats. Through the narrow streets, packed with excited 'Varsitymen it went, until stopped and dispersed on Market-hill....

[*Cambridge Daily News*, 21 May 1897]

After the Senate House scenes yesterday afternoon there was a brief respite. It was the calm before the storm. About seven o'clock there was a grand gathering of the clans. Undergraduates began trooping through the streets to what was evidently a pre-arranged rendezvous — the Market-hill. Before the exodus took place from Caius the exceedingly lively young bloods of that college had summed up the situation in one word, which was worked out in fairy lamps and hung in a conspicuous place, and that word was

"SAVED!"

By common consent town and gown converged on Market-hill and commenced to start the ball. The upper windows of the houses overlooking the hill were crowded with undergraduates, who commenced operations very mildly by throwing confetti on the people below. These retaliated by pelting the window men with fireworks, and then matters began to get decidedly lively. From the four corners of the square a fierce fire was opened upon everybody and everything within range. Crackers were tied together in bunches and flung haphazard into the crowd, through open windows into the rooms of the houses, from whence they were hastily ejected, leaving behind them clouds of smoke and fire. Bombs, hand-rockets, and every description of firework manufactured followed suit, until the scene resembled nothing so much as the bombardment of a hostile camp. It is no exaggeration to say that hundreds of pounds worth of stuff were got rid of in this way during the five hours the proceedings lasted. Perhaps the most effective missiles used were a firework that projected balls of fire of various colours. These were aimed with marvellous accuracy at the windows, ball after ball of fire passing through into the rooms, where the occupants were kept exceedingly busy stamping out the fire and preventing outbreaks. As dusk came on the scene became a very brilliant one. The air was literally filled with flying fire, the dense crowd of people, estimated at 15,000 or 20,000, bobbing, ducking, and dodging the unpleasant projectiles....

[*Cambridge Daily News*, 22 May 1897]

4. An Undergraduate at Newnham College, 1896–99

[C. Crowther (née Kenyon) was an undergraduate at Newnham College from 1896 to 1899, about the time that Vivie would have been there. An account of her experiences is given in *A Newnham Anthology*, edited by Ann Phillips (Cambridge: Cambridge UP, 1979) 37–39.]

... Women students in Cambridge were there at that time more or less on sufferance. We were allowed to take the Tripos examinations, but we had no status as undergraduates and were not granted a degree. We were given certificates to show that we had passed the Tripos examination and had resided in College the required number of terms, so that if and when degrees were granted we should be qualified to receive them. Many members of the University disapproved of women's colleges and of higher education for women generally, so the authorities of Newnham and Girton liked us to be as unobtrusive as possible. We did not take much part in the life of the University, and we suffered many restrictions. We were asked always to wear gloves in the town (and of course hats!); we must not ride a bicycle in the main streets, nor take a boat out on the river in the daytime unless accompanied by a chaperon who must be either a married woman or one of the College dons. In the May Term we could be on the river in the early morning, without chaperon, between the hours of six and nine, and as some of my friends were keen on rowing we often left the Silver Street boathouse soon after six o'clock, rowed to Baitsbite[1] where we had breakfast, and were back in College by nine o'clock. It was very lovely gliding along the Backs[2] past Queens', Clare, King's, John's, Trinity, etc., under the beautiful bridges in the quiet of an early summer morning. During the Long Vacation we could go on the river at any time unchaperoned and we had several lovely long days taking lunch and tea with us, idling along quiet backwaters. When we watched the Lent and May Races[3] on the river we were not supposed to go on the towing path, but to stand in the meadows on the opposite side.

We were not allowed to entertain any men friends in our own rooms. When fathers or brothers visited us, we could give them tea, but could not invite any of our friends into our room to meet them, not even if our mother were there as well. Smoking was forbidden and so were amateur theatricals in term-time; but acting was allowed in the 'Long'....

I was a keen hockey player and we had to wear navy blue serge skirts that must come down to within twelve inches of the ground, to hide our legs as much as possible. Tennis was played in long white piqué skirts that almost touched the ground. But I have never seen better women's hockey than was played at Newnham in the years from 1896 to 1899. These restrictions did not trouble us much; they were all part of the general Victorian attitude to women, and College life was full of interest and in many ways was a very free life in comparison with our home life....

---

1   The site of a lock on the River Cam, about two miles out of Cambridge.
2   That part of the River Cam that flows past the "backs" (the rear) of several Colleges.
3   College rowing races.

Appendix H: The New Woman

1. From Grant Allen, "Plain Words on the Woman Question," *Fortnightly Review*, 46 (October 1889)[1]

[The 1880s and 1890s witnessed intense debates about the "Woman Question"—i.e. the role, rights, and responsibilities of women in late Victorian England. Many of the issues raised in the debates relate to *Mrs Warren's Profession*, particularly Vivie Warren's decision to pursue a professional career rather than the conventional route of marriage, motherhood, and domesticity. Novelist, teacher, essayist, and Fabian Society member Grant Allen (1848-99) supported the extension of women's rights, arguing, in the essay quoted here, that the situation of women for much of the nineteenth century could not bear scrutiny:"Their education was inadequate; their social status was humiliating; their political power was nil; their practical and personal grievances were innumerable; above all, their relations to the family—to their husbands, their children, their friends, their property—was simply unsupportable." Allen also, however, held firm to the belief that marriage and child-bearing were a woman's prime function and responsibility, and he would have condemned Vivie, destined, by choice, to become a "self-supporting spinster," as an "an abnormality, not the woman of the future."]

... Now I have the greatest sympathy with the modern woman's demand for emancipation. I am an enthusiast on the Woman Question. Indeed, so far am I from wishing to keep her in subjection to man, that I should like to see her a great deal more emancipated than she herself as yet at all desires. Only, her emancipation must not be of a sort that interferes in any way with this prime natural necessity. To the end of all time, it is mathematically demonstrable that most women must become the mothers of a at least four children, or else the race must cease to exist. Any supposed solution of the woman-problem, therefore, which fails to look this fact straight in the face, is a false solution. It cries "Peace, peace!" where there is no peace. It substitutes a verbal juggle for a real way out of the difficulty. It withdraws the attention of thinking women from the true problem of their sex to fix it on side-issues of comparative unimportance.

---

1   From Carolyn Christensen Nelson, ed., *A New Woman Reader: Fiction, Articles, and Drama of the 1890s* (Peterborough, ON: Broadview Press, 2001) 210-24.

And this, I believe, is what almost all the Woman's Rights women are sedulously doing at the present day. They are pursuing a chimæra,[1] and neglecting to perceive the true aim of their sex. They are setting up a false and unattainable ideal, while they omit to realise the true and attainable one which alone is open to them....

For what is the ideal that most of these modern women agitators set before them? Is it not clearly the ideal of an unsexed woman? Are they not always talking to us as though it were not the fact that most women must be wives and mothers? Do they not treat any reference to that fact as something ungenerous, ungentlemanly, and almost brutal? Do they not talk about our "casting their sex in their teeth"?—as though any man ever resented the imputation of manliness. Nay, have we not even, many times lately, heard those women who insist upon the essential womanliness of women described as "traitors to the cause of their sex"? Now, we men are (rightly) very jealous of our own virility. We hold it a slight not to be borne that anyone should impugn our essential manhood. And we do well to be angry: for virility is the keynote to all that is best and most forcible in the masculine character. Women ought equally to glory in their femininity. A woman ought to be ashamed to say she has no desire to become a wife and mother. Many such women there are no doubt—it is to be feared, with our existing training, far too many: but instead of boasting of their sexlessness as a matter of pride, they ought to keep it dark, and to be ashamed of it—as ashamed as a man in alike predicament would be of his impotence. They ought to feel they have fallen short of the healthy instincts of their kind, instead of posing as in some sense the cream of the universe, on the strength of what is really a functional aberration.

Unfortunately, however, just at the present moment, a considerable number of the ablest women have ben misled into taking this unfeminine side, and becoming real "traitors to their sex" in so far as they endeavour to assimilate women to men in everything, and to put upon their shoulders, as a glory and privilege, the burden of their own support. Unfortunately, too, they have erected into an ideal what is really an unhappy necessity of the passing phase. They have set before them as an aim what ought to be regarded as a *pis-aller.*[2] And the reasons why they have done so are abundantly evident to anybody who takes a wide and extended view of the present crisis—for a crisis it undoubtedly is—in the position of women.

---

1   A fanciful, unrealistic idea.
2   A course of action followed for want of a better; a last resort.

[For example], the movement for the Higher education of Women, in itself an excellent and most praiseworthy movement, has at first, almost of necessity, taken a wrong direction, which has entailed in the end much of the present uneasiness. Of course, nothing could well be worse than the so-called education of women forty of fifty years ago. Of course, nothing could be narrower than the view of their sex then prevalent as eternally predestined to suckle fools and chronicle small beer.[1] But when the need for some change was first felt, instead of reform taking a rational direction—instead of women being educated to suckle strong and intelligent children, and to order well a wholesome, beautiful, reasonable household, the mistake was made of educating them like men—giving a like training for totally unlike functions. The result was that many women became unsexed in the process, and many others acquired a distaste, an unnatural distaste, for the functions which nature intended them to perform. At the present moment, a great majority of the ablest women are wholly dissatisfied with their own position as women, and with the position imposed by the facts of the case upon women generally: and this as the direct result of their false education. They have no real plan to propose for the future of women as a sex: but in a vague and formless way they protest inarticulately against the whole feminine function in women, often even going the length of talking as though the world could get along permanently without wives and mothers....

.... Almost all the Woman's Rights women have constantly spoken, thought, and written as though it were possible and desirable for the mass of women to support themselves, and to remain unmarried for ever. The point of view they all tacitly take is the point of view of the self-supporting spinster. Now, the self-supporting spinster is undoubtedly a fact—a deplorable accident of the passing moment. Probably, however, even the most rabid of the Woman's Rights people would admit, if hard pressed, that in the best-ordered community almost every woman should marry at twenty or thereabouts. We ought, of course, frankly to recognise the existence of the deplorable accident; we ought for the moment to make things as easy and smooth as possible for her; we ought to remove all professional barriers, to break down the absurd jealousies and prejudices of men, to give her fair play, and if possible a little more than fair play, in the struggle for existence. So much our very chivalry ought to make obligatory upon us. That we should try to handicap her heavily in the race for life is a shame to our manhood.

---

1   Deal with trivial matters.

But we ought at the same time fully to realise that she is an abnormality, not the woman of the future. We ought not to erect into an ideal what is in reality a painful necessity of the present transitional age. We ought always clearly to bear in mind—men and women alike—that to all time the vast majority of women must be wives and mothers; that on those women who become wives and mothers depends the future of the race; and that if either class must be sacrificed to the other, it is the spinsters whose type perishes with them that should be sacrificed to the matrons who carry on the life and quality of the species.

For this reason a scheme of female education ought to be mainly a scheme for the education of wives and mothers. And if women realised how noble and important a task it is that falls upon mothers, they would ask no other. If they realised how magnificent a nation might be moulded by mothers who devoted themselves faithfully and earnestly to their great privilege, they would be proud to carry out the duties of their maternity. Instead of that, the scheme of female education now in vogue is a scheme for the production of literary women, schoolmistresses, hospital nurses, and lecturers on cookery. All these things are good in themselves, to be sure—I have not a word to say against them; but they are not of the centre. They are side-lines off the main stream of feminine life, which must always consist of the maternal element. "But we can't know beforehand," say the advocates of the mannish training, "which women are going to be married, and which to be spinsters." Exactly so; and therefore you sacrifice the many to the few, the potential wives to the possible lady-lecturers. You sacrifice the race to a handful of barren experimenters. What is thus true of the blind groping after female education is true throughout almost all of the Woman Movement. It gives precedence to the wrong element in the problem. What is essential and eternal it neglects in favour of what is accidental and temporary. What is feminine in women it neglects in favour of what is masculine. It attempts to override the natural distinction of the sexes, and to make women men—in all but virility....

2. From Sarah Grand, "The New Aspect of the Woman Question," *North American Review* 158 (March 1894)[1]

[Sarah Grand (the pseudonym of Frances Elizabeth Clarke McFall, 1854-1943), novelist, lecturer, and women's rights advocate, coined the

---

1   From Carolyn Christensen Nelson, ed., *A New Woman Reader: Fiction, Articles, and Drama of the 1890s* (Peterborough, ON: Broadview Press, 2001) 142-43.

phrase "new woman" in this *North American Review* essay to reflect the values—principally social, political, and educational equality with men, as well as economic independence—of the generation represented by Vivie in *Mrs Warren's Profession*. While Vivie nowhere in the play displays Sarah Grand's zeal and the rhetorical power, her values and choices fit well with the principles expressed so forcefully by Grand.]

... What [the new woman] perceived at the outset was the sudden and violent upheaval of the suffering sex in all parts of the world. Women were awakening from their long apathy, and, as they woke, like healthy hungry children unable to articulate, they began to whimper for they knew not what. They might have been easily satisfied at that time had not society, like an ill-conditioned and ignorant nurse, instead of finding out what they lacked, shaken them and beaten them and stormed at them until what was once a little wail became convulsive shrieks and roused up the whole human household. Then man, disturbed by the uproar, came upstairs all anger and irritation, and, without waiting to learn what was the matter, added his own old theories to the din, but, finding they did not act rapidly, formed new ones, and made an intolerable nuisance of himself with his opinions and advice. He was in the state of one who cannot comprehend because he has no faculty to perceive the thing in question, and that is why he was so positive. The dimmest perception that you may be mistaken will save you from making an ass of yourself.

We must look upon man's mistakes, however, with some leniency, because we are not blameless in the matter ourselves. We have allowed him to arrange the whole social system and manage or mismanage it all these ages without ever seriously examining his work with a view to considering whether his abilities or motives were sufficiently good to qualify him for the task. We have listened without a smile to his preachments, about our place in life and all we are good for, on the text that "there is no understanding a woman." We have endured most poignant misery for his sins, and screened him when we should have exposed him and had him punished. We have allowed him to exact all things of us, and have been content to accept the little he grudgingly gave us in return. We have meekly bowed our heads when he called us bad names instead of demanding proofs of the superiority which alone would give him a right to do so. We have listened much edified to man's sermons on the subject of virtue, and have acquiesced uncomplainingly in the convenient arrangement by which this quality has come to be altogether practised for him by us vicariously. We have seen him set up Christ as an example for all men to follow, which argues his belief in the possibility of doing so, and have not only allowed his weakness and hypocrisy in the matter to pass without comment, but, until lately, have not even seen the humor of his pretensions when contrasted with his practices, nor held him up to that wholesome ridicule which is a stimulating corrective. Man deprived us of all proper education, and then jeered at us because we had no knowledge. He narrowed our outlook on life so that our view of it should be all distorted, and then declared that our mistaken impression of it proved us to be senseless creatures. He cramped our minds so that there was no room for reason in them, and then made merry at our want of logic. Our divine intuition was not to be controlled by him, but he did his best to damage it by sneering at it as an inferior feminine method of arriving at conclusions; and finally, after having had his own way until he lost his head completely, he set himself up as a sort of god and required us to worship him, and to our eternal shame be it said, we did so. The truth has all along been in us, but we have cared more for man than for truth, and so the whole human race has suffered. We have failed of our effect by neglecting our duty here, and have deserved much of the obloquy that was cast upon us. All that is over now, however, and while on the one hand man has shrunk to his true proportions in our estimation, we, on the other, have been expanding to our own; and now we come confidently forward to maintain, not that this or that was "intended," but that there are in ourselves, in both sexes, possibilities hitherto suppressed or abused, which, when properly developed, will supply to either what is lacking in the other.

The man of the future will be better, while the woman will be stronger and wiser. To bring this about is the whole aim and object of the present struggle, and with the discovery of the means lies the solution of the Woman Question. Man, having no conception of himself as imperfect from the woman's point of view, will find this difficult to understand, but we know his weakness, and will be patient with him, and help him with his lesson. It is the woman's place and pride and pleasure to teach the child, and man morally is in his infancy. There have been times when there was a doubt as to whether he was to be raised or woman was to be lowered, but we have turned that corner at last; and now woman holds out a strong hand to the child-man, and insists, but with infinite tenderness and pity, upon helping him up....

3. From Alys W. Pearsall Smith, "A Reply from the Daughters," *Nineteenth Century* 35 (March 1894)[1]

[An essay in the January 1894 issue of *Nineteenth Century* spoke of the "hidden disease" of mother-daughter conflicts, and criticized young women—such perhaps as Vivie Warren—who "revolt" against their mothers: "For inner barrenness of spirit, manifesting itself in ugly outside action, few things can match the ruthless young daughter pulling her own way against her mother, and generally getting it too. She is, by reason of her youth, perfectly insensible to, absolutely regardless of, the agony she is causing and the wounds she is inflicting. For the time being she presents to the observer a curious mental compound of which the fundamental basis is egoism."[2] The essay prompted a response—much more sympathetic to the Vivie Warrens of Victorian England—by Alys W. Pearsall Smith (1867?-1951), a member of the Fabian Society (and also first wife of philosopher Bertrand Russell (1872-1970).]

... Let every girl then claim her right to individual development, not merely for her own welfare and enjoyment or for that of her family, but chiefly that she may become a more perfect instrument to perform her allotted part in the world's work. It must be a matter of principle, not a matter of self-indulgence. She must be able to say not merely, "I want to do this or that," but "I believe I ought to do it." It is as fatal to a woman to live her life merely for her own enjoyment as it is for her to sacrifice her own life to other people's enjoyment. She must sacrifice herself, not *to* people, but *for* principles. She must ask herself frankly and honestly, "Have I any worthy purpose in my life? Am I doing the best with such powers as God has given me, or am I allowing them to be unused and wasted? Am I growing stronger and better with each year, or am I narrowing and deteriorating? Shall I be able rightly to fulfil my duties to the world in which I live if I allow myself to be frittered away in little nothings, and fail to strengthen and develop all my powers? Is it not my duty, even for the sake of others, to realise my best and highest self, and to make the most of all my capacities?"

If the community were only alive to its own high interests, it would hail with heartiest welcome the advent of girls such as these, and all true

---

1   From Carolyn Christensen Nelson, ed., *A New Woman Reader: Fiction, Articles, and Drama of the 1890s* (Peterborough, ON: Broadview Press, 2001) 275-76.

2   B.A. Crackenthorpe, "The Revolt of the Daughters," *Nineteenth Century* 35 (January 1894), in Nelson 261-69.

lovers of humanity would reach out a hand to help them break through the trammels of prejudice or conventionality that have hitherto held them in check.

Hundreds of avenues are opening for girls of to-day in which they can get the development and find the work they need. It ought, therefore, to be a matter of principle for every girl who has reached maturity to consider what is her own special gift or capability; and having discovered it, she ought to be as conscientious in trying to carry it out as she would be conscientious in carrying out the domestic duties which hitherto may have seemed to her to have been the only career allowed her.

The revolt of the daughter is not, if I understand it, a revolt against any merely surface conventionalities, that are after all of not much account one way or another, but it is a revolt against a bondage that enslaves her whole life. In the past she has belonged to other people, now she demands to belong to herself. In the past other people have decided her duties for her, now she asks that she may decide them for herself. She asks simply and only for freedom to make out of her own life the highest that can be made, and to develop her own individuality as seems to her the wisest and the best. She claims only the ordinary rights of a human being, and humbly begs that no one will hinder her.

Select Bibliography

Works by Shaw and Other Editions of *Mrs Warren's Profession*

An Autobiography. Selected from his Writings by Stanley Weintraub. 2 vols. New York: Weybright and Talley, 1969-70.

Collected Letters. Ed. Dan H. Laurence. 4 vols. New York: Viking Penguin, 1985-88.

Collected Plays with Their Prefaces. Under the editorial supervision of Dan H. Laurence. 7 vols. London: Max Reinhardt, The Bodley Head, 1970-74.

Complete Prefaces. Ed. Dan H. Laurence and Daniel J. Leary. 3 vols. London: Allen Lane, the Penguin Press, 1993-97.

Diaries 1885-1897. Ed. Stanley Weintraub. 2 vols. University Park, PA: Pennsylvania State UP, 1986.

The Drama Observed. Ed. Bernard F. Dukore. 4 vols. University Park, PA: Pennsylvania State UP, 1993.

George Bernard Shaw's Plays. Ed. Sandie Byrne. New York: Norton, 2002. [Includes *Mrs Warren's Profession, Man and Superman, Major Barbara, Pygmalion*.]

Interviews and Recollections. Ed. A.M. Gibbs. Iowa City: U of Iowa P, 1990.

Man and Superman and Three Other Plays. Introduction and Notes by John A. Bertolini. New York: Barnes & Noble, 2004. [Includes *Mrs Warren's Profession, Candida, The Devil's Disciple*.]

Mrs Warren's Profession. A Facsimile of the Holograph Manuscript. Introduction by Margot Peters. New York & London: Garland, 1981.

Platform and Pulpit. Ed. Dan H. Laurence. New York: Hill and Wang, 1961. [Lectures and Broadcasts.]

Plays Unpleasant. Under the editorial supervision of Dan H. Laurence. Introduction by David Edgar. London: Penguin, 2000. [Includes *Widowers' Houses, The Philanderer, Mrs Warren's Profession*.]

Shaw on Theatre. Ed. E.J. West. New York: Hill and Wang, 1958.

Shaw's Music: The Complete Musical Criticism. Ed. Dan H. Laurence. 3 vols. London: The Bodley Head, 1981.

Works of Bernard Shaw: Collected Edition. 33 vols. London: Constable, 1930-38.

Works on *Mrs Warren's Profession*

Allett, John. "*Mrs Warren's Profession* and the Politics of Prostitution." *SHAW: The Annual of Bernard Shaw Studies* 19 (1999): 23-39.

Bermel, Albert. "A Shavian Whodunit: The Mysterious Mrs Warren." *Independent Shavian* 38.1 (2000): 6-15.

Bullough, Geoffrey. "Literary Relations of Shaw's Mrs Warren." *Philological Quarterly* 41.1 (1962): 339-58.

Chen, Wendi. "The First Shaw Play on the Chinese Stage: the Production of *Mrs Warren's Profession* in 1921." *SHAW: The Annual of Bernard Shaw Studies* 19 (1999): 99-118.

Conolly, L.W. "*Mrs Warren's Profession* and the Lord Chamberlain." *SHAW: The Annual of Bernard Shaw Studies* 24 (2004): 46-95.

Crane, Gladys M. "Directing Early Shaw: Acting and Meaning in *Mrs Warren's Profession.*" *SHAW: The Annual of Bernard Shaw Studies* 3 (1983): 29-39.

Dolid, William A. "Vivie Warren and the Tripos." *Shaw Review* 23.2 (1980): 52-56.

Fisher, James. "Edy Craig and the Pioneer Players' Production of *Mrs Warren's Profession.*" *SHAW: The Annual of Bernard Shaw Studies* 15 (1995): 37-56.

Greer, Germaine. "A Whore in Every Home." *Fabian Feminist. Bernard Shaw and Woman.* Ed. Rodelle Weintraub. University Park, PA: Pennsylvania State UP, 1977. 163-66.

Kapelke, Randy. "Preventing Censorship: The Audience's Role in *Sapho* (1900) and *Mrs Warren's Profession* (1905)." *Theatre History Studies* 18 (1998): 117-33.

Knepper, B.G. "Shaw Rewriting Shaw: A Fragment." *Shaw Review* 12.3 (1969): 104-10.

Laurence, Dan H. "Victorians Unveiled: Some Thoughts on *Mrs Warren's Profession.*" *SHAW: The Annual of Bernard Shaw Studies* 24 (2004): 38-45.

Mudford, Peter. "*Mrs Warren's Profession.*" *The Shavian* 6 (1987): 4-10.

Nelson, Raymond S. "*Mrs Warren's Profession* and English Prostitution." *Journal of Modern Literature* 2.3 (1971-72): 357-66.

Nethercot, Arthur H. "*Mrs Warren's Profession* and *The Second Mrs Tanqueray.*" *Shaw Review* 13.1 (1970): 26-28.

———. "The Vivie-Frank Relationship in *Mrs Warren's Profession.*" *The Shavian* 15 (June 1959): 7-9.

Radford, F.L. "The Educative Sequel: *Lady Chatterley's Second Husband* and *Mrs Warren's Daughter.*" *Shaw Review* 23.2 (1980): 57-62.

Salih, Sabah A. "The *New York Times* and Arnold Daly's Production of *Mrs Warren's Profession*." *Independent Shavian* 26.3 (1988): 57-59.

Shaw, Mary. "My 'Immoral' Play." *McClure's Magazine* 38 (April 1912): 684-94.

Stafford, Tony J. "*Mrs Warren's Profession*: In the Garden of Respectability." *SHAW: The Annual of Bernard Shaw Studies* 2 (1982): 3-11.

Wasserman, Marlie Parker. "Vivie Warren: A Psychological Study." *Fabian Feminist. Bernard Shaw and Woman*. Ed. Rodelle Weintraub. University Park, PA: Pennsylvania State UP, 1977. 168-73.

Wellwarth, George E. "Mrs Warren Comes to America, or the Blue-Noses, the Politicians and the Procurers." *Shaw Review* 2.8 (1959): 8-16.

Works on Shaw

Baker, Stuart E. *Bernard Shaw's Remarkable Religion. A Faith that Fits the Facts*. Gainesville: U of Florida P, 2002.

Bentley, Eric. *Bernard Shaw*. London: Methuen, 1967.

Berst, Charles A. *Bernard Shaw and the Art of Drama*. Urbana: U of Illinois P, 1973.

Bertolini, John A. *The Playwrighting Self of Bernard Shaw*. Carbondale: Southern Illinois UP, 1991.

Bevan, E. Dean. *A Concordance to the Plays and Prefaces of Bernard Shaw*. 10 vols. Detroit: Gale Research, [1972].

Carpenter, Charles A. *Bernard Shaw & the Art of Destroying Ideals: The Early Plays*. Madison: U of Wisconsin P, 1969.

Conolly, L.W., and Ellen M. Pearson, eds. *Bernard Shaw on Stage. Papers from the 1989 International Shaw Conference*. Guelph: U of Guelph, 1991.

Crompton, Louis. *Shaw the Dramatist*. London: George Allen & Unwin, 1971.

Davis, Tracy C. *George Bernard Shaw and the Socialist Theatre*. Westport, CT: Greenwood Press, 1994.

Dukore, Bernard F. *Bernard Shaw, Director*. London: George Allen & Unwin, 1971.

———. *Money & Politics in Ibsen, Shaw, and Brecht*. Columbia: U of Missouri P, 1980.

Evans, T.F., ed. *Shaw: The Critical Heritage*. London: Routledge, 1976.

Gainor, J. Ellen. *Shaw's Daughters: Dramatic and Narrative Constructions of Gender*. Ann Arbor: U of Michigan P, 1991.

Gibbs, A.M. *A Bernard Shaw Chronology*. Basingstoke: Palgrave, 2001.

Grene, Nicholas. *Bernard Shaw: A Critical View*. New York: St Martin's Press, 1984.

Holroyd, Michael. *Bernard Shaw*. 5 vols. London: Chatto & Windus, 1988-92.

Hugo, Leon. *Edwardian Shaw. The Writer and His Age*. London: Macmillan, 1999.

Innes, Christopher, ed. *The Cambridge Companion to George Bernard Shaw*. Cambridge: Cambridge UP, 1998.

Laurence, Dan. H. *Bernard Shaw: A Bibliography*. 2 vols. Oxford: Clarendon P, 1983.

———. *Shaw: An Exhibit*. [Catalogue of an exhibit at the University of Texas at Austin, 11 September 1997-28 February 1978.] Austin: U of Texas, 1977.

Mander, Raymond, and Joe Mitchenson. *Theatrical Companion to Shaw*. New York: Pitman, 1955.

Meisel, Martin. *Shaw and the Nineteenth-Century Theater*. Princeton: Princeton UP, 1963.

Morgan, Margery M. *The Shavian Playground. An Exploration of the Art of George Bernard Shaw*. London: Methuen, 1972.

Peters, Margot. *Bernard Shaw and the Actresses*. New York: Doubleday, 1980.

———, Sally. *Bernard Shaw: The Ascent of the Superman*. New Haven: Yale UP, 1996.

Pharand, Michel. *Bernard Shaw and the French*. Gainesville: U Press of Florida, 2000.

Smith, J. Percy. *The Unrepentant Pilgrim. A Study of the Development of Bernard Shaw*. Boston: Houghton Mifflin, 1965.

Turco, Alfred. *Shaw's Moral Vision. The Self and Salvation*. Ithaca: Cornell UP, 1976.

Tyson, Brian F. "Shaw Among the Actors: Theatrical Additions to *Plays Unpleasant*." *Modern Drama* 14 (1971-72): 264-75.

Valency, Maurice. *The Cart and the Trumpet. The Plays of George Bernard Shaw*. New York: Oxford UP, 1973.

Watson, Barbara Bellow. *A Shavian Guide to the Intelligent Woman*. London: Chatto & Windus, 1964.

Weintraub, Rodelle, ed. *Fabian Feminist. Bernard Shaw and Woman*. University Park, PA: Pennsylvania State UP, 1977.

Whitman, Robert F. *Shaw and the Play of Ideas*. Ithaca: Cornell UP, 1977.

Wisenthal, J. L. *The Marriage of Contraries: Bernard Shaw's Middle Plays*. Cambridge, MA: Harvard UP, 1974.

———. *Shaw's Sense of History*. Oxford: Clarendon Press, 1988.

Works on the Contexts of *Mrs Warren's Profession*

Acton, William. *Prostitution*. Ed. Peter Fryer. New York: Praeger, 1969.

Bartley, Paula. *Prostitution. Prevention and Reform in England, 1860-1914*. London and New York: Routledge, 2000.

Bennett, Daphne. *Emily Davis and the Liberation of Women 1830-1921*. London: Deutsch, 1990.

Bird, M. Mostyn. *Woman at Work. A Study of the Different Ways of Earning a Living Open to Women*. London: Chapman & Hall, 1911.

Black, Clementina. *Sweated Industry and the Minimum Wage*. London: Duckworth, 1907.

——, ed. *Married Women's Work. Being the Report of the Enquiry Undertaken by the Women's Industrial Council*. London: Virago, 1983.

Booth, General [William]. *In Darkest England and the Way Out*. London: Salvation Army, 1890.

Brooke, Christopher N.L. *A History of the University of Cambridge*. Volume IV, 1870-1990. Cambridge: Cambridge UP, 1993.

Burnett, John. *A History of the Cost of Living*. Harmondsworth: Penguin Books, 1969.

Chothia, Jean, ed. *The New Woman and Other Emancipated Woman Plays*. Oxford: Oxford UP, 1998.

Conolly, L.W. *The Censorship of English Drama 1737-1824*. San Marino: Huntington Library, 1976.

de Jongh, Nicholas. *Politics, Prudery & Perversions: The Censoring of the English Stage 1901-1968*. London: Methuen, 2000.

Dyhouse, Carol. *No Distinction of Sex? Women in British Universities, 1870-1939*. London: UCL Press, 1995.

Eschbach, Elizabeth Seymour. *The Higher Education of Women in England and America, 1865-1920*. New York: Garland, 1993.

Fisher, Trevor. *Prostitution and the Victorians*. New York: St Martin's Press, 1997.

Hamilton, Mary Agnes. *Newnham: An Informal Biography*. London: Faber, 1936.

Haney, Robert W. *Comstockery in America: Patterns of Censorship and Control*. Boston: Beacon Press, 1960.

Hellerstein, Erna Olafson, Leslie Parker Hume, and Karen M. Offen, eds. *Victorian Women. A Documentary Account of Women's Lives in Nineteenth-Century England, France, and the United States*. Stanford: Stanford UP, 1981.

Houchin, John H. *Censorship of the American Theatre in the Twentieth Century*. Cambridge: Cambridge UP, 2003.

Innes, Christopher, ed. *A Sourcebook on Naturalist Theatre*. London and New York: Routledge, 2000.

Johnston, John. *The Lord Chamberlain's Blue Pencil*. London: Hodder & Stoughton, 1990.

Leedham-Green, Elizabeth. *A Concise History of the University of Cambridge*. Cambridge: Cambridge UP, 1996.

McHugh, Paul. *Prostitution and Victorian Social Reform*. London: Croom Heln, 1980.

McWilliams-Tullberg, Rita. *Women at Cambridge*. London: Gollancz, 1975.

Nelson, Carolyn Christensen, ed. *A New Woman Reader: Fiction, Articles, and Drama of the 1890s*. Peterborough, ON: Broadview Press, 2001.

Nicholson, Steve. *The Censorship of British Drama 1900-1968*. Volume One: 1900-1932. Exeter: U of Exeter P, 2003.

Nield, Keith, ed. *Prostitution in the Victorian Age. Debates on the Issue from 19th Century Critical Journals*. Farnborough: Gregg International, 1973.

Phillips, Ann, ed. *A Newnham Anthology*. Cambridge: Cambridge UP, 1979.

Powell, Kerry. *Women and Victorian Theatre*. Cambridge: Cambridge UP, 1997.

Redmond, James, ed. *Women in Theatre*. Cambridge: Cambridge UP, 1989.

Roydon, A. Maude. *Downward Paths. An Inquiry into the Causes which Contribute to the Making of the Prostitute*. London: G. Bell & Sons, 1916.

Simon, Louis. *Shaw on Education*. New York: Columbia UP, 1958.

Stephens, John Russell. *The Censorship of English Drama 1824-1901*. Cambridge: Cambridge UP, 1980.

Thompson, E.P., and Eileen Yeo, eds. *The Unknown Mayhew. Selections from the Morning Chronicle 1849-1850*. London: Merlin Press, 1971.

Walkowitz, Judith R. *Prostitution and Victorian Society. Women, Class, and the State*. Cambridge: Cambridge UP, 1980.

Waller, P.J., ed. *Politics and Social Change in Modern Britain*. Brighton: Harvester Press, 1987.

Weinreb, Ben, and Christopher Hibbert, eds. *The London Encyclopedia*. Revised ed. London: Macmillan, 1993.

Wiley, Catherine. "The Matter with Manners: the New Woman and the Problem Play." *Women in Theatre*. Ed. James Redmond. Cambridge: Cambridge UP, 1989. 109-27.

Website

The website of the International Shaw Society has current information on Shavian research projects, publications, awards, conferences, symposia, and productions: <http://chuma.cas.usf.edu/~dietrich/iss.htm>.